A CELLO CHRISTMAS

CRAIG DUNCAN

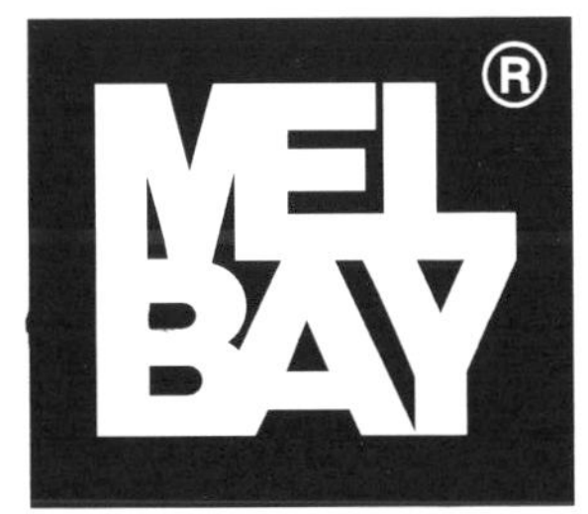

WWW.MELBAY.COM

Index of Tunes

Preface

A Cello Christmas contains Christmas and holiday tunes from a wide variety of sources. Old English, French, German, Austrian, Irish, American and Ukranian carols are included alongside the traditional hymn carols. All of these melodies are arranged for cello solo and have suggested bowings, guitar chords, piano accompaniment and background information. A second cello part included with each tune makes this a useful cello duet book. The collection is a great resource of traditional Christmas music for cellists.

Angels, from the Realms of Glory

James Montgomery first published "Angels, from the Realms of Glory" in his newspaper the *Sheffield Iris,* on Christmas Eve 1816. It has been sung to several melodies since that time. Henry Smart composed this hymn tune entitled "Regent Square" for publication in 1867. It is now the most popular tune for this carol.

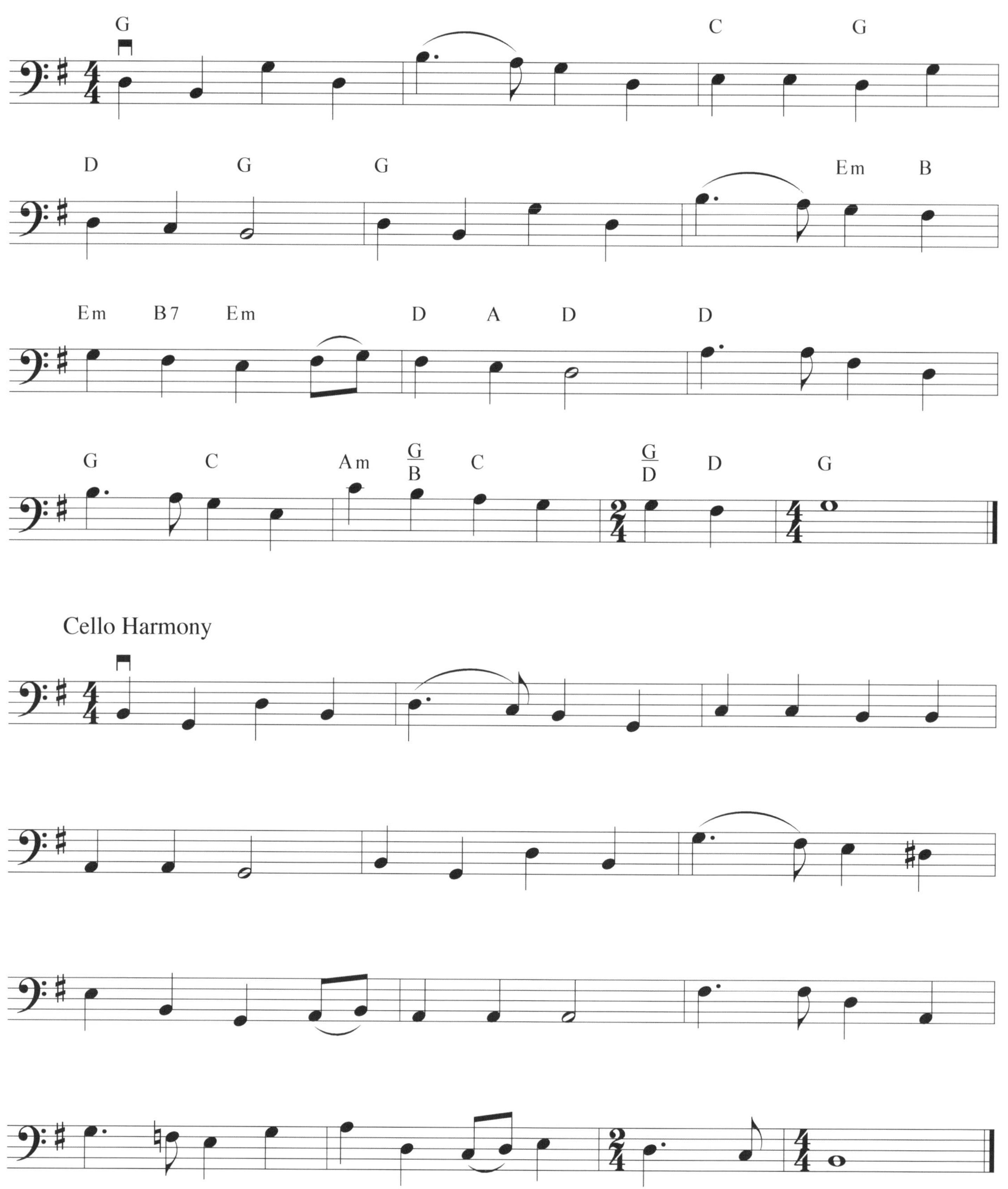

Angels We Have Heard on High

Originally a French carol printed in 1842, this carol appeared in 1860 as an English tune in *The Holy Family Hymns*. It is one of the most popular carols today.

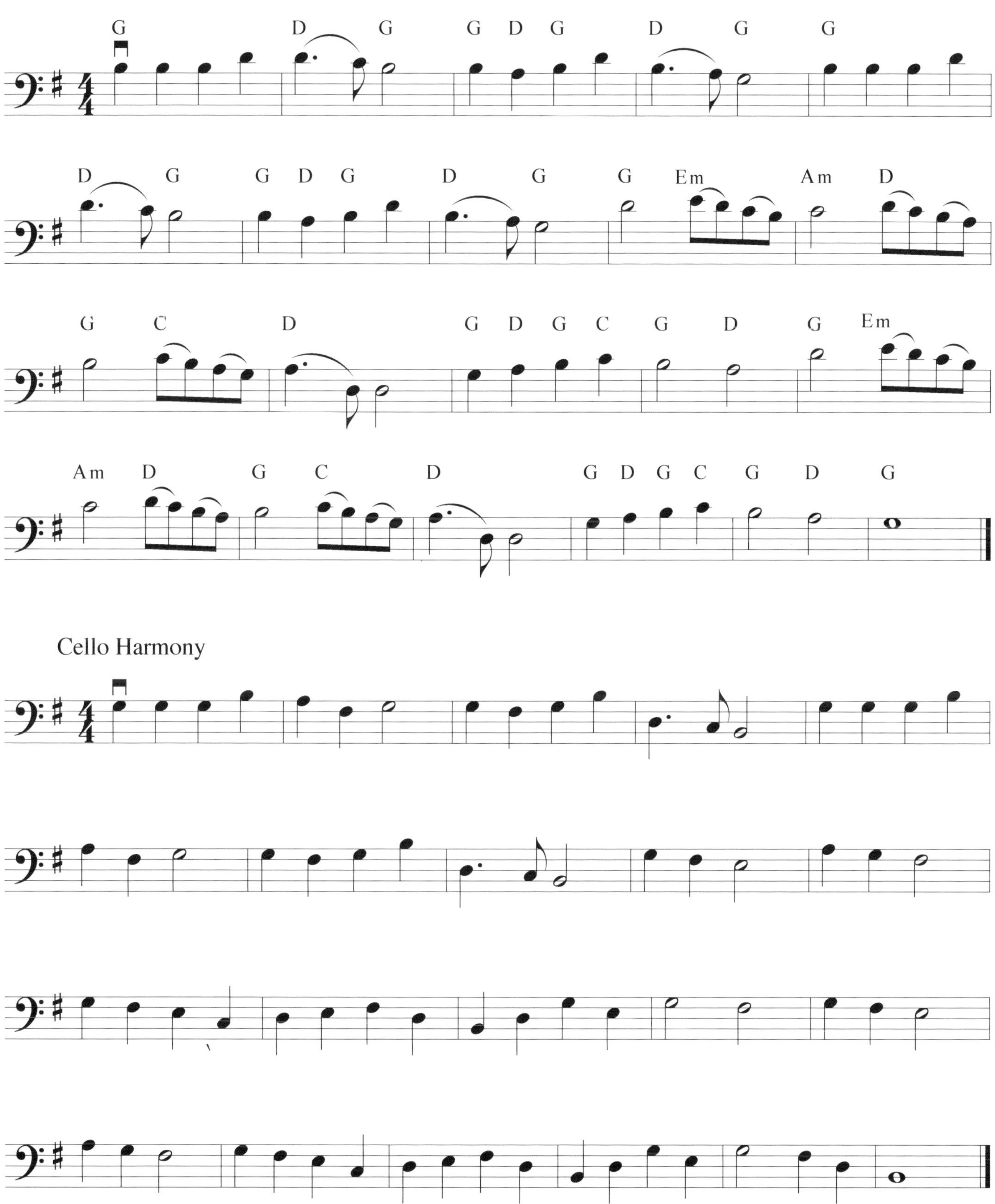

As Lately We Watched

Although this carol has an "Old English" sound and feeling, it comes from nineteenth century Austria. The name of the carol tune is "Austrian Carol".

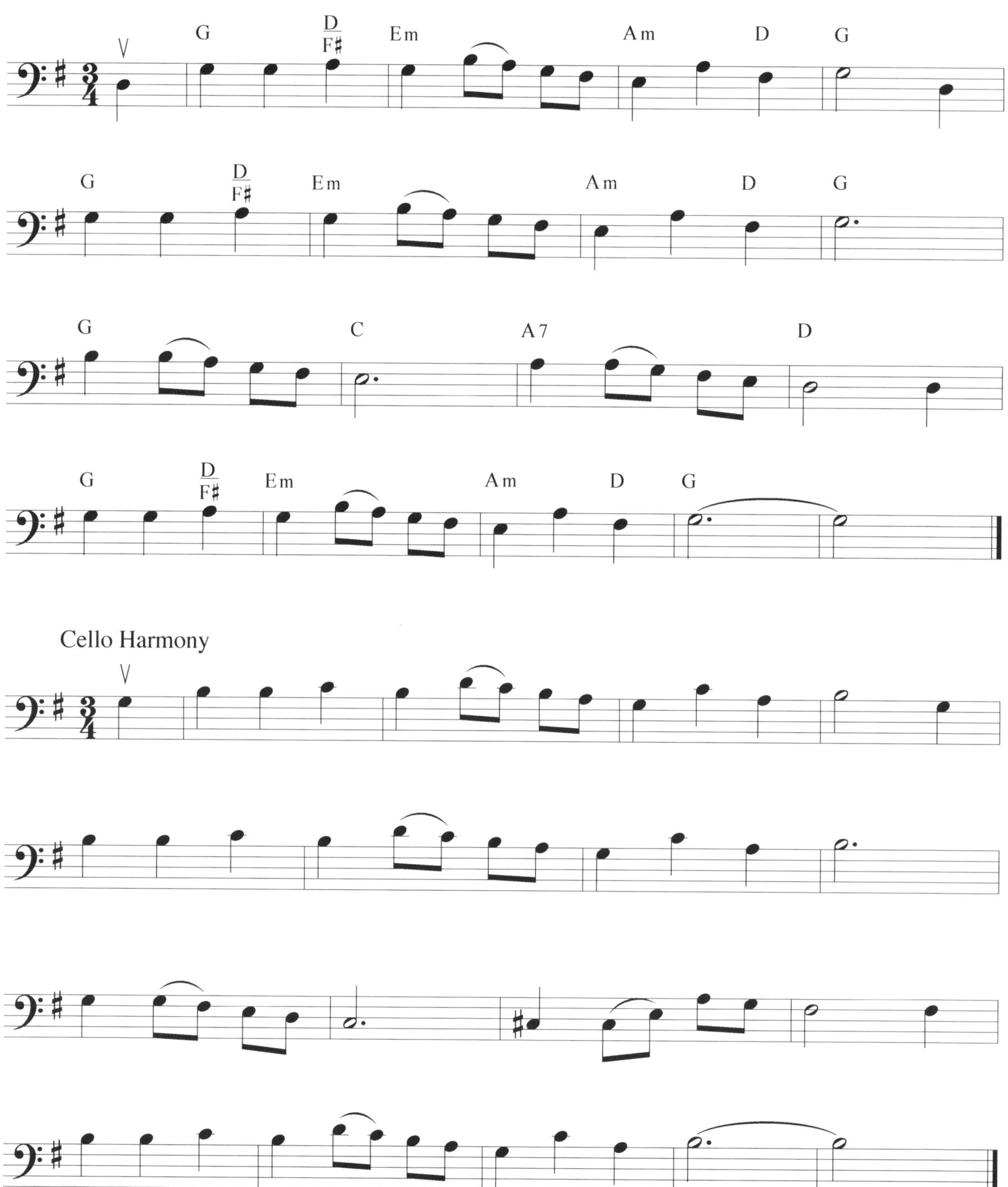

Away in a Manger

This melody of "Away in a Manger" was published first in 1895 in Cincinnati, Ohio. It is the most popular melody associated with the carol in England.

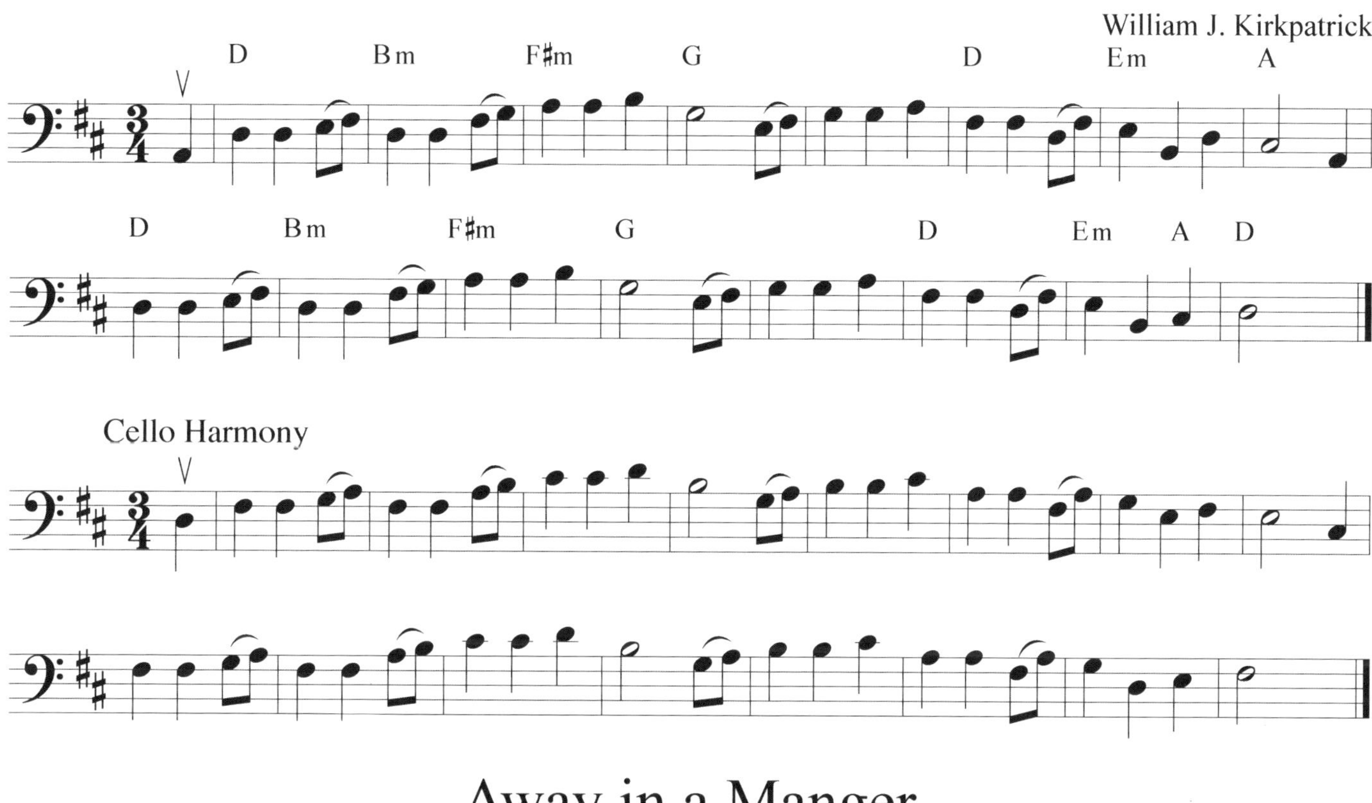

Away in a Manger

The text of "Away in a Manger" was first published in 1885 with a different tune. James Murray wrote and published this melody in 1887, as "Luther's Cradle Hymn." It is now the standard American tune sung with this carol.

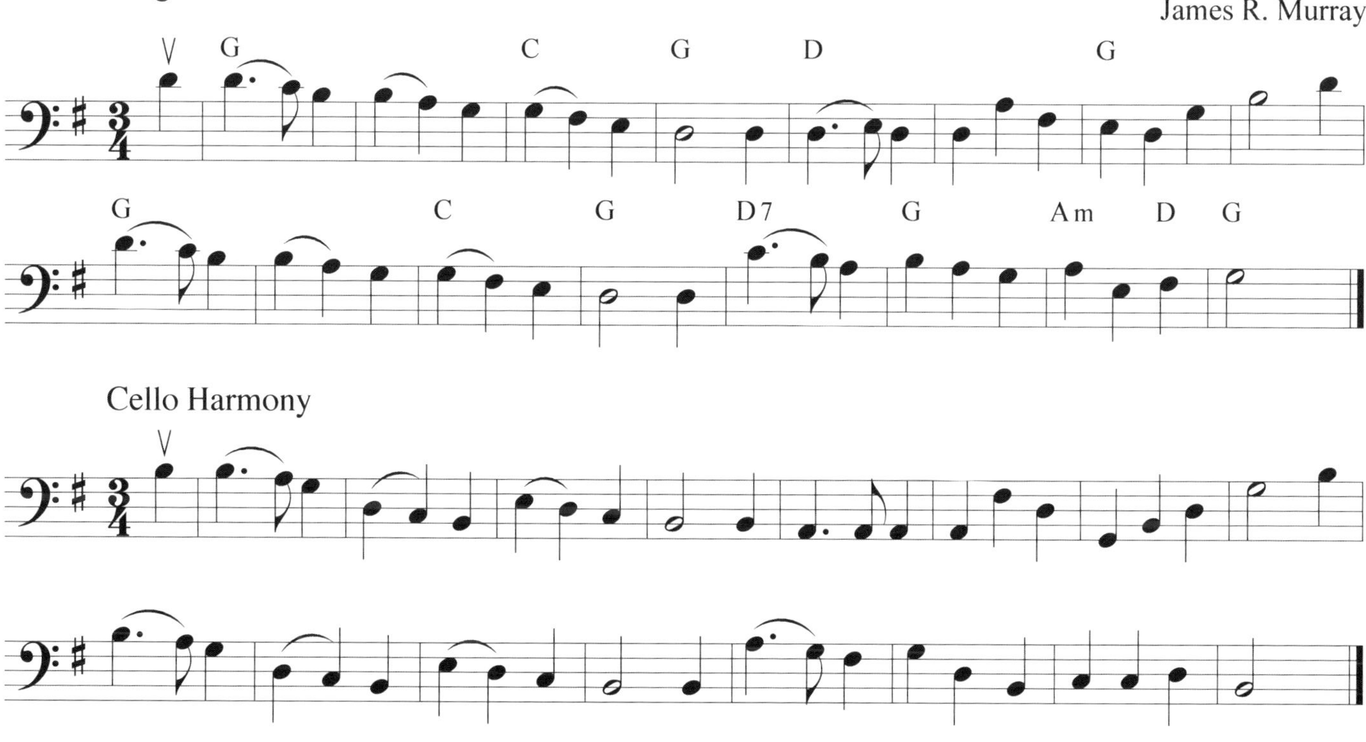

Blessed Be That Maid Marie

The melody to this English carol was taken from *William Ballet's Lute Book* written in 1600. The lyric by Rev. Charles Lewis Hutchins was published in *Carols Old and New* in 1916.

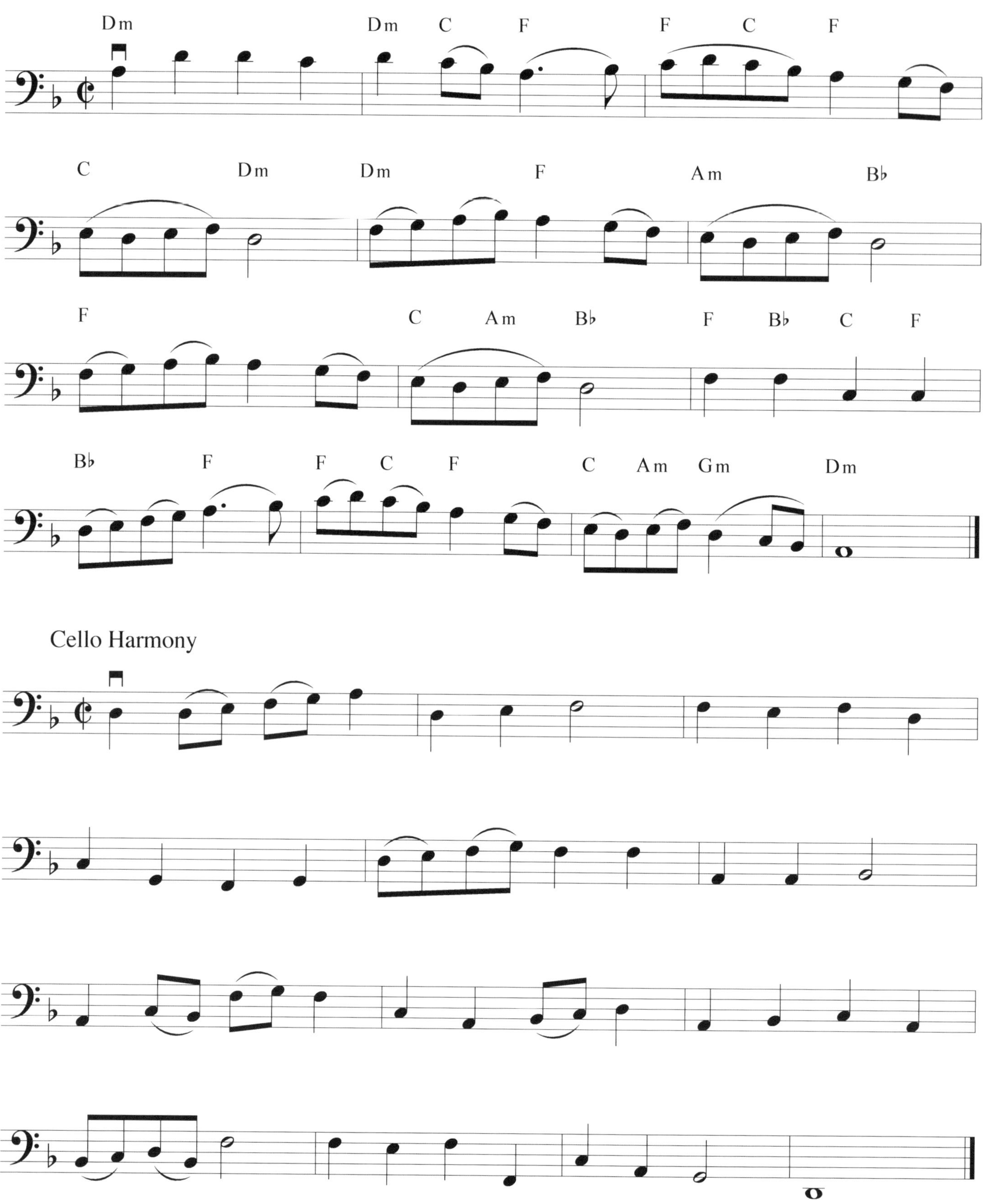

The Boar's Head Carol

"The Boar's Head Carol" was printed in William Wallace Fyfe's *Christmas, It's Customs and Carols* in 1860. The carol comes from the popularity of boar's head feasts during the Christmas season in England.

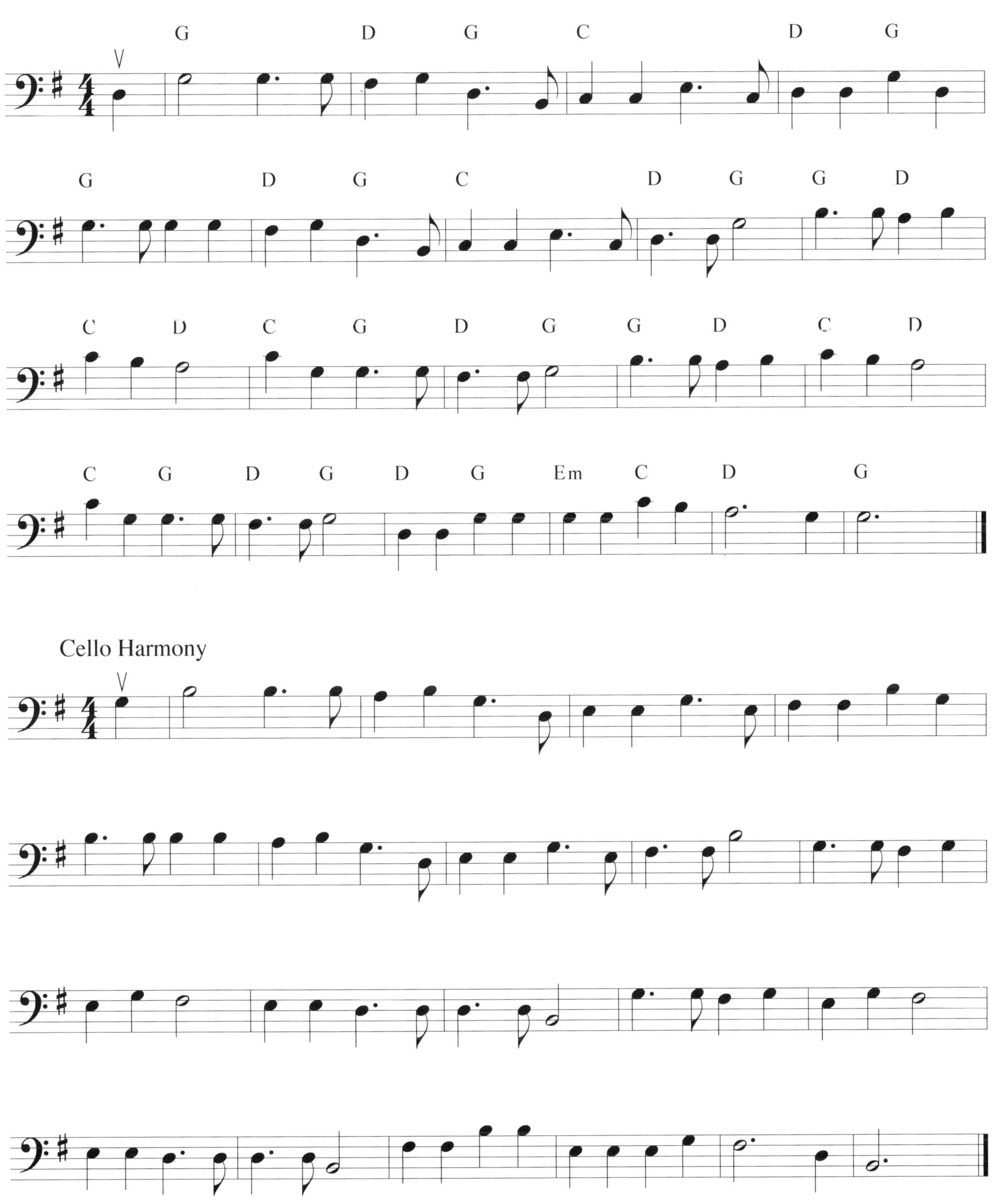

Bring a Torch, Jeanette, Isabella

This is a traditional French melody which can be traced back to Marc-Antione Charpentier. The carol was first published in France in the seventeenth century and was translated into English in the eighteenth century.

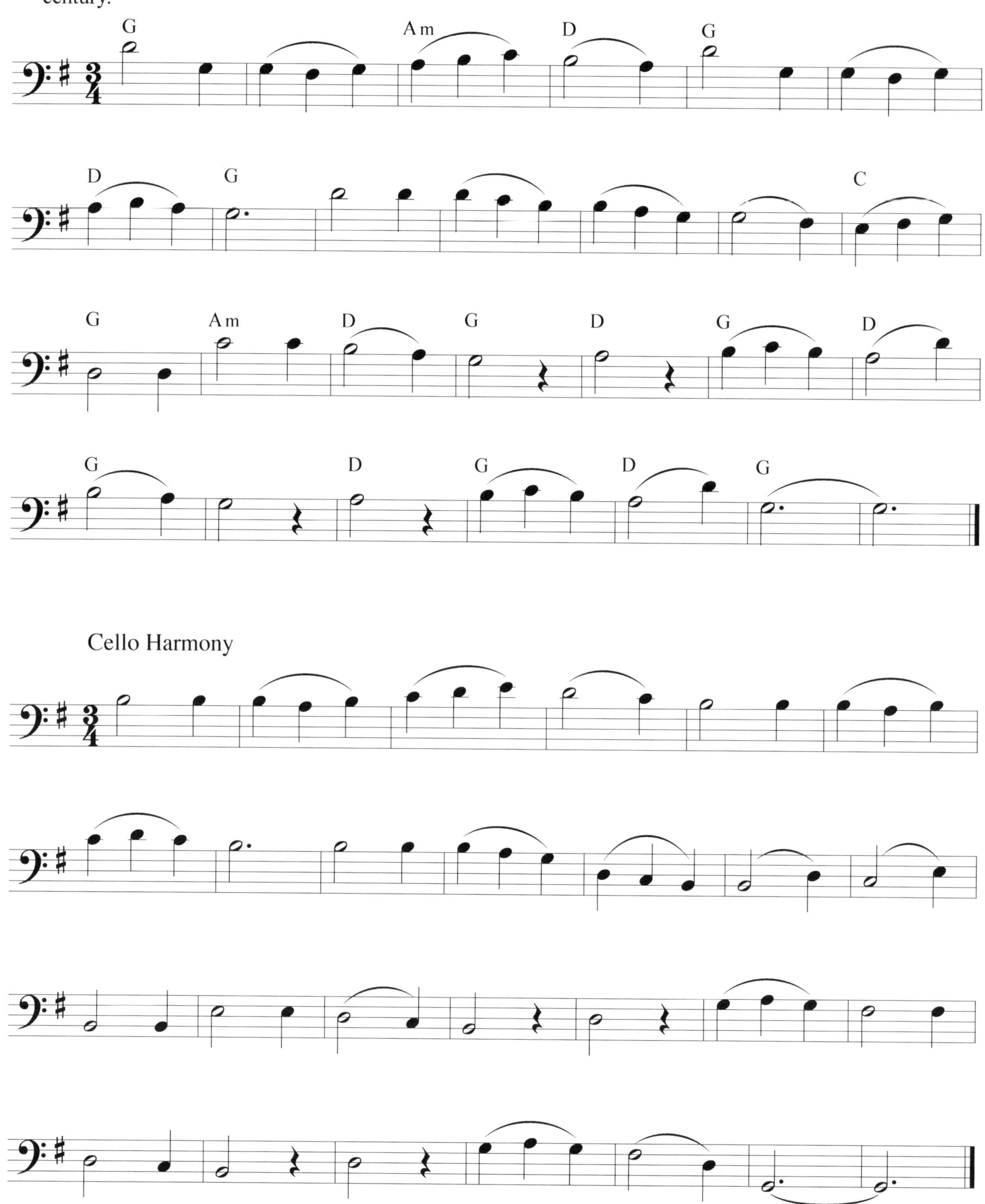

The Cherry Tree Carol

The text of "The Cherry Tree Carol" dates back to the fifteenth century. This arrangement combines two traditional melodies. The first melody dates back to the seventeenth century and the second melody is from *The New Oxford Book of Carols*.

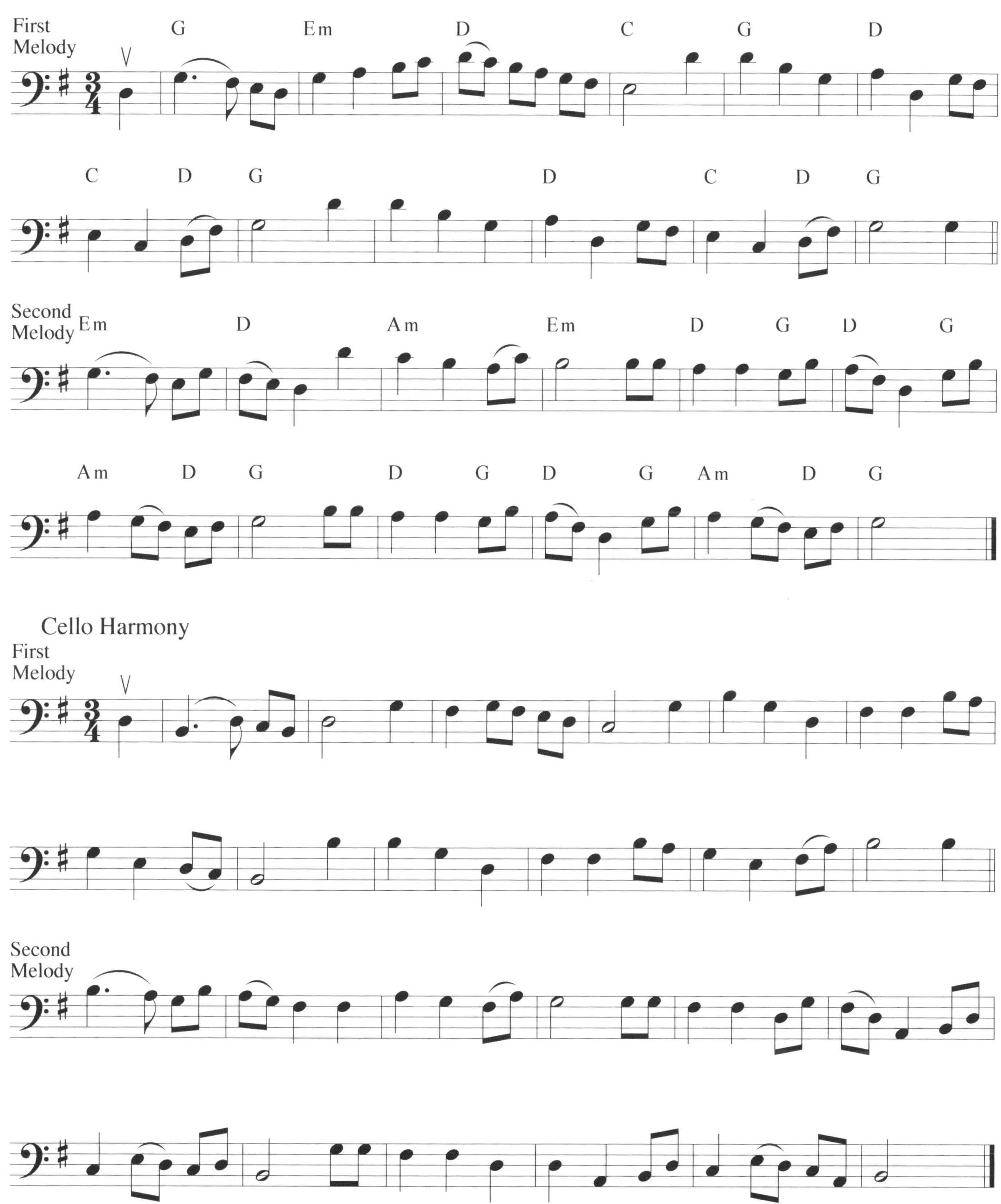

Carol of the Bells

Ukranian Bell Carol

The melody of this carol is based on the Ukranian folk chant, "Shchedryk", and was written by Mykola Leontovych in 1914. When performing this arrangement as a duet, the cellists could swap parts during the repeat section and could repeat more than once.

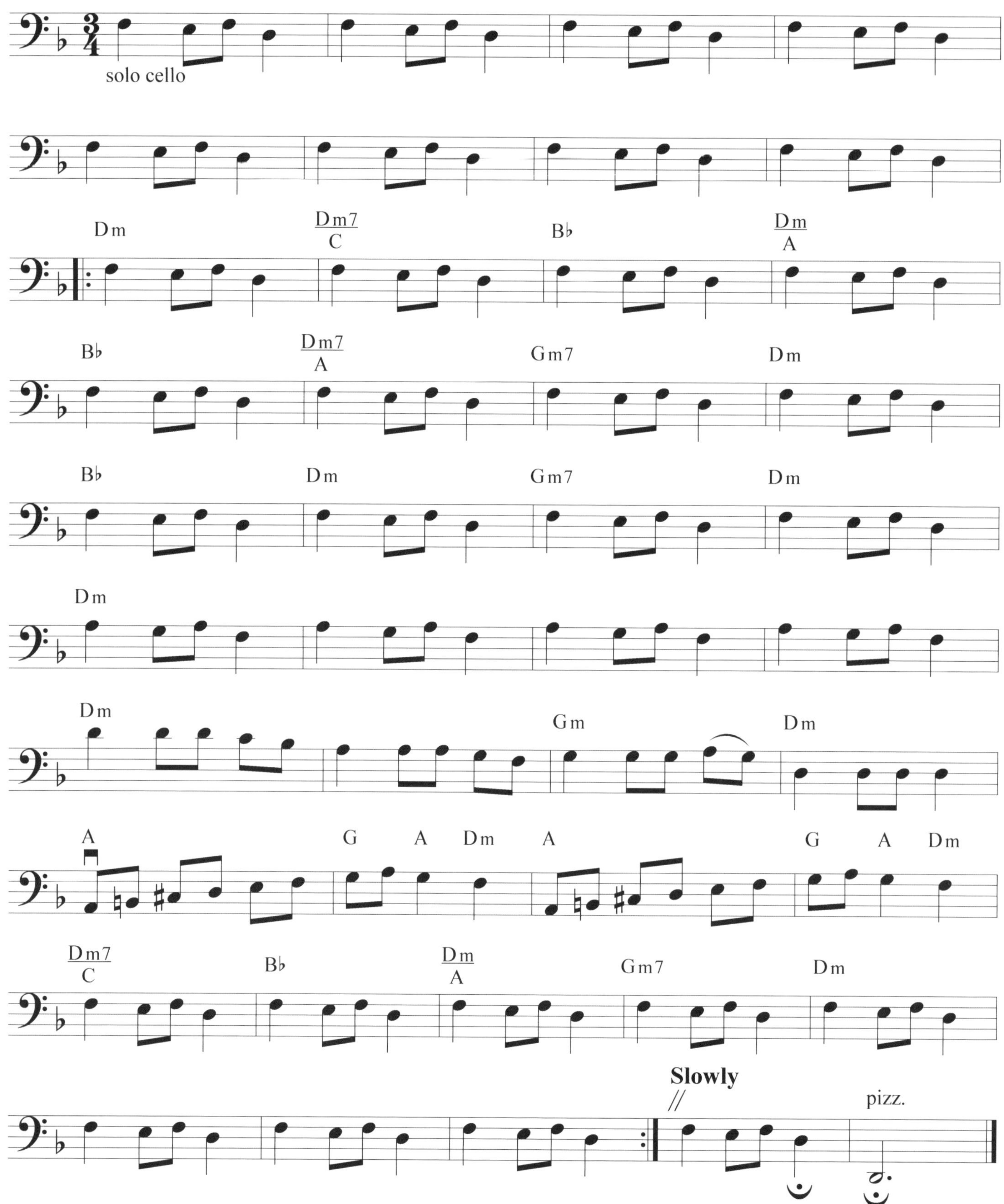

Carol of the Bells

Ukranian Bell Carol

Cello Harmony

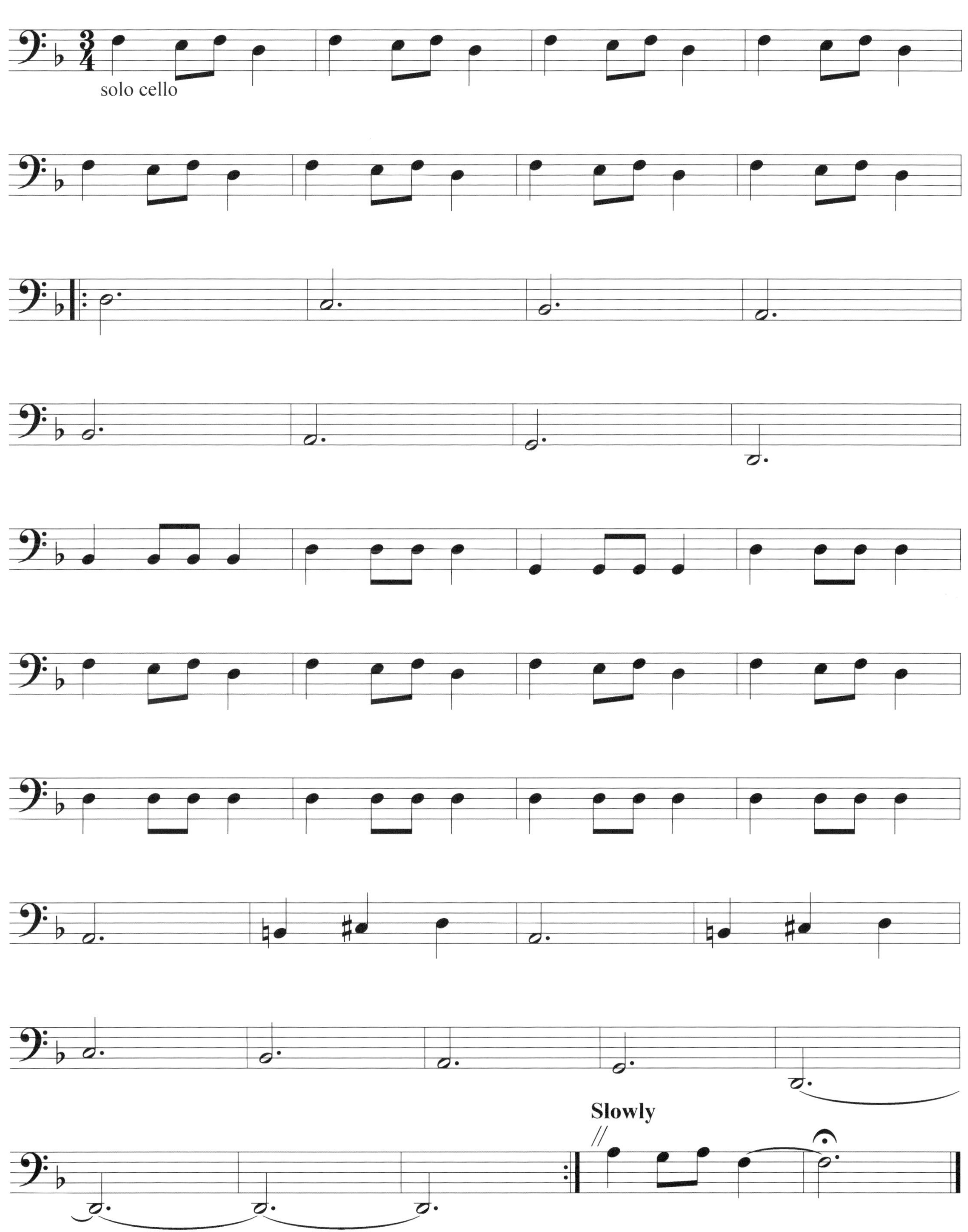

Christmas Day in the Morning

This is a medley of two tunes. The first tune is a traditional two-part fiddle tune. A *DC* is marked in the music for the tune to be played twice with repeats. The second tune is a Shetland fiddle tune entitled "Christmas Day Ida Moarning". It is marked with a *DS* for the tune to be played twice. The Coda restates the first part.

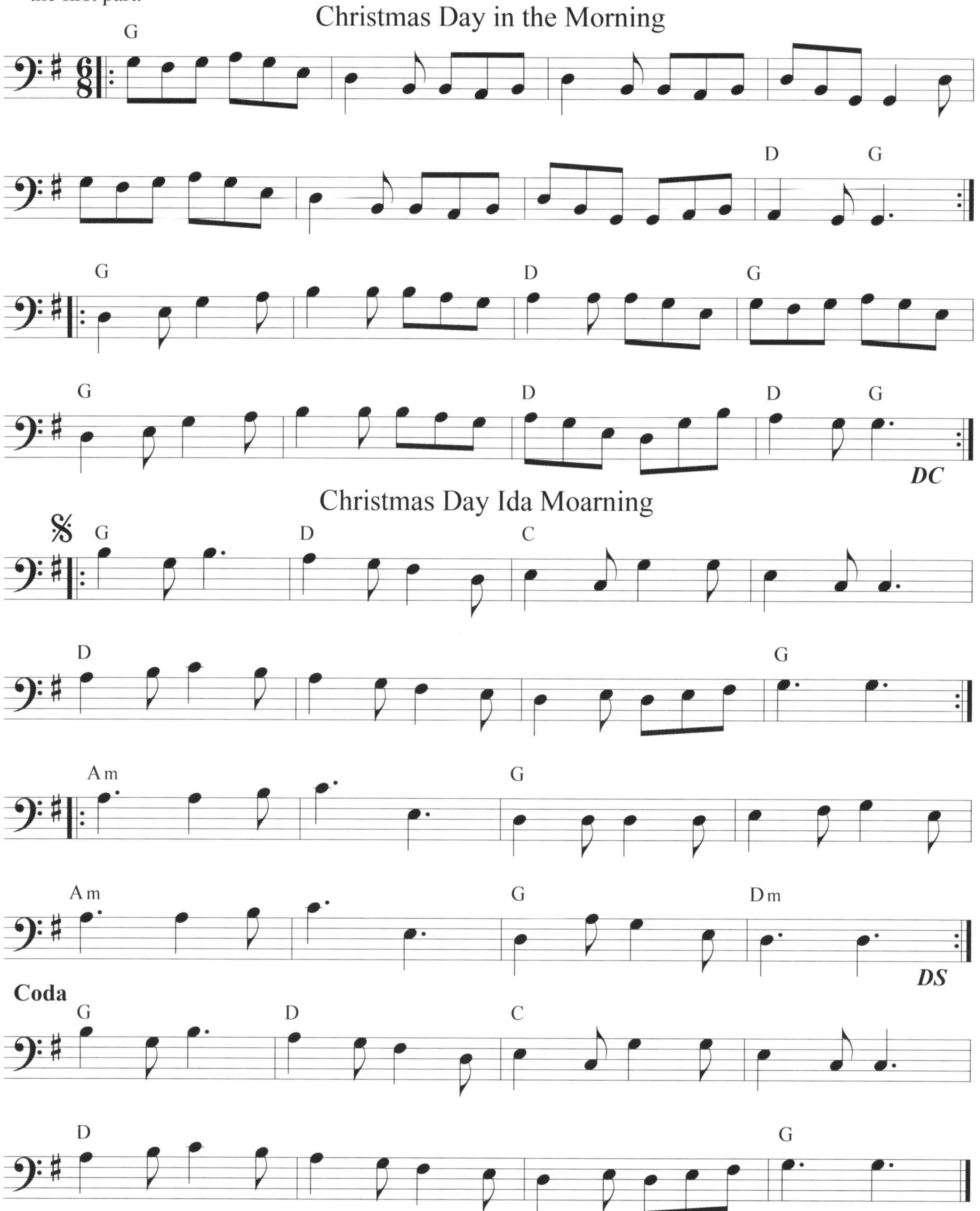

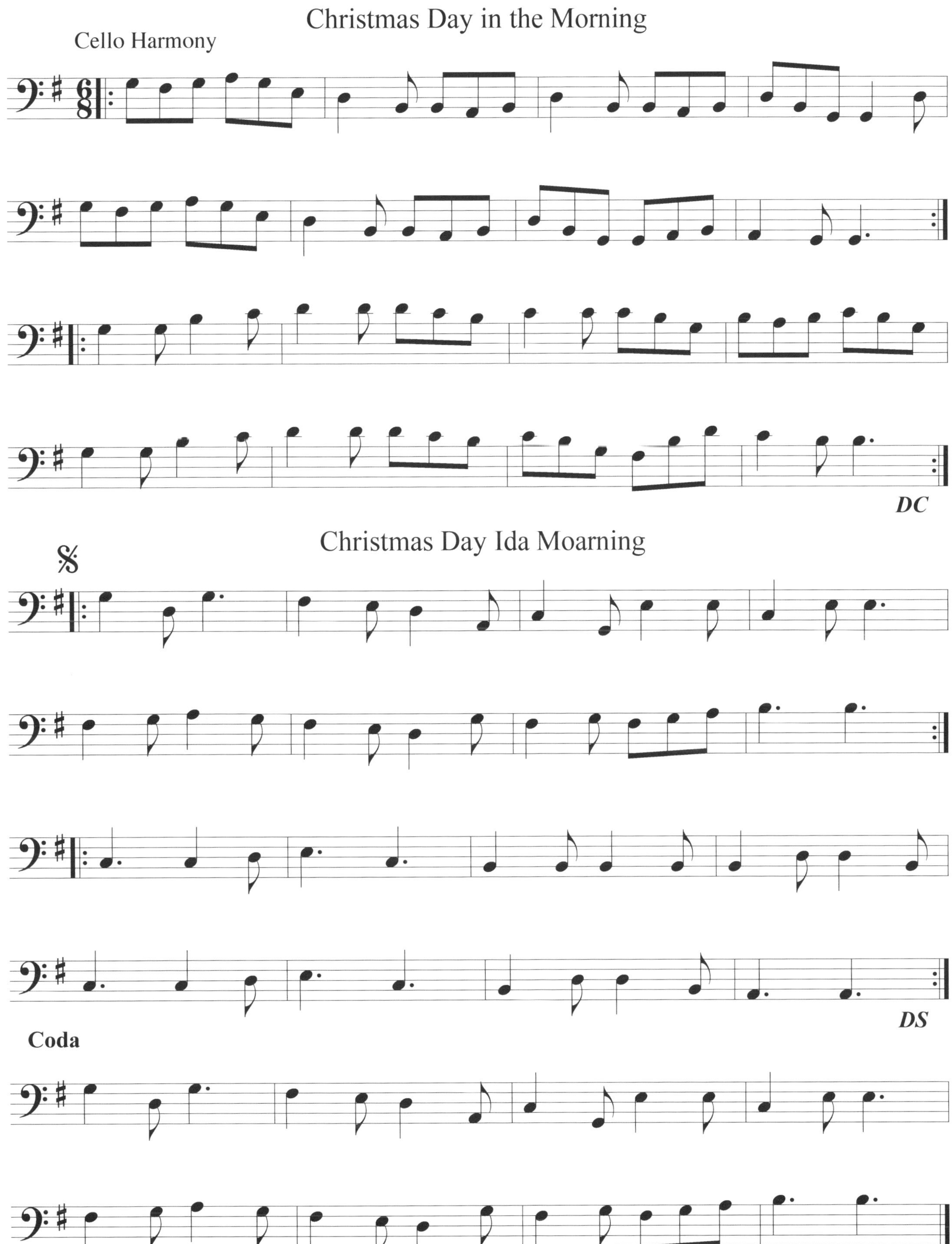
Christmas Day in the Morning
Cello Harmony
DC
Christmas Day Ida Moarning
DS
Coda

Come, Thou Long Expected Jesus

The text of this carol was written by Charles Wesley. The tune is an English hymn tune from the nineteenth century entitled "Hyfrydol". It was written by Rowland Prichard.

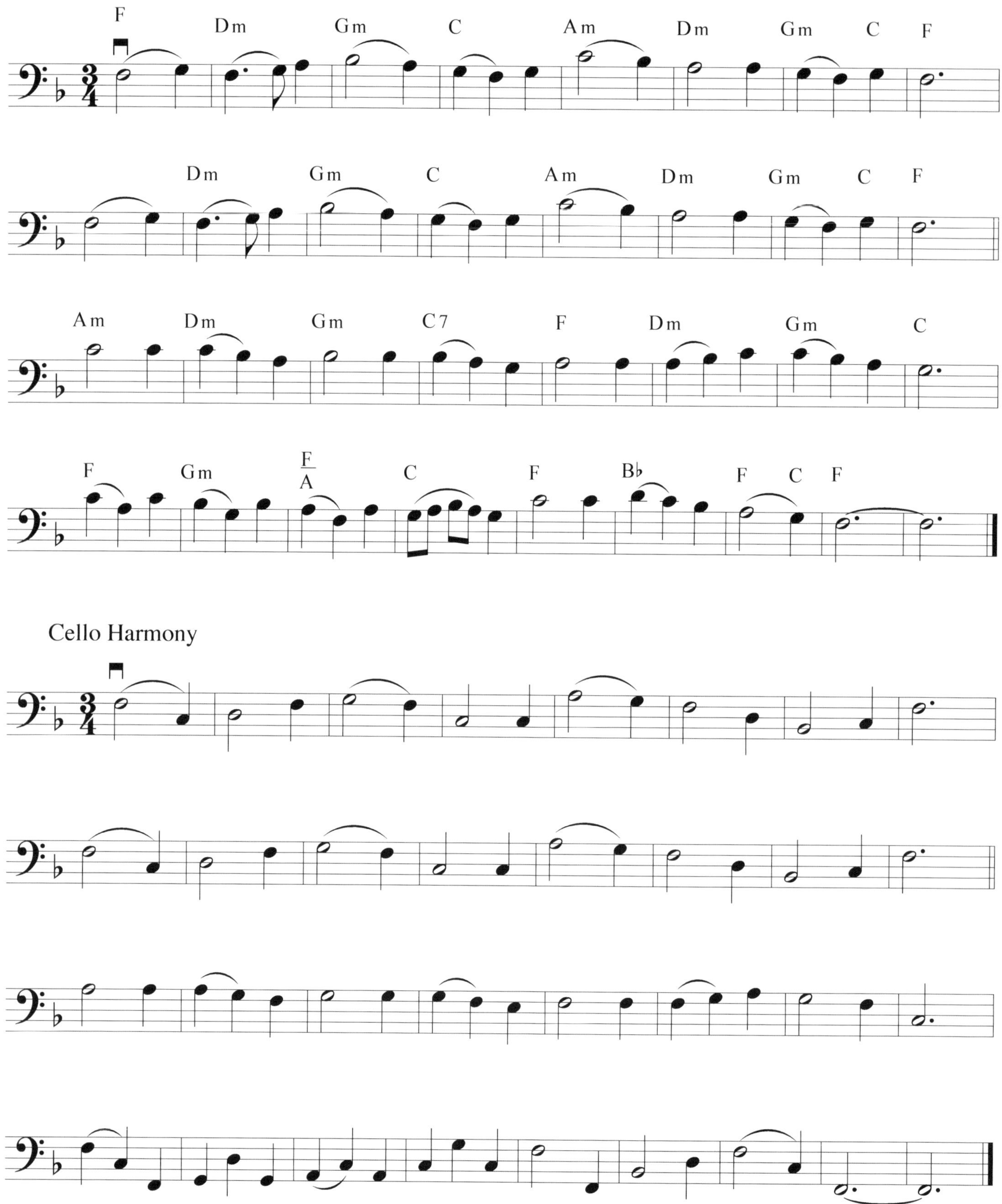

The Coventry Carol

The *Pageant of the Shearman and Tailors* was part of the cycle of mystery plays performed in Coventry in the sixteenth century. This plaintive carol was part of the pageant. It was sung by the mothers trying to keep their babies asleep when Herod's soldiers were killing all of the young males.

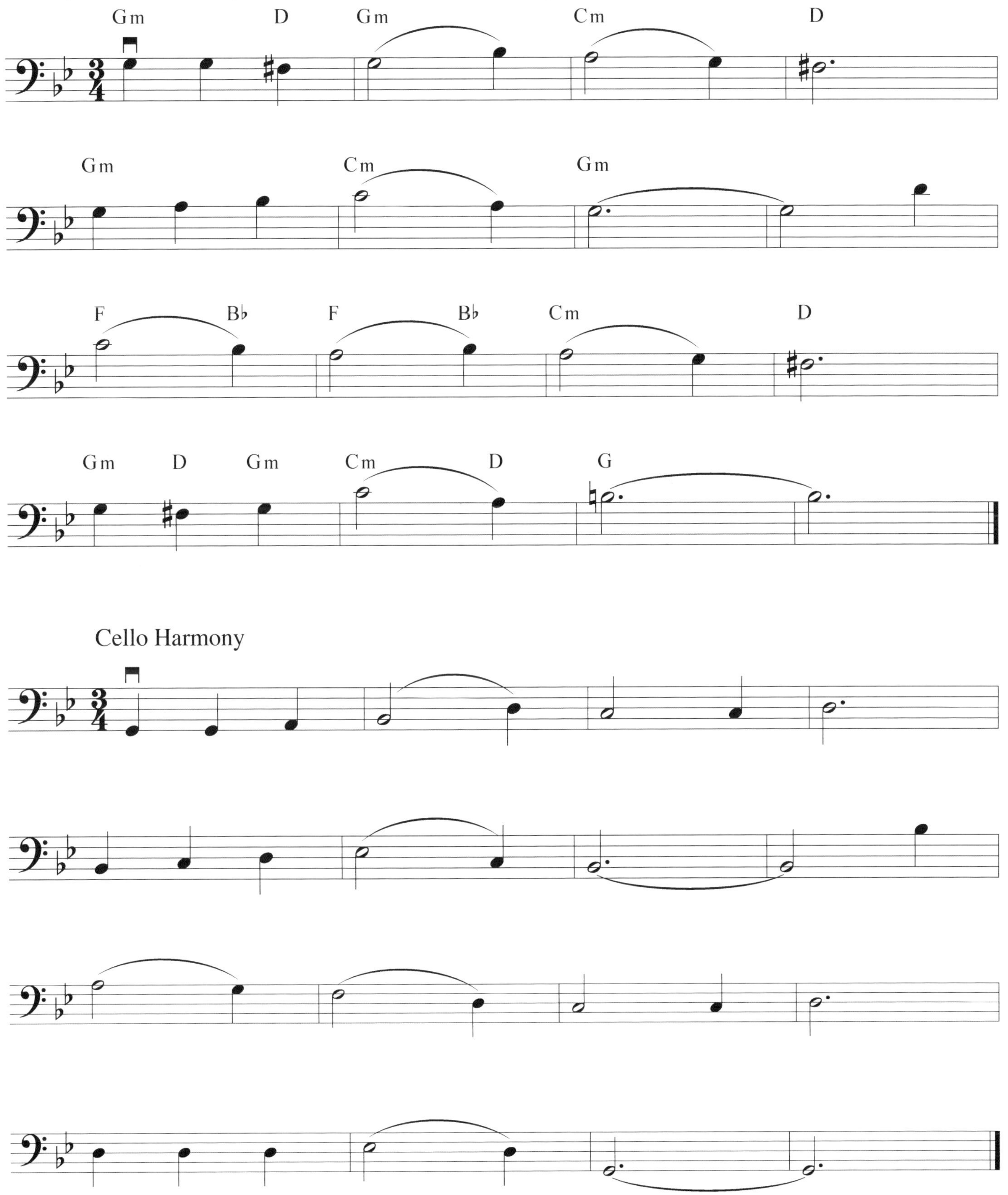

Deck the Halls

The original title of this tune is "Nos Galan", which is Welsh for New Year's Eve. It first appeared in 1784 in *Musical and Poetical Relicks of the Welsh Bards* by harpist, Edward Jones. In 1881 the tune was published as "Deck the Halls" in the *Franklin Square Song Collection*.

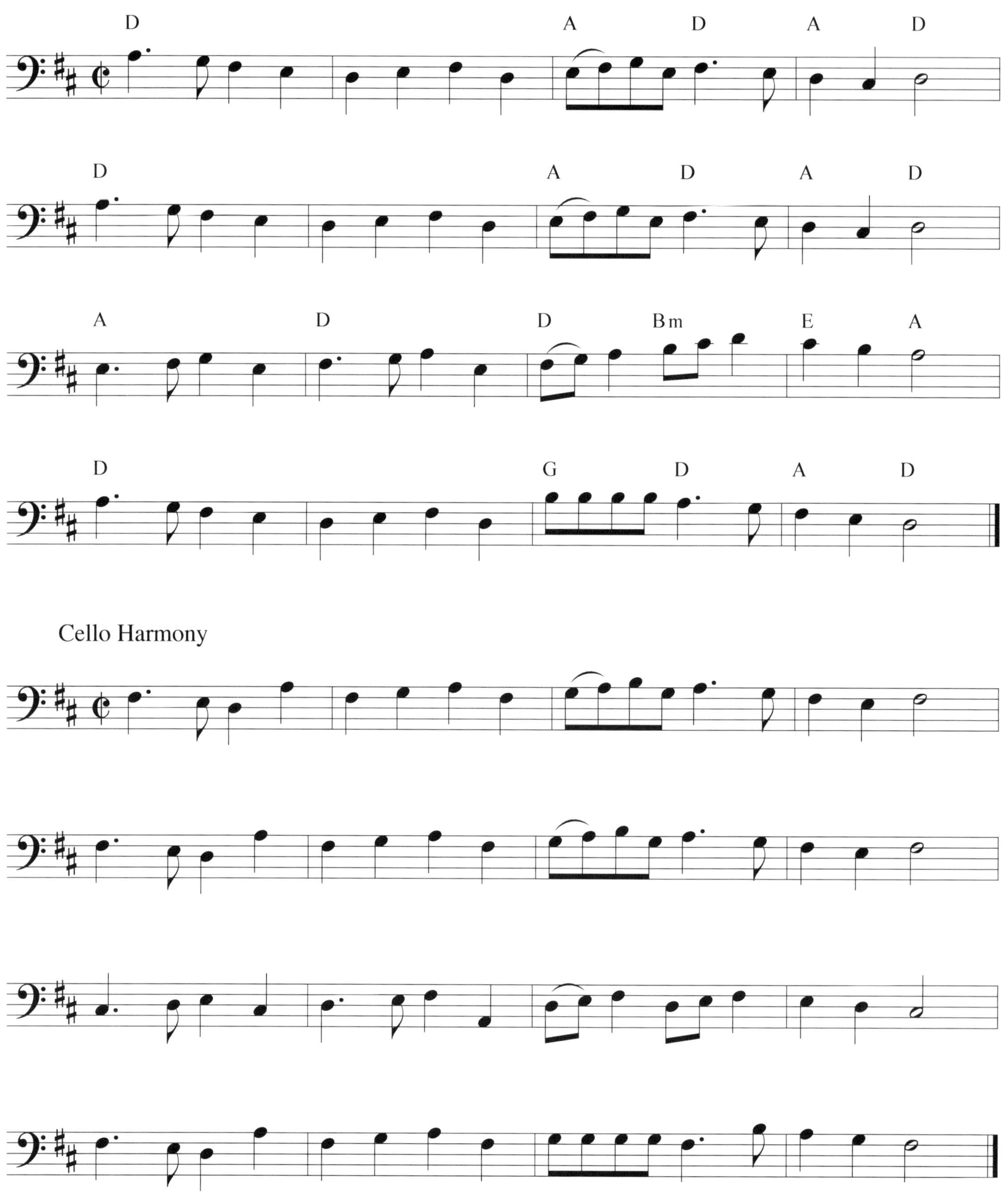

Ding! Dong! Merrily on High

Originally a dance tune called a "branle", this tune was published in 1589 and 1596 in the *Orchésographie* of Thoinot Arbeau. George R. Woodward wrote the text and published it as a carol in 1924 in *The Cambridge Carol Book.*

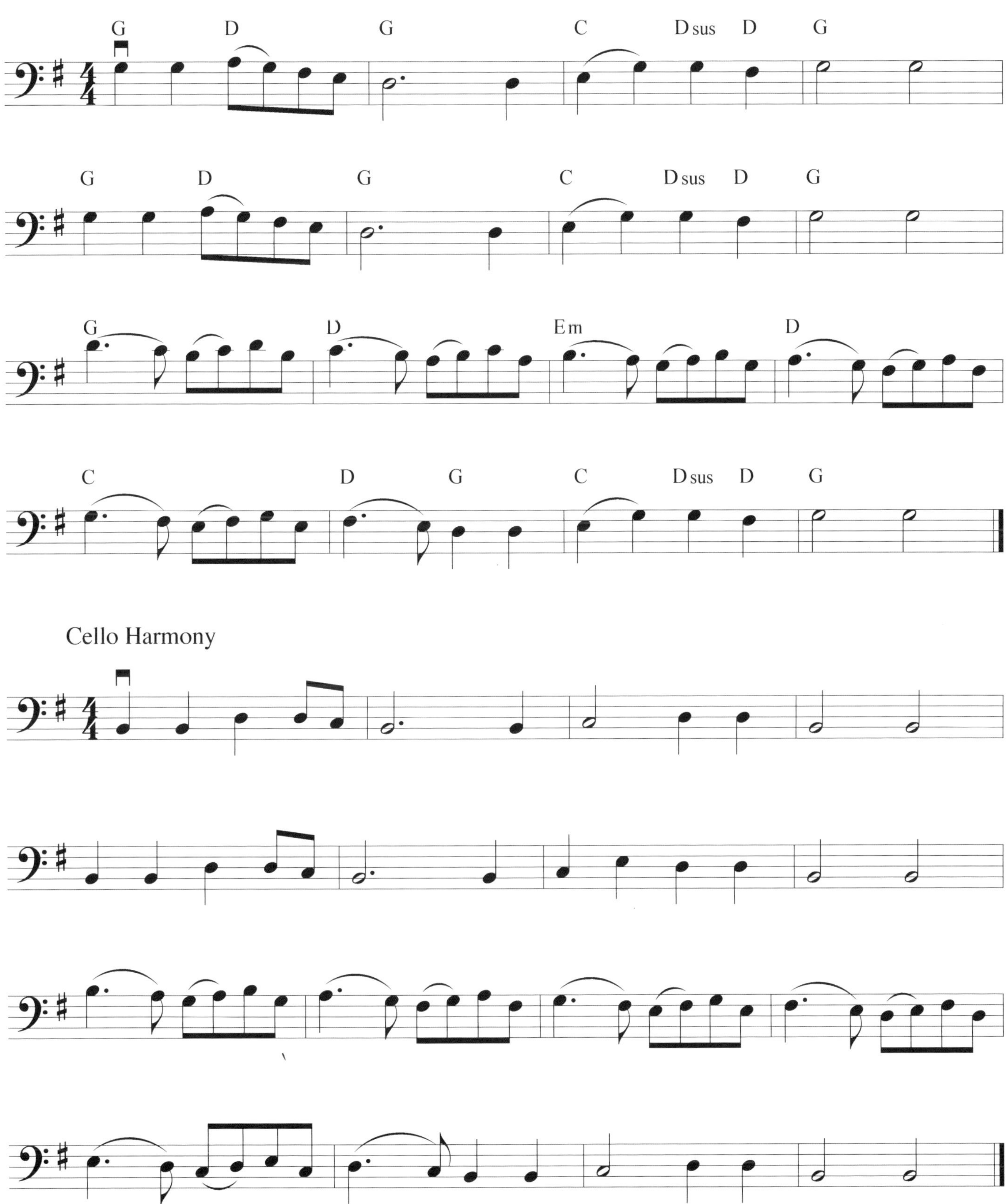

Drive the Cold Winter Away

All Hail to the Days

This melody is found in John Playford's *The Dancing Master*. The lyric entitled "All Hail to the Days" dates from a broadside published in 1625. Other lyrics are also sung to this melody, including "The Praise of Christmas".

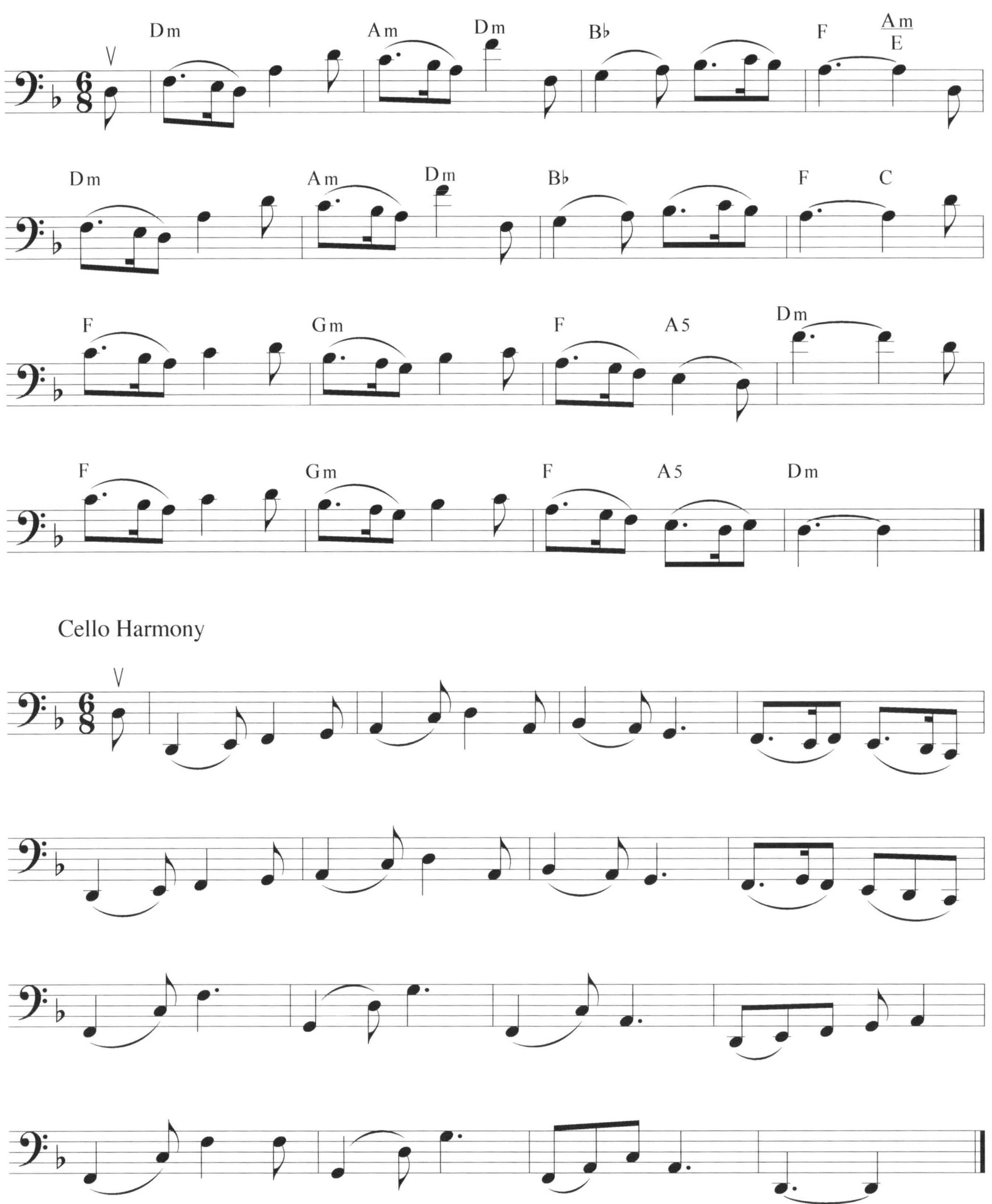

The First Noel

This carol was first published in 1833 in William Sandys *Christmas Carols Ancient and Modern.* It is a traditional English carol of the sixteenth or seventeenth century. Noel is often spelled Nowell.

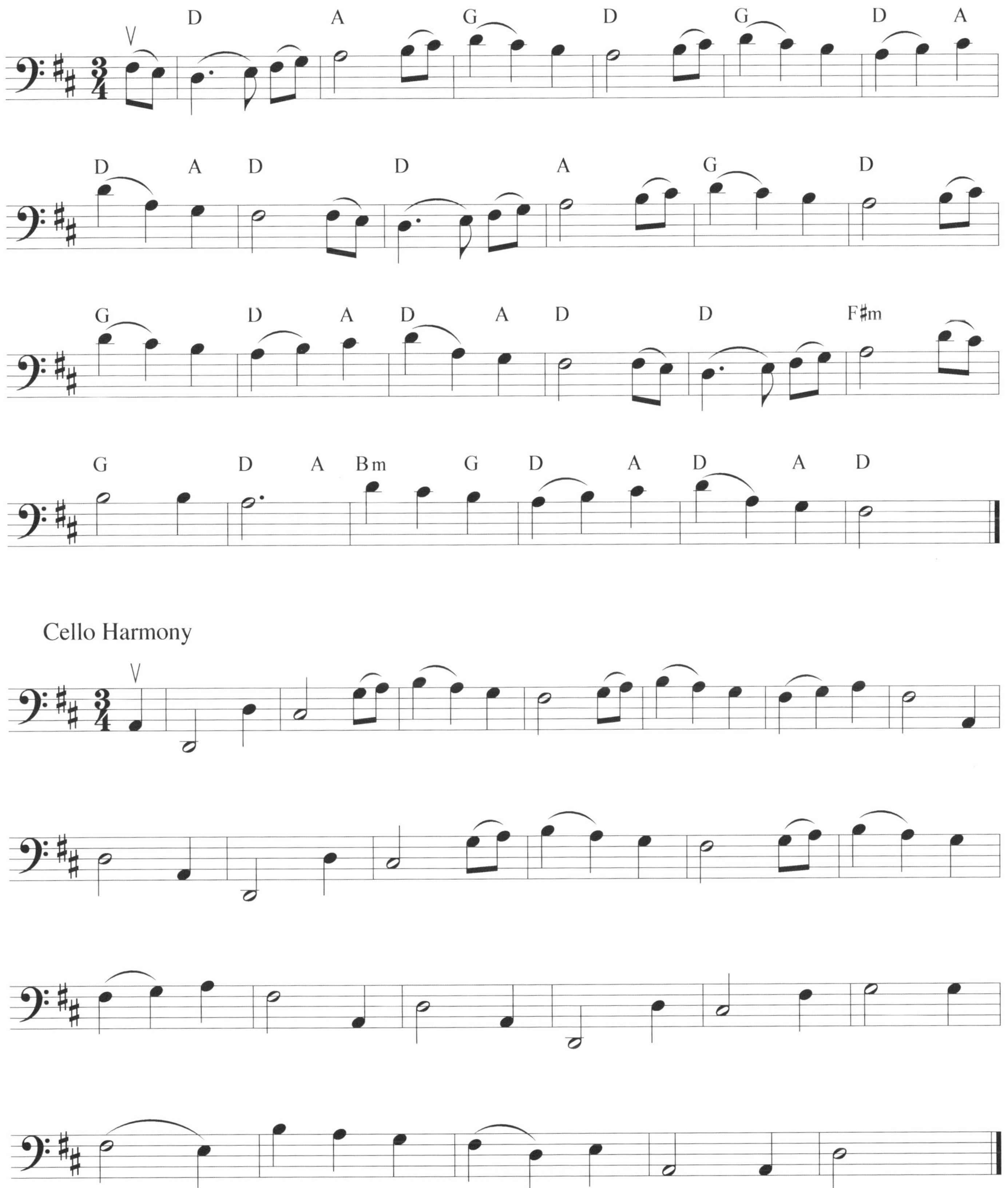

Frost and Snow

This traditional hornpipe is found in *O'Neill's Music of Ireland.* It is in Dorian mode, which is a minor key with a raised sixth degree. This gives the tune a special beauty. The harmony part is written in traditional "fiddle" style, a third or fourth above the melody.

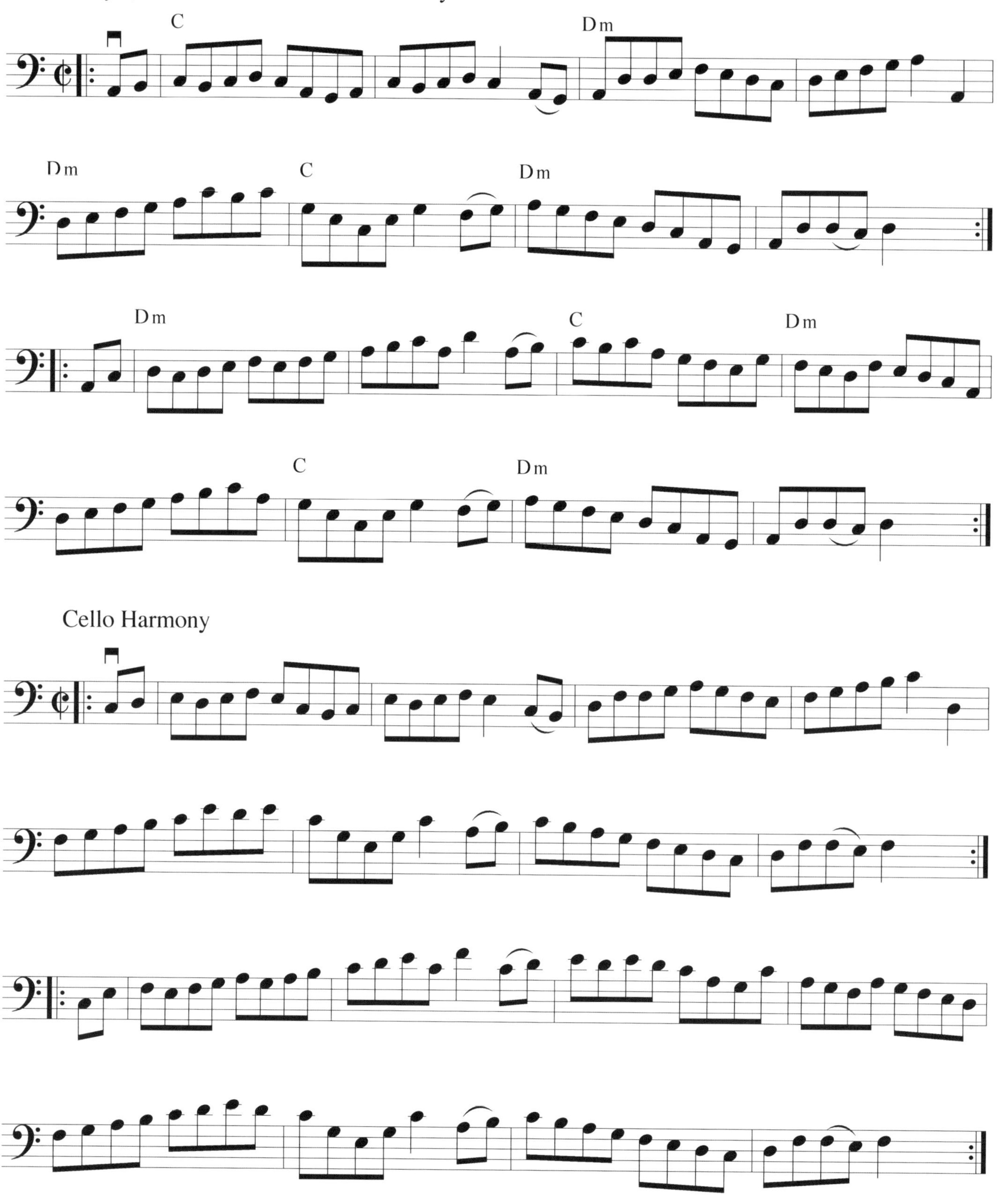

Go Tell It on the Mountain

This is a traditional American spiritual, sung and played in a lively manner. It should be performed in a swing style, so the dotted eighth-sixteenth rhythms sound as quarter-eighth triplets. In this arrangement, the first section is repeated, giving an overall AABA form to the instrumental version. The cello harmony part is written as a jazz bass line.

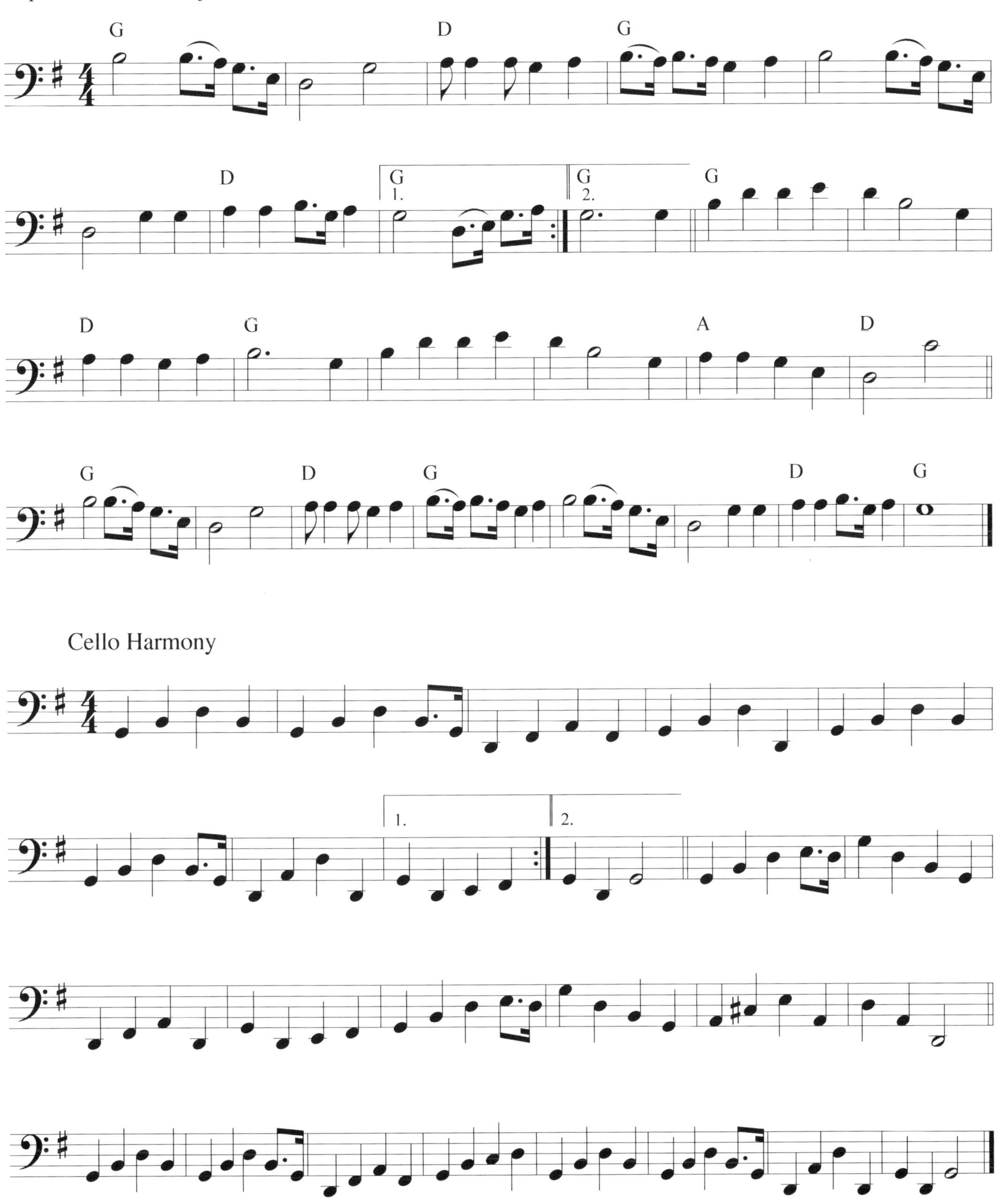

God Rest Ye Merry Gentlemen

"Chestnut" is the name of this tune, which goes back to John Playford's 1651 publication of *The English Dancing Master*. It is the standard melody associated with "God Rest Ye Merry Gentlemen".

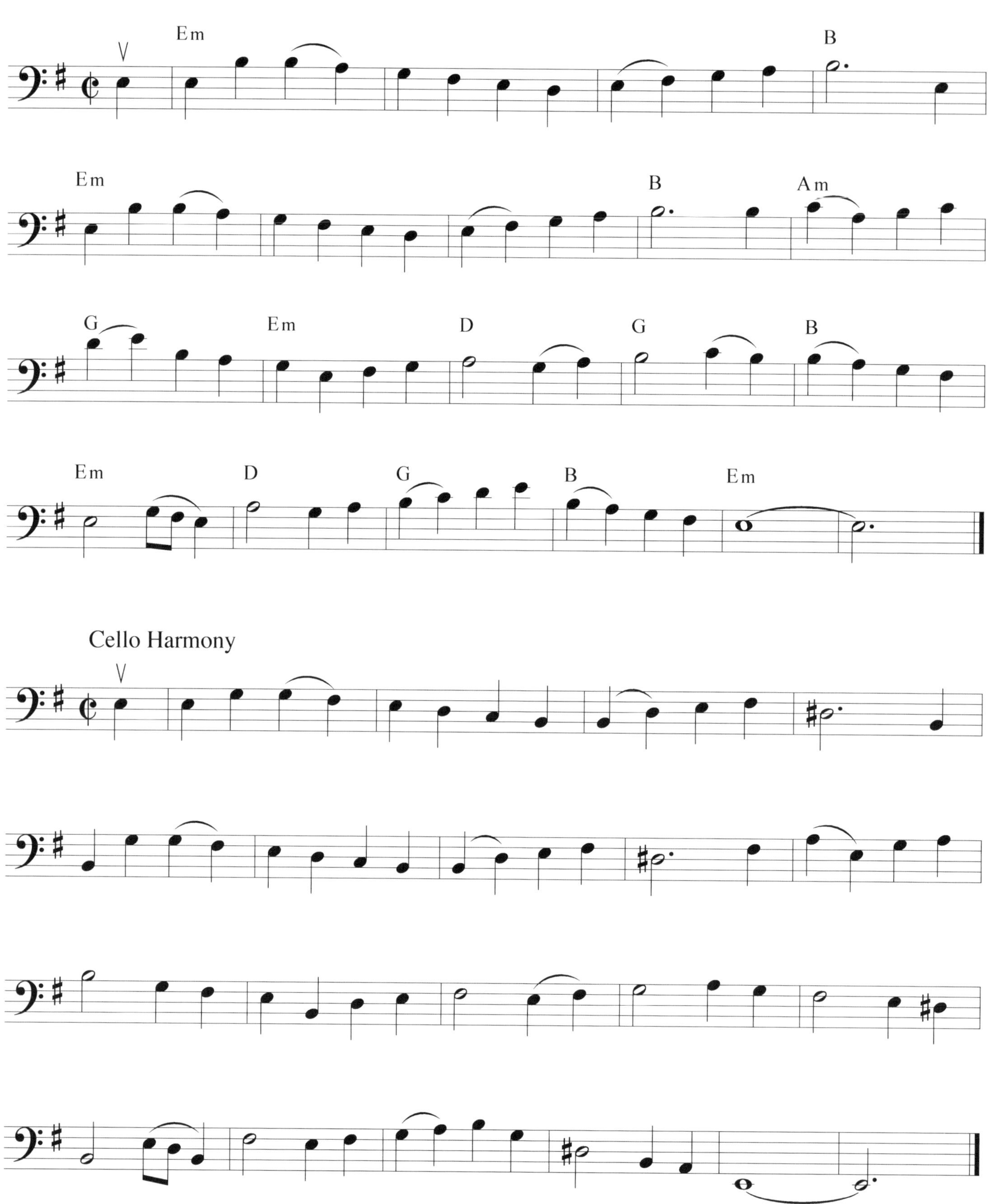

The Golden Carol of the Wisemen

Although this traditional Old English carol is not often heard, it is very lyrical and quite fun to play. It was published in Boston in 1916 in *Carols Old and Carols New*.

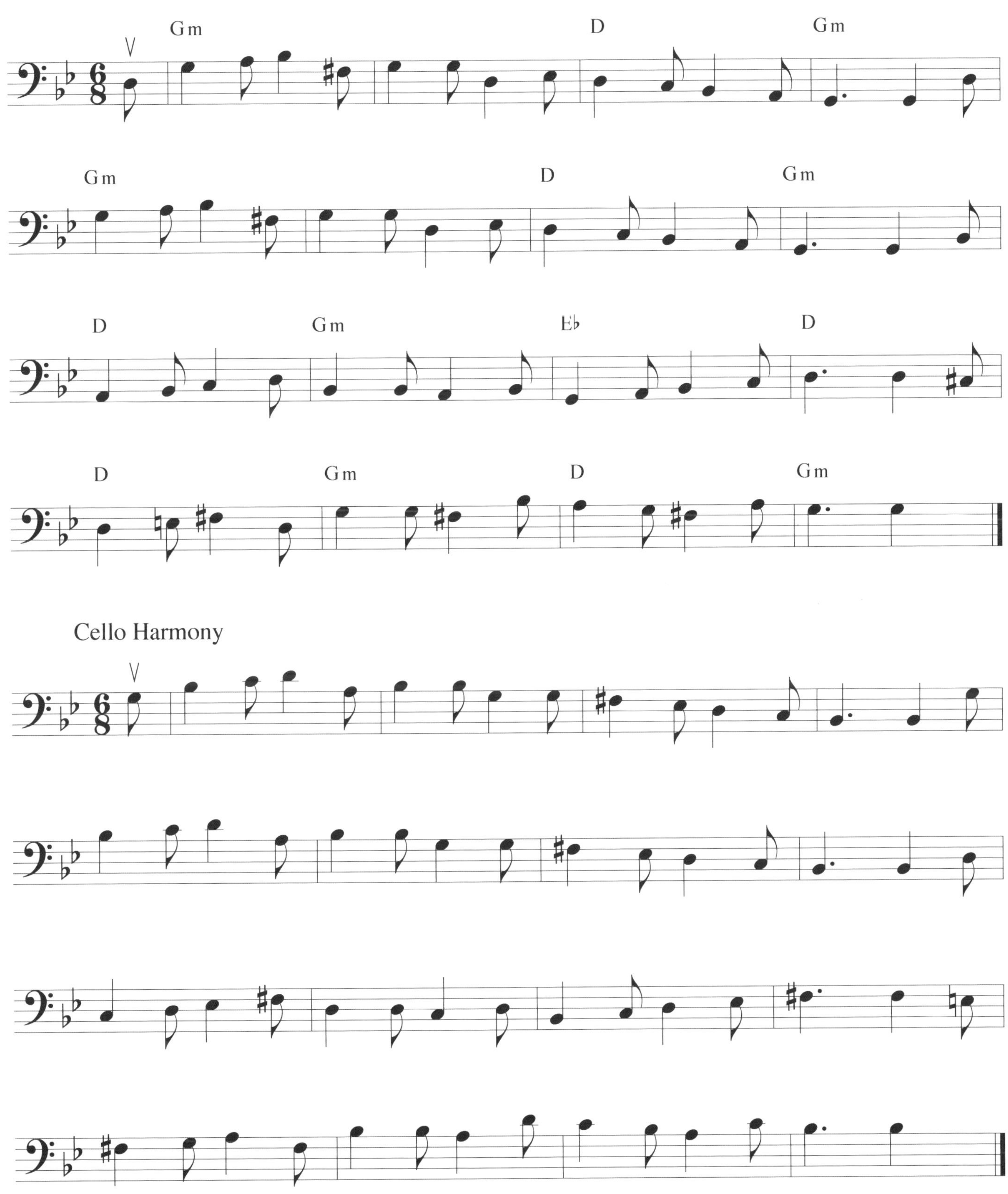

Good Christian Men Rejoice

The original title of this carol is "In dulci jubilo". It is said that it was taught to Heinrich Seuse, a German Dominican monk, by angels. The earliest source of the carol is a Leipzig University manuscript from around 1400.

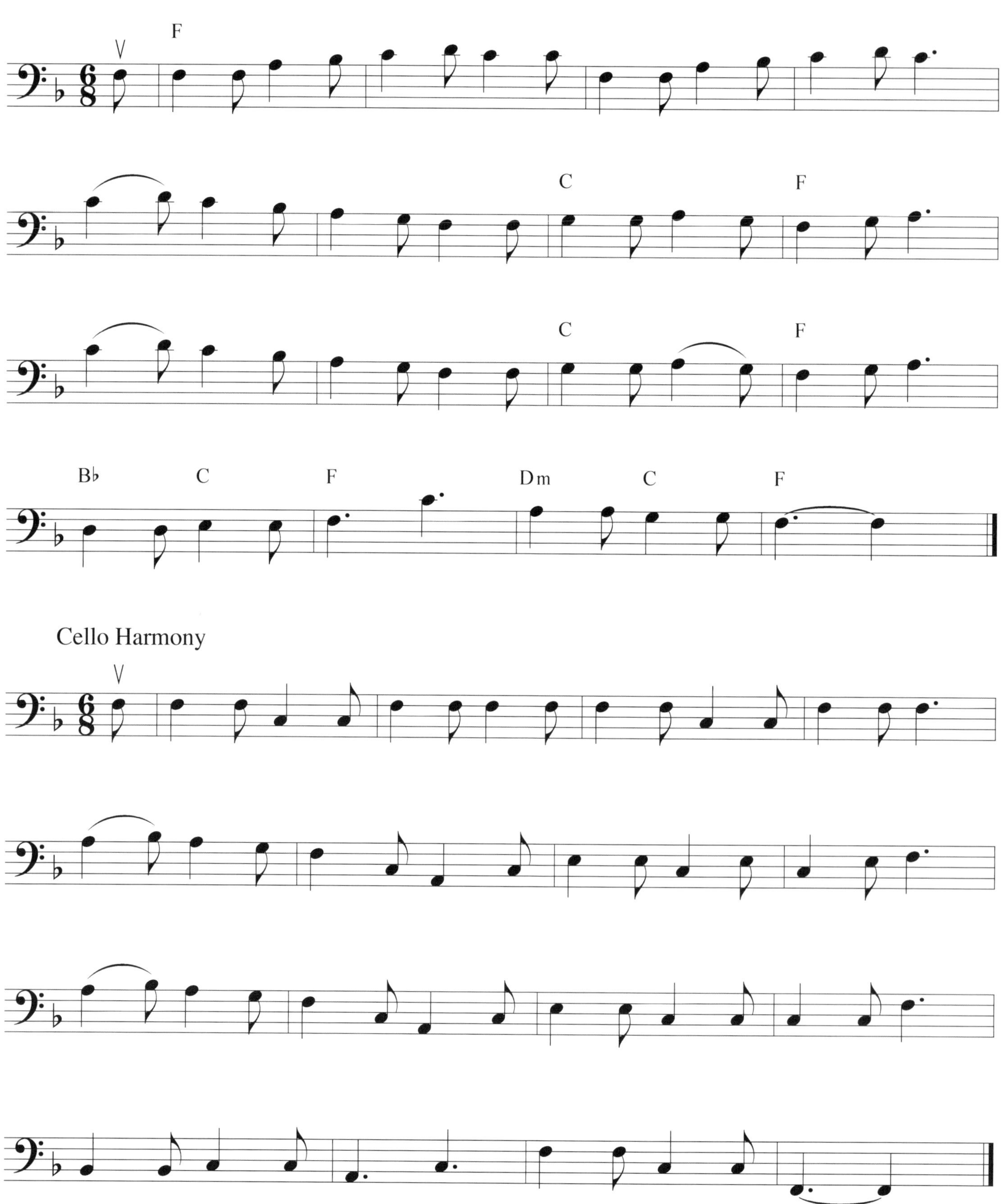

Good King Wenceslas

Gentle Mary Laid Her Child

"Good King Wenceslas" refers to Václav the Good, who reigned in Bohemia from 922 to 929. J. M. Neale wrote the text in 1853 and used a "spring song" tune found in *Piae Cantiones* written in 1582. The lullaby "Gentle Mary Laid Her Child" is also sung to this melody.

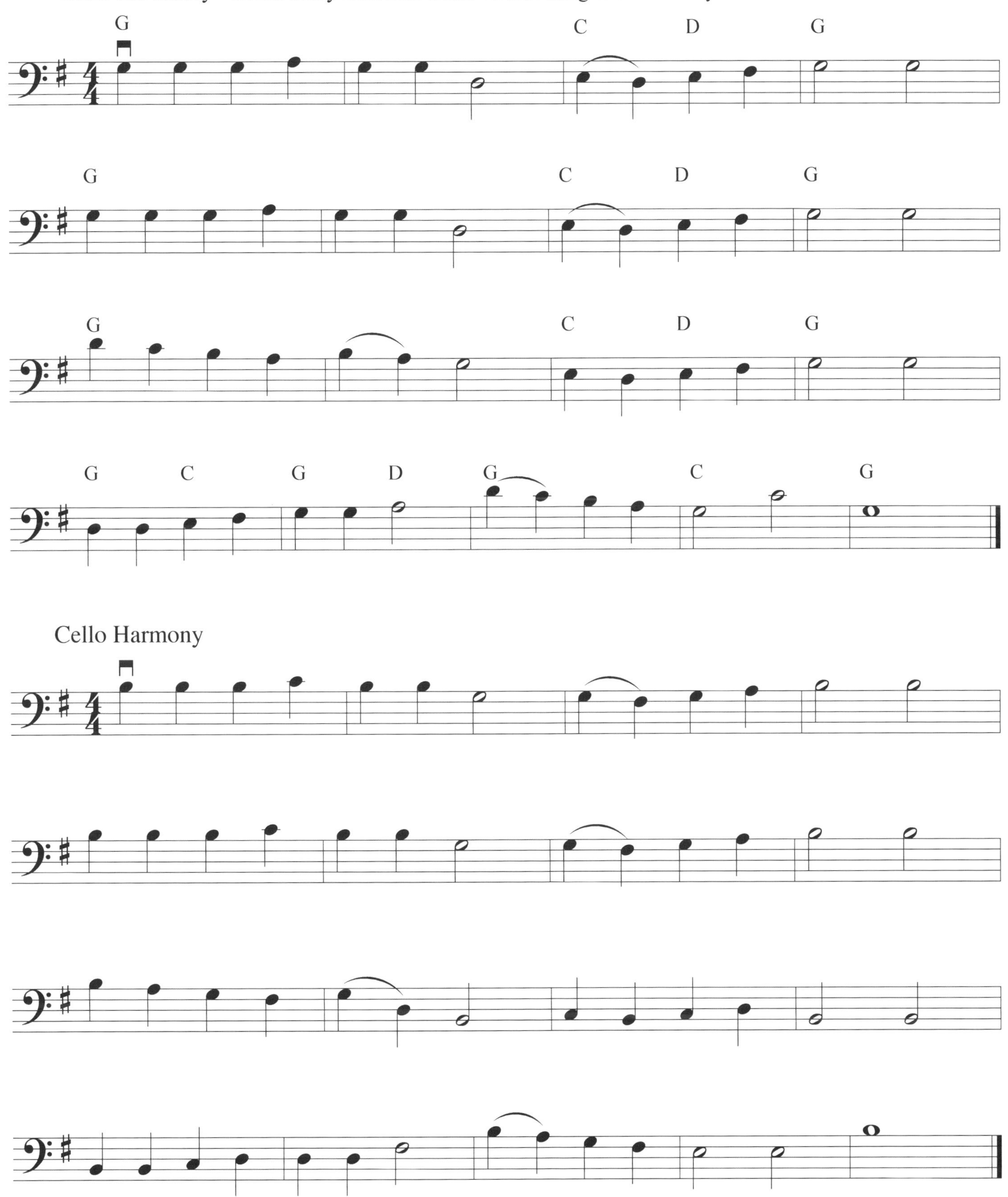

The Gooding Carol

This is a traditional English carol about the passing of the Christmas season. To "go a-gooding" is to pay a good luck visit, traveling from door to door singing carols such as this one.

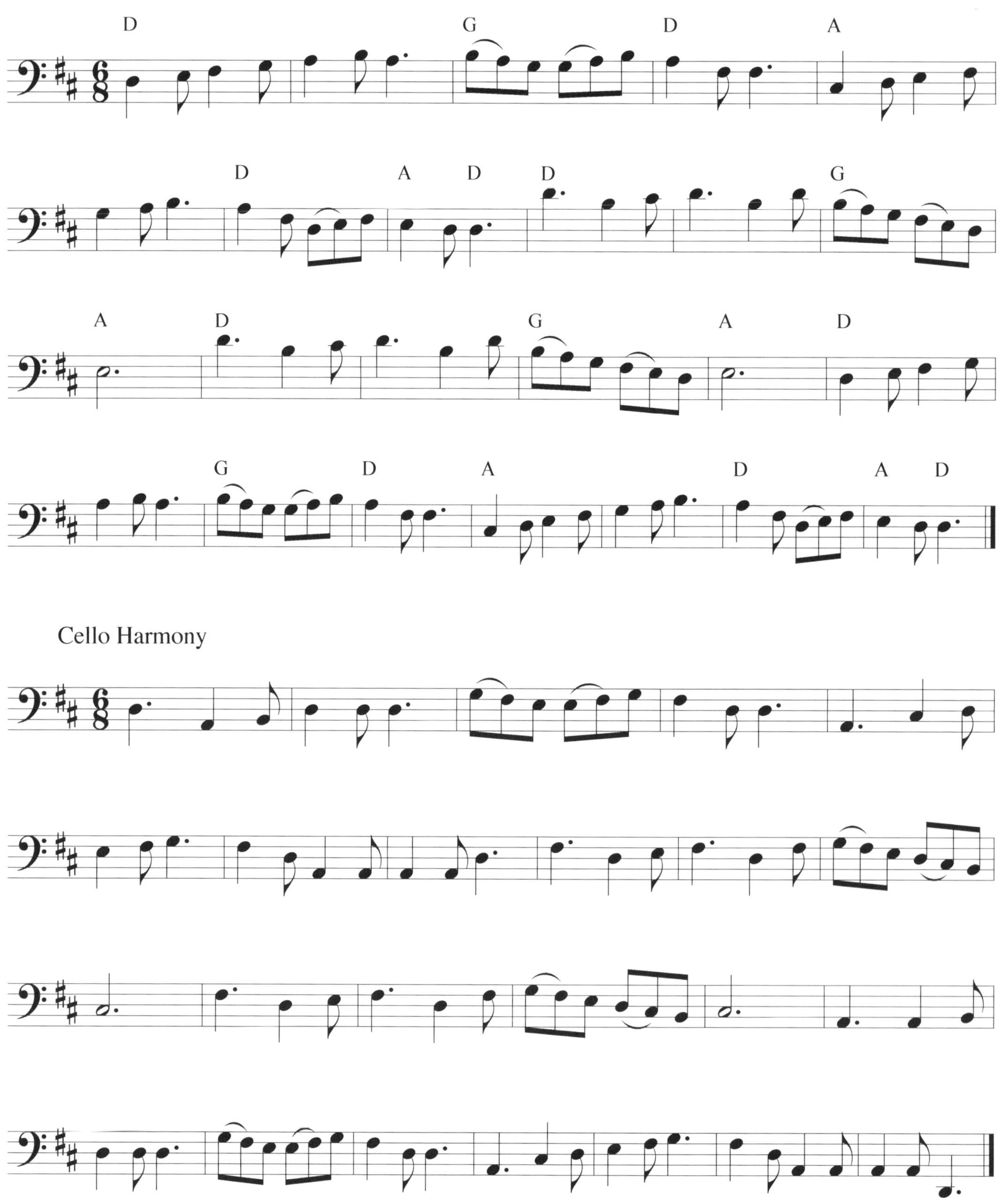

Hark! The Herald Angels Sing

Charles Wesley titled the text to this carol "Hymn for Christmas Day" when he published it in 1739. Felix Mendelssohn wrote the tune in 1840 as part of a piece for the Gutenberg Festival in Leipzig. William Cummings adapted Wesley's text to Mendelssohn's melody in 1856 and "Hark! The Herald" became a classic carol.

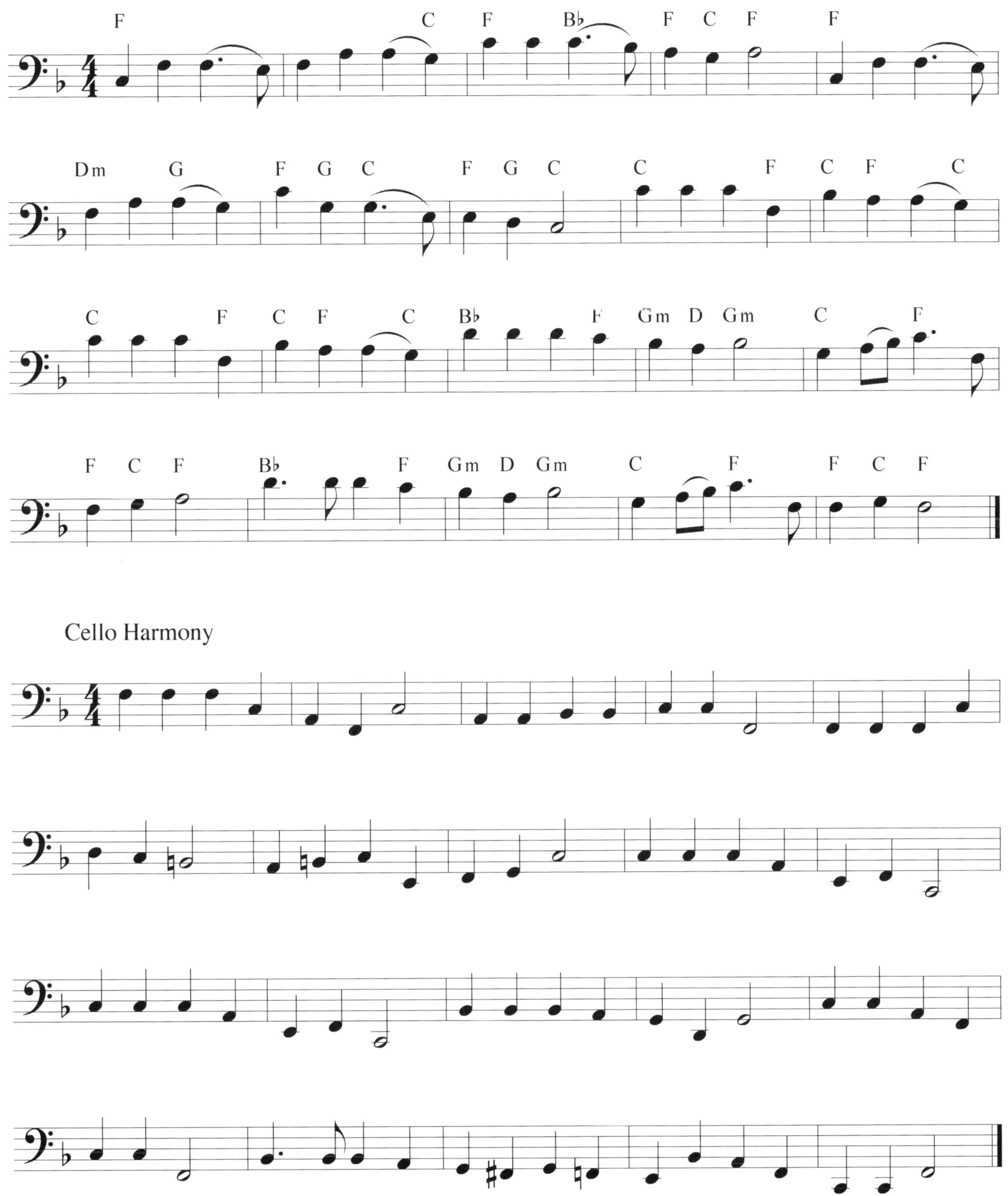

He is Born, the Divine Christ Child

This is a traditional French tune also known as "Christ is Born a Child on Earth". It first appeared in print in 1862 as "Ancien air de chasse" in Grosjean's *Airs des nöels lorrain.*

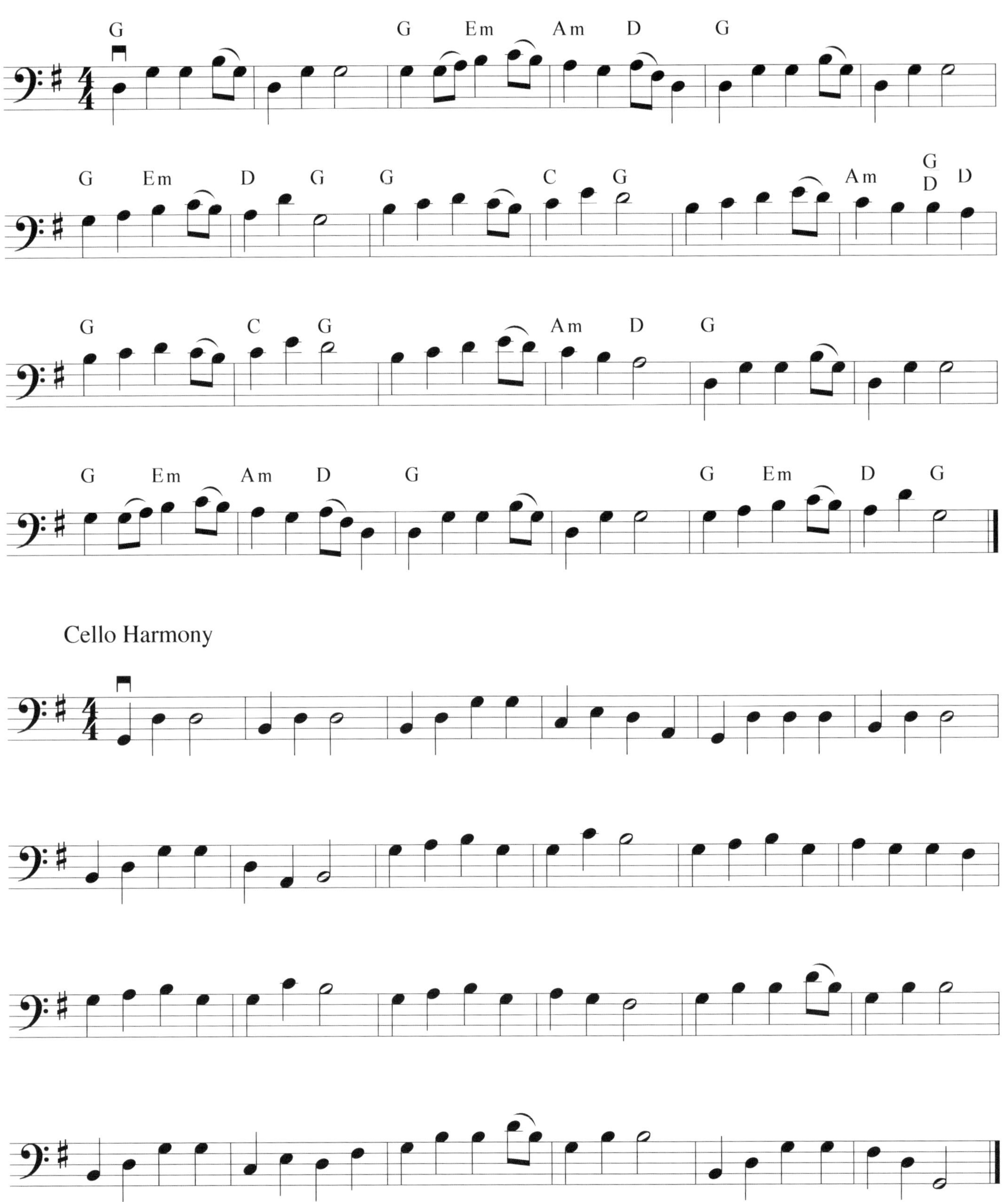

The Holly and the Ivy

This ancient English carol is based on medieval symbols of good and evil. The eight measure melody is presented here with the lyric rhythms of the verse followed by the rhythms of the chorus. The second eight uses a variation on the chord changes.

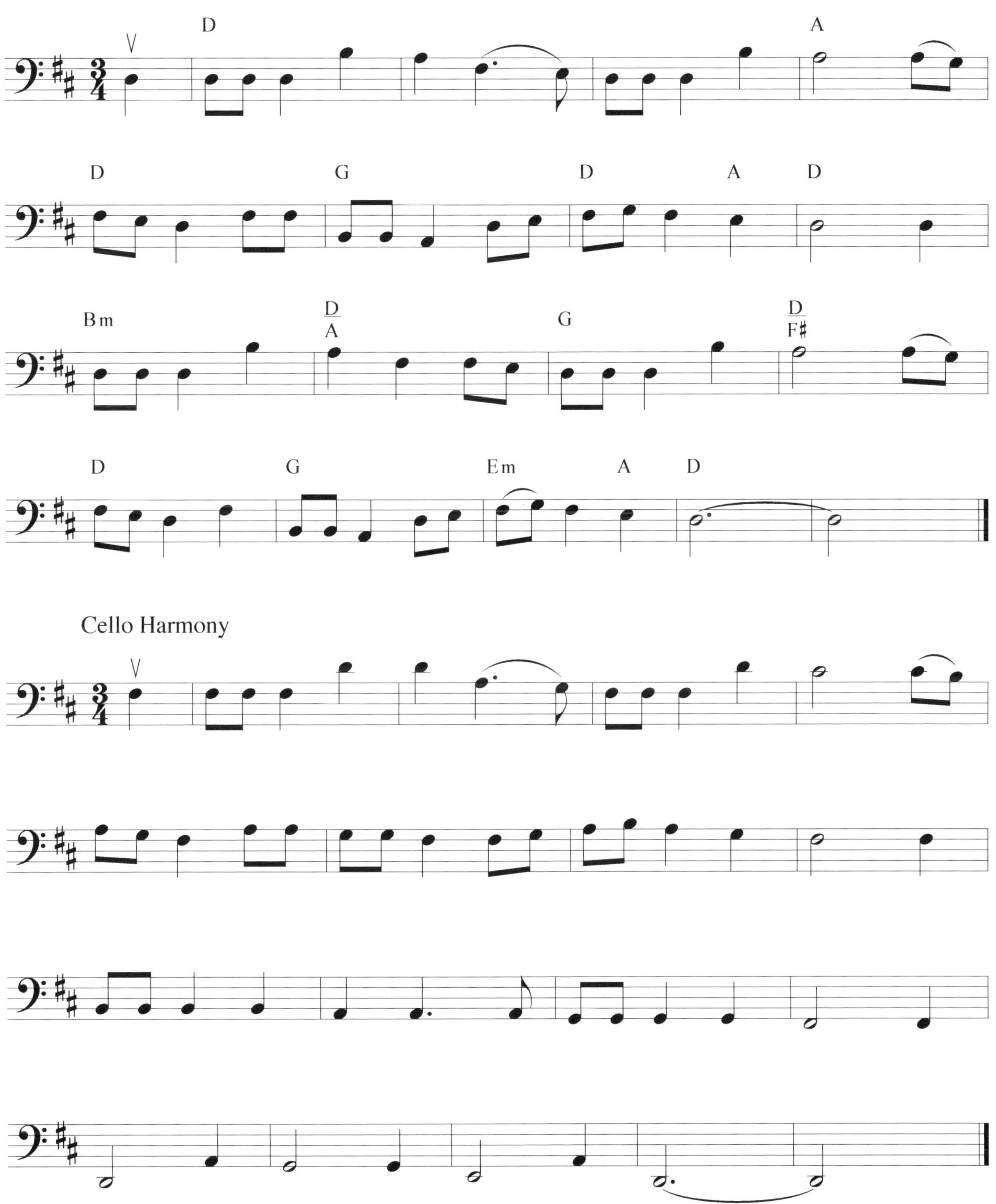

The Holly Bears a Berry

The Saint Day Carol

"The Holly Bears a Berry" is also known as the "Saint Day Carol" because Reverend G. H. Doble transcribed it from singers in Saint Day, England. The eighth notes are performed in swing style.

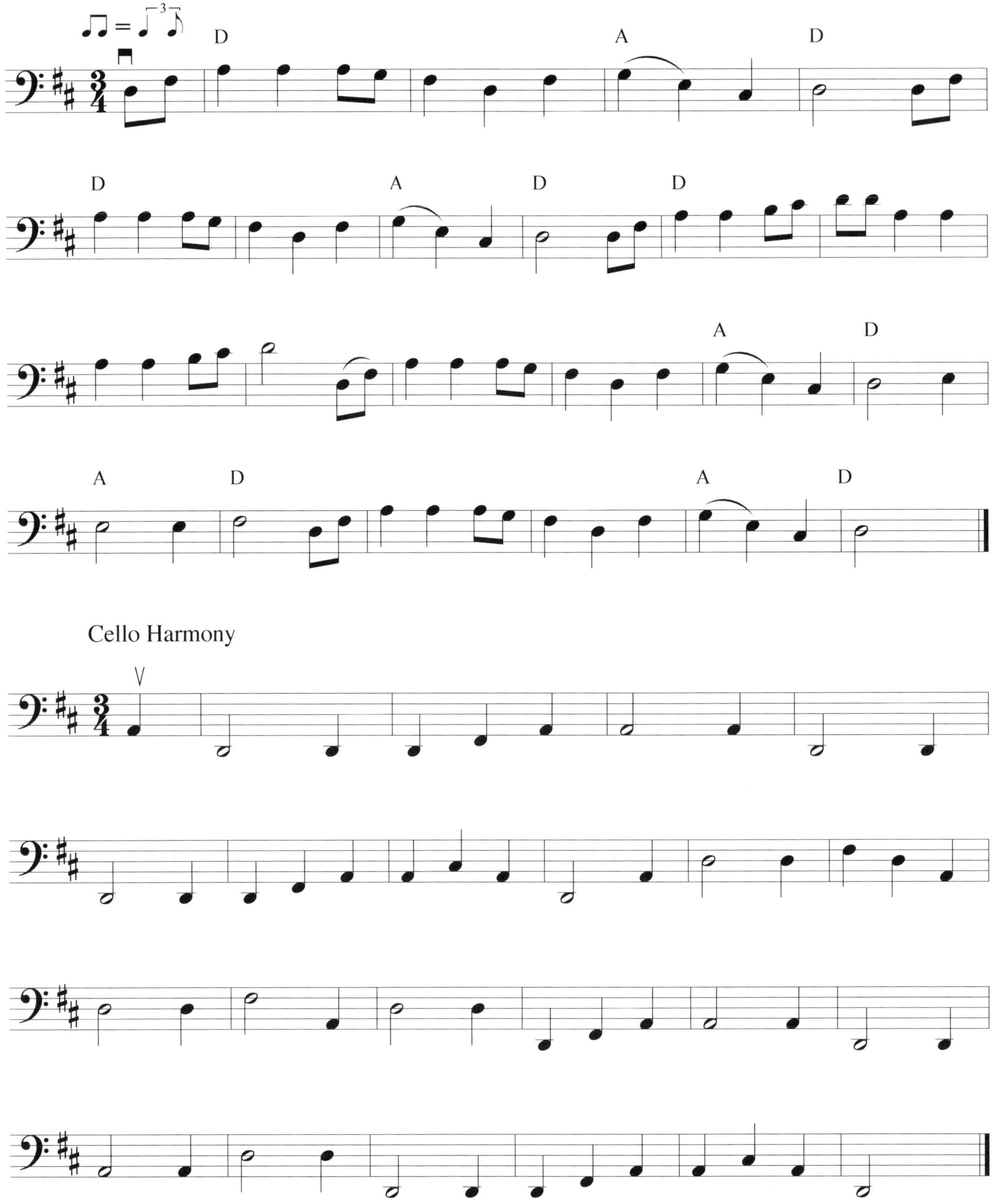

A CELLO CHRISTMAS

CRAIG DUNCAN

Piano Accompaniment

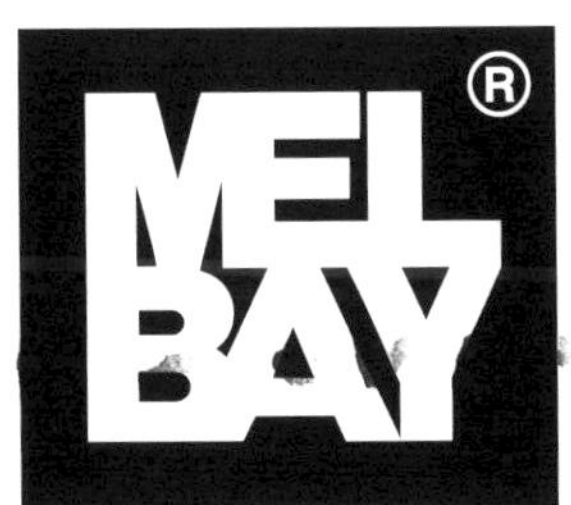

WWW.MELBAY.COM

Index of Tunes

Preface

A Cello Christmas contains Christmas and holiday tunes from a wide variety of sources. Old English, French, German, Austrian, Irish, American and Ukranian carols are included alongside the traditional hymn carols. All of these melodies are arranged for cello solo and have suggested bowings, guitar chords, piano accompaniment and background information. A second cello part included with each tune makes this a useful cello duet book. The collection is a great resource of traditional Christmas music for cellists.

Angels, from the Realms of Glory

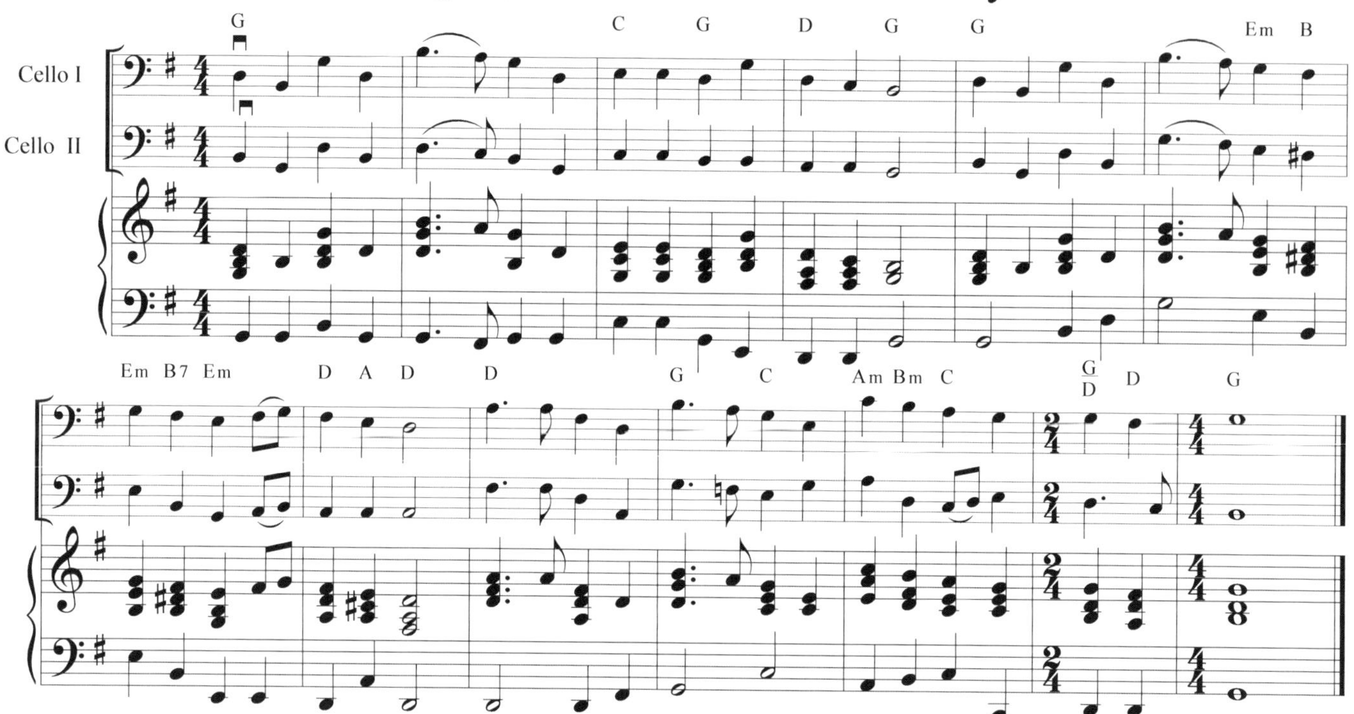

Angels We Have Heard on High

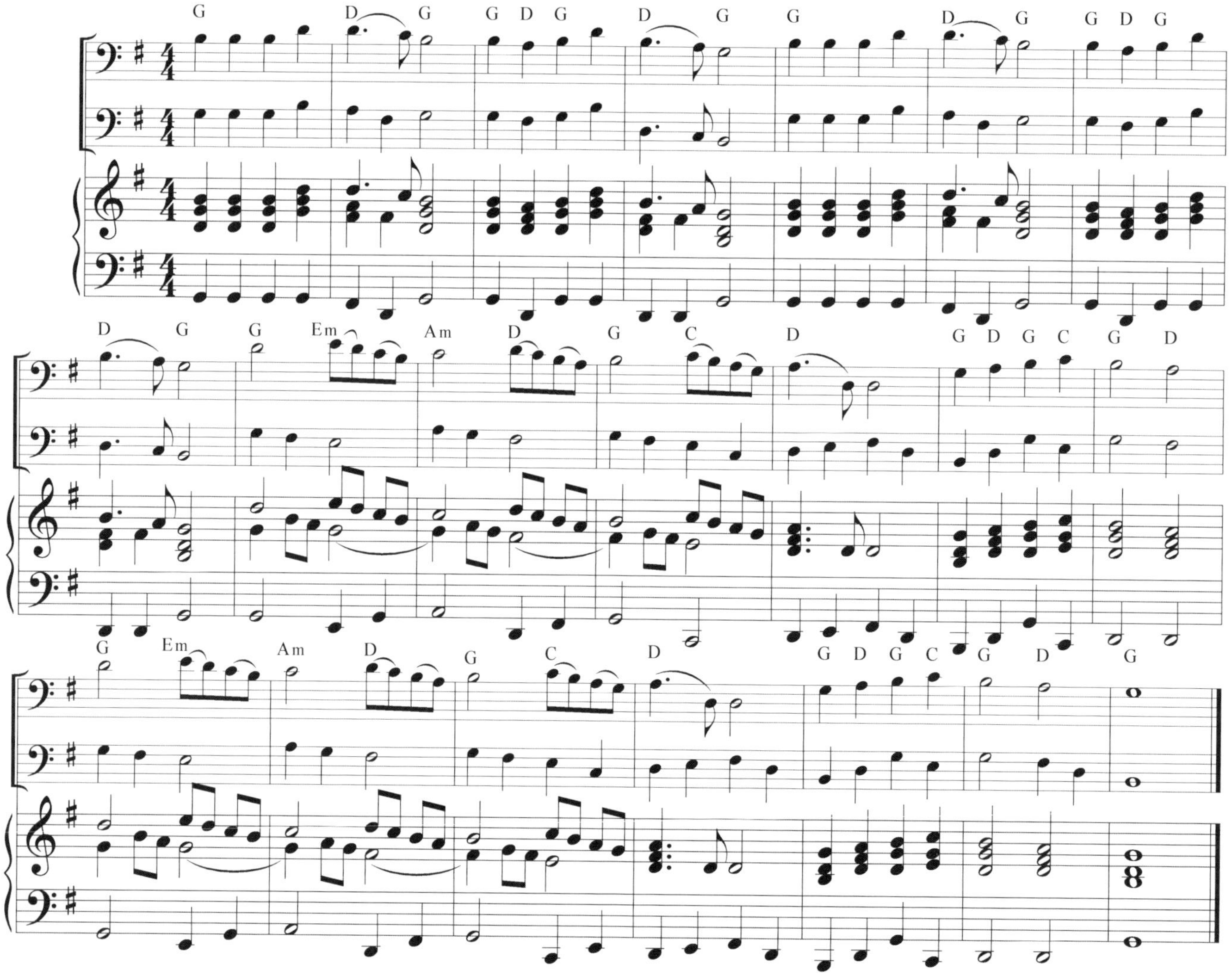

G D G G D G D G G D G G D G

D G G Em Am D G C D G D G C G D

G Em Am D G C D G D G C G D G

As Lately We Watched

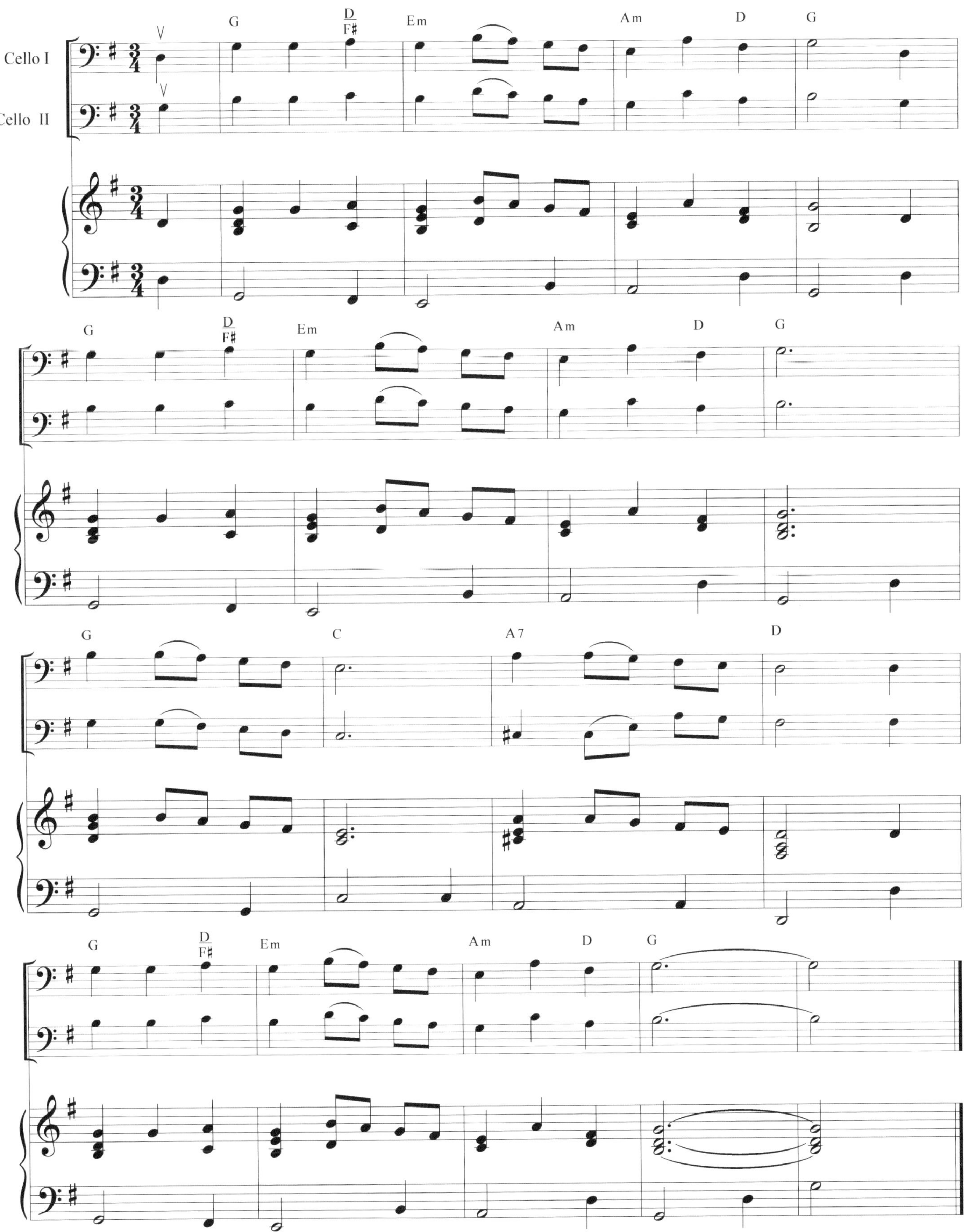

Away in a Manger

William J. Fitzpatrick

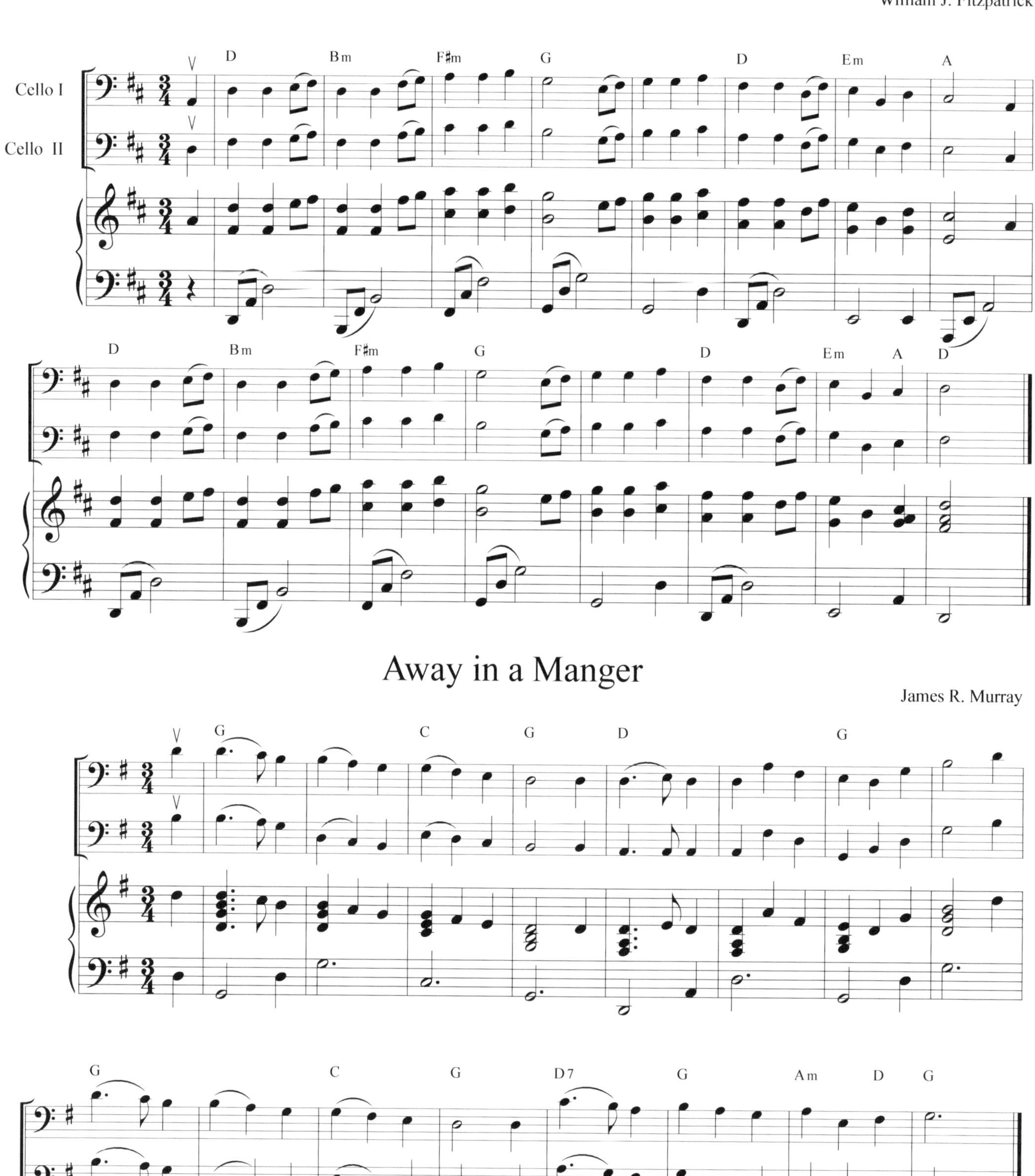

Away in a Manger

James R. Murray

Blessed Be That Maid Marie

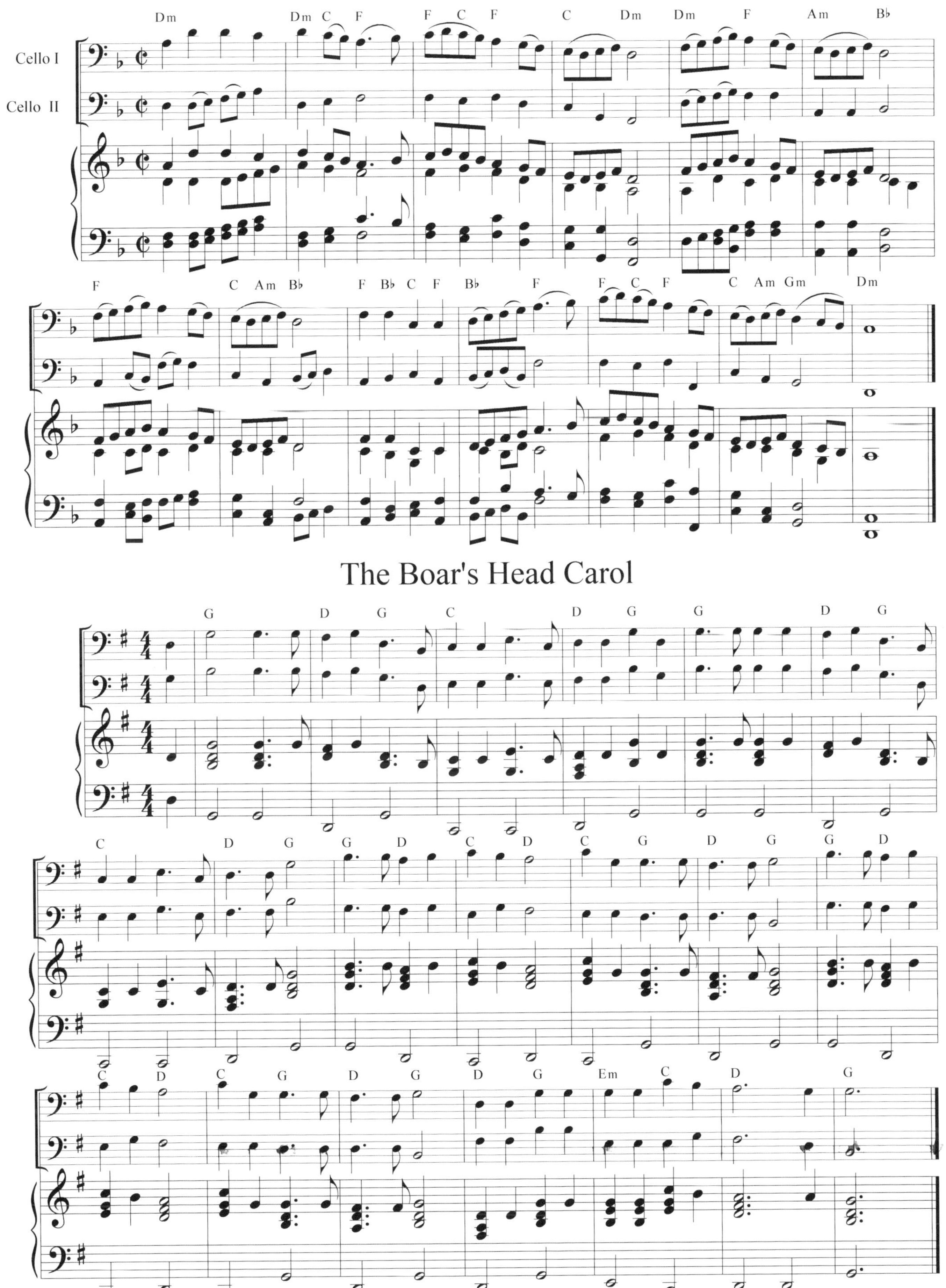

Bring a Torch, Jeanette, Isabella

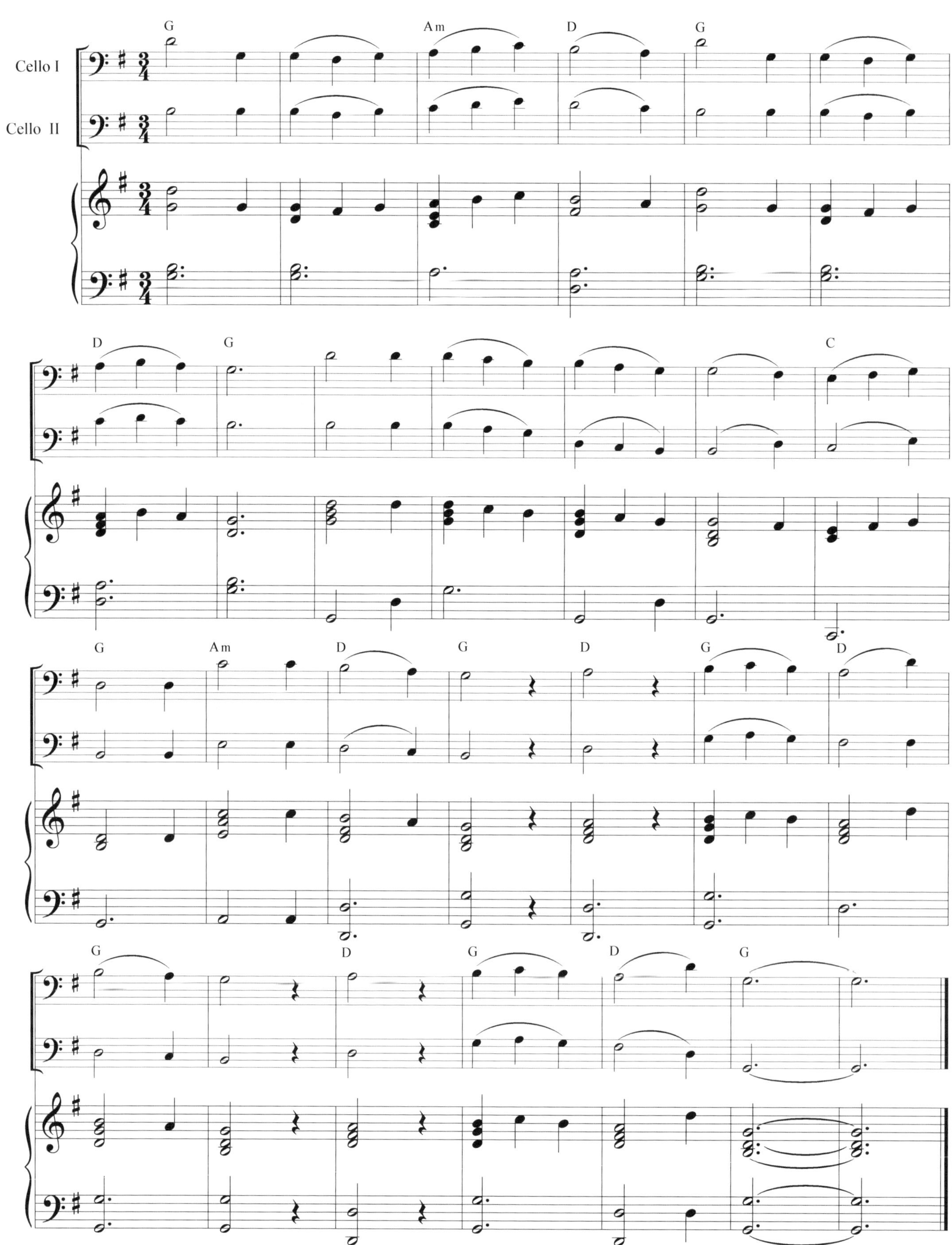

Carol of the Bells - Ukranian Bell Carol

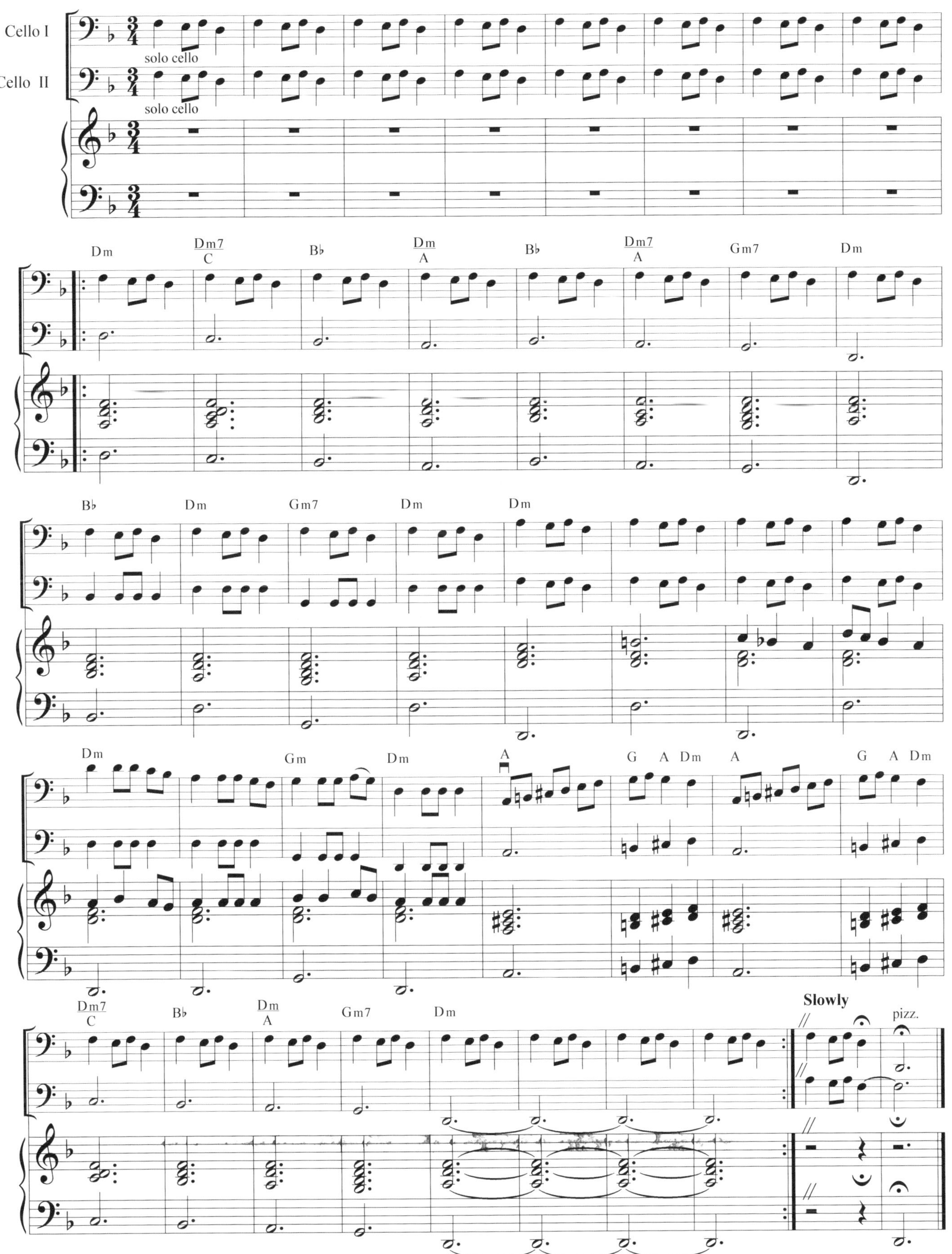

The Cherry Tree Carol

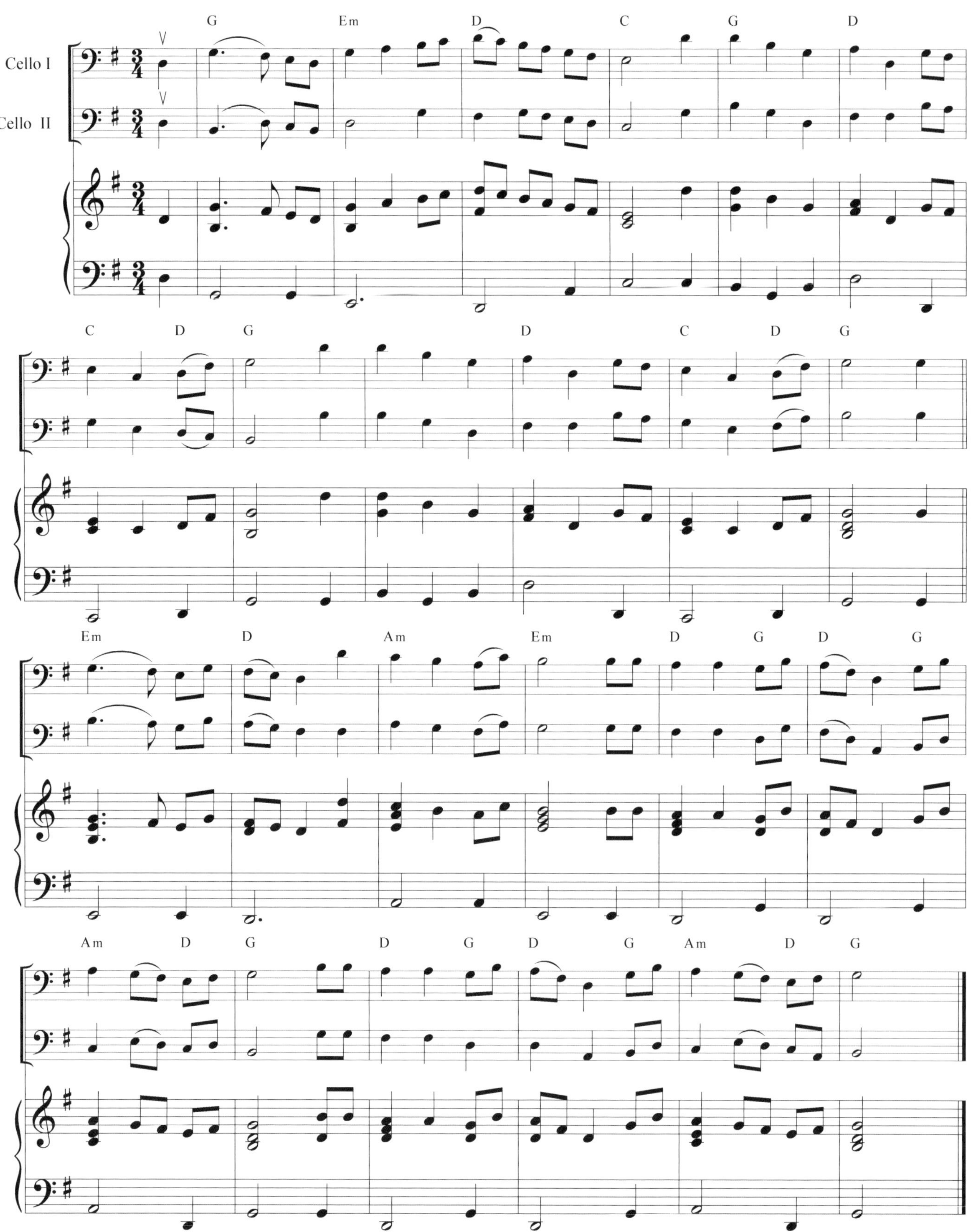

Christmas Day in the Morning-Christmas Day Ida Moarning

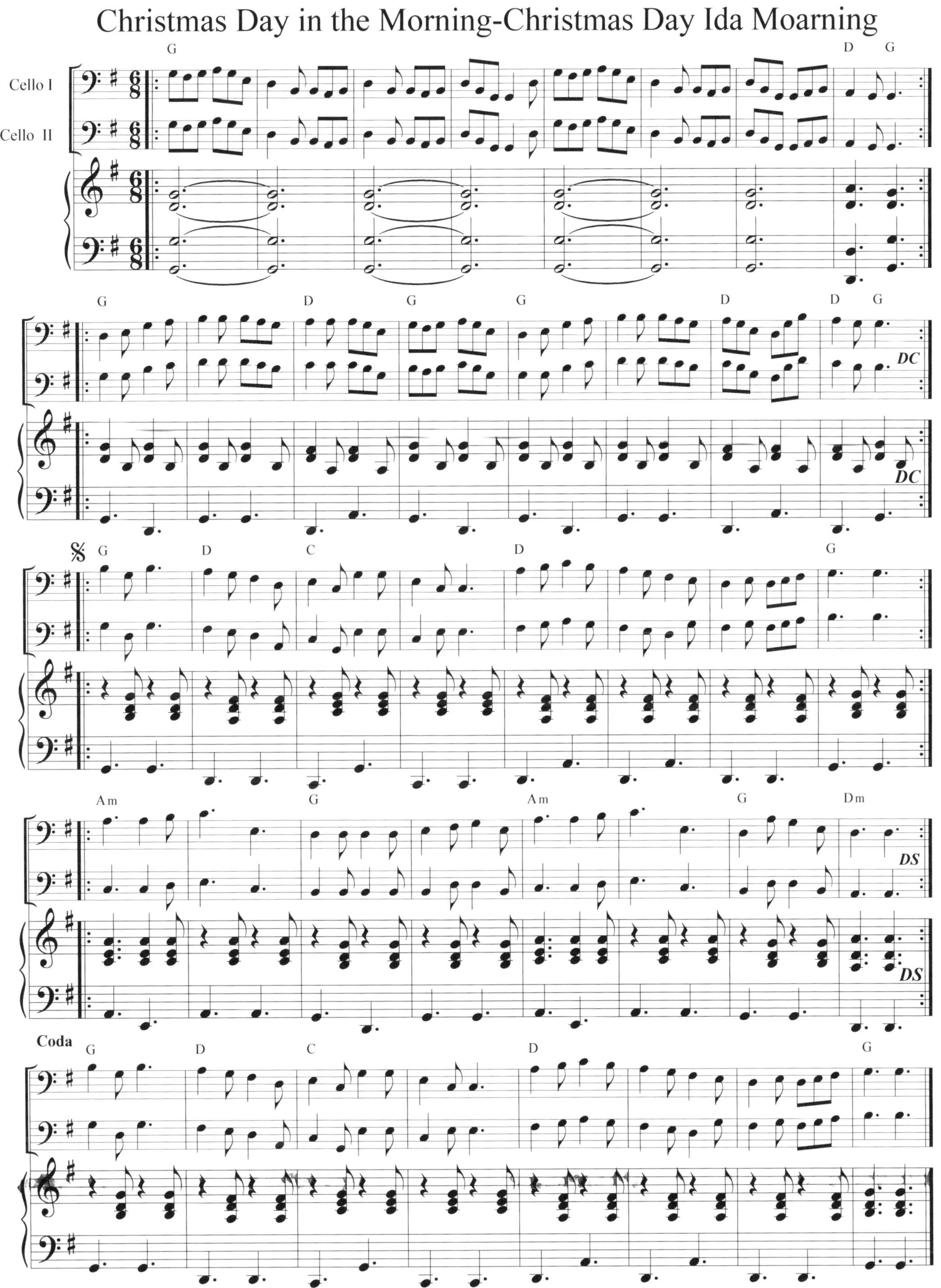

Come, Thou Long Expected Jesus

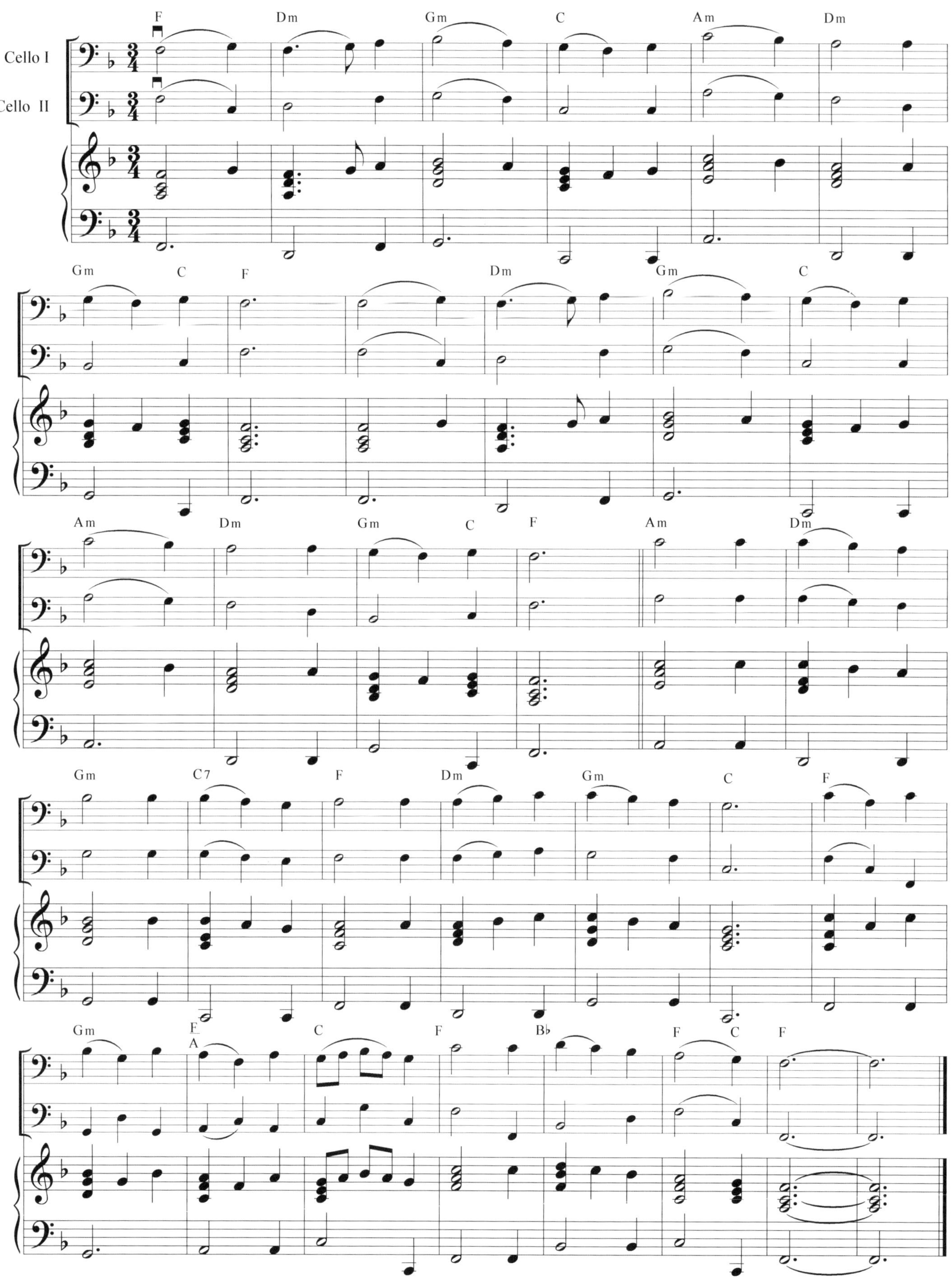

The Coventry Carol

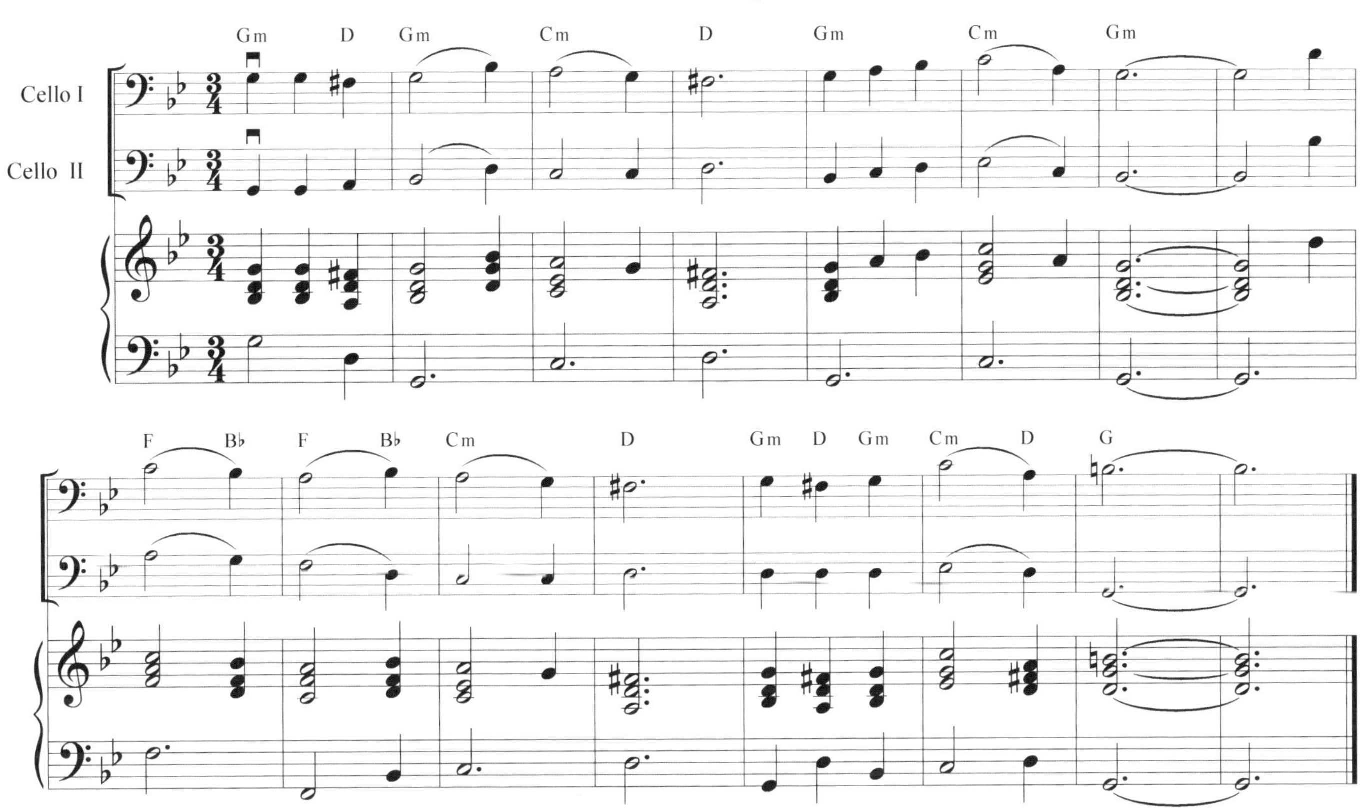

Deck the Halls

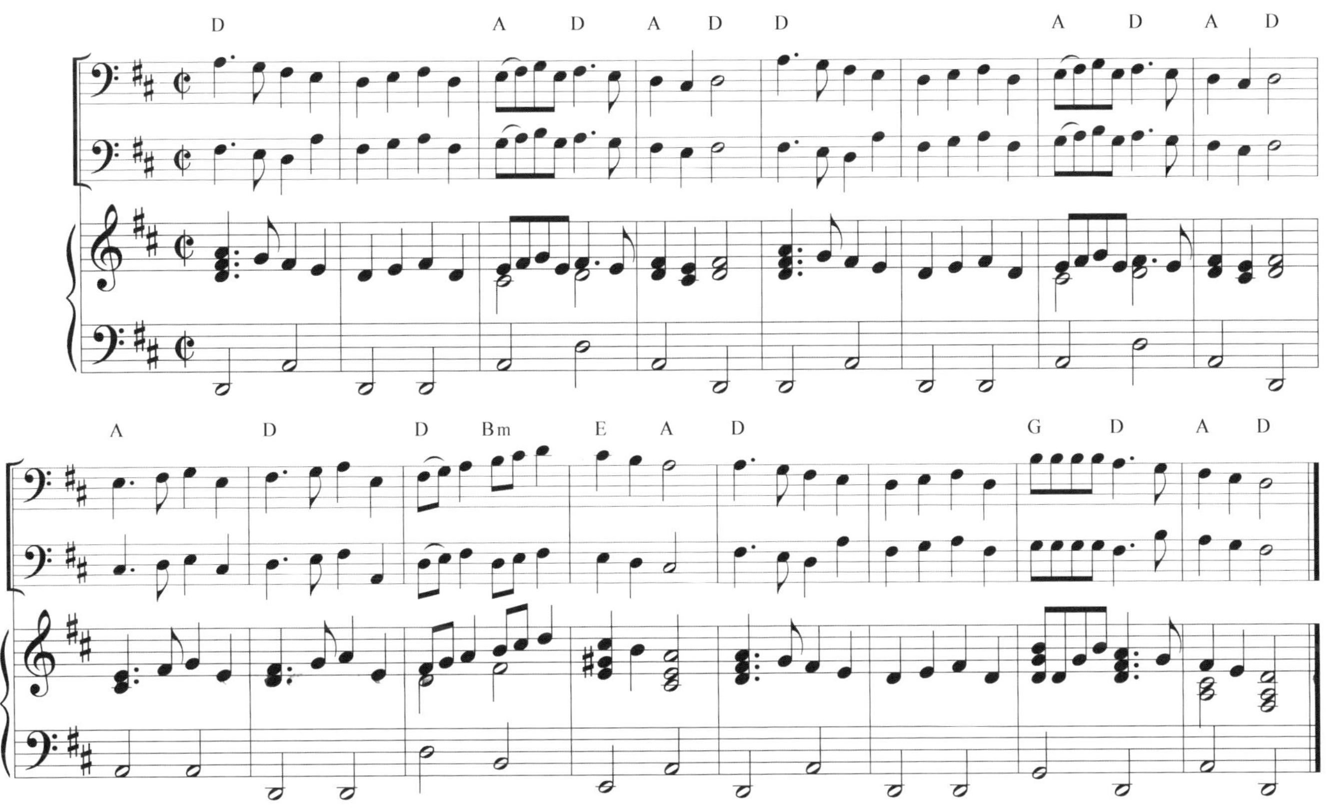

Ding! Dong! Merrrily on High

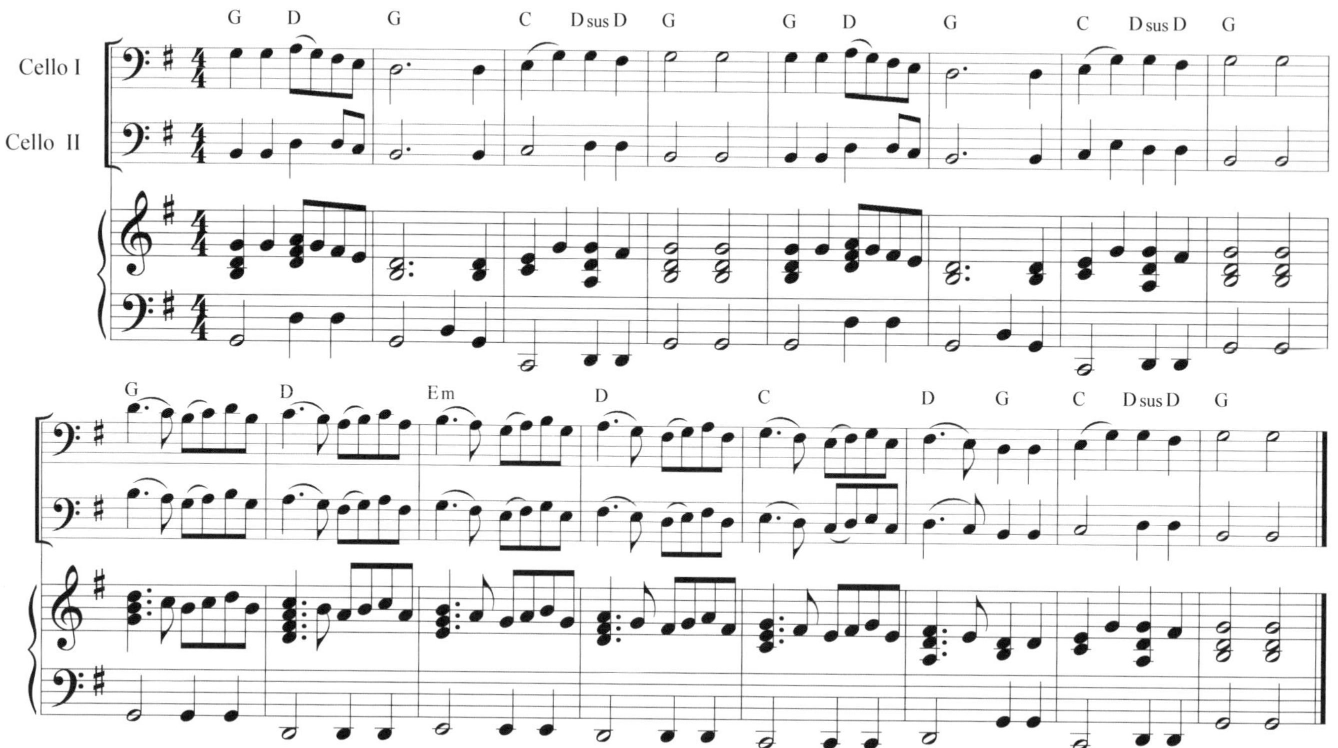

Drive the Cold Winter Away

All Hail to the Days

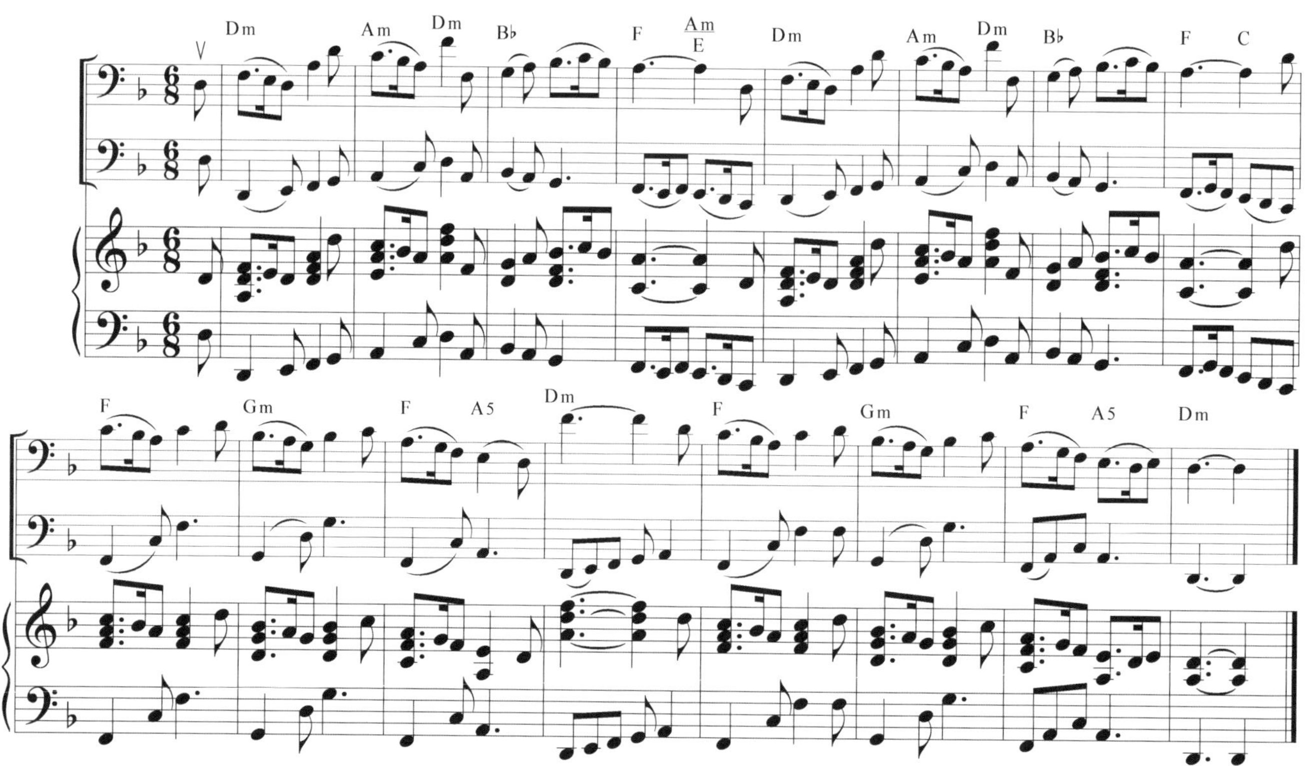

The First Noel

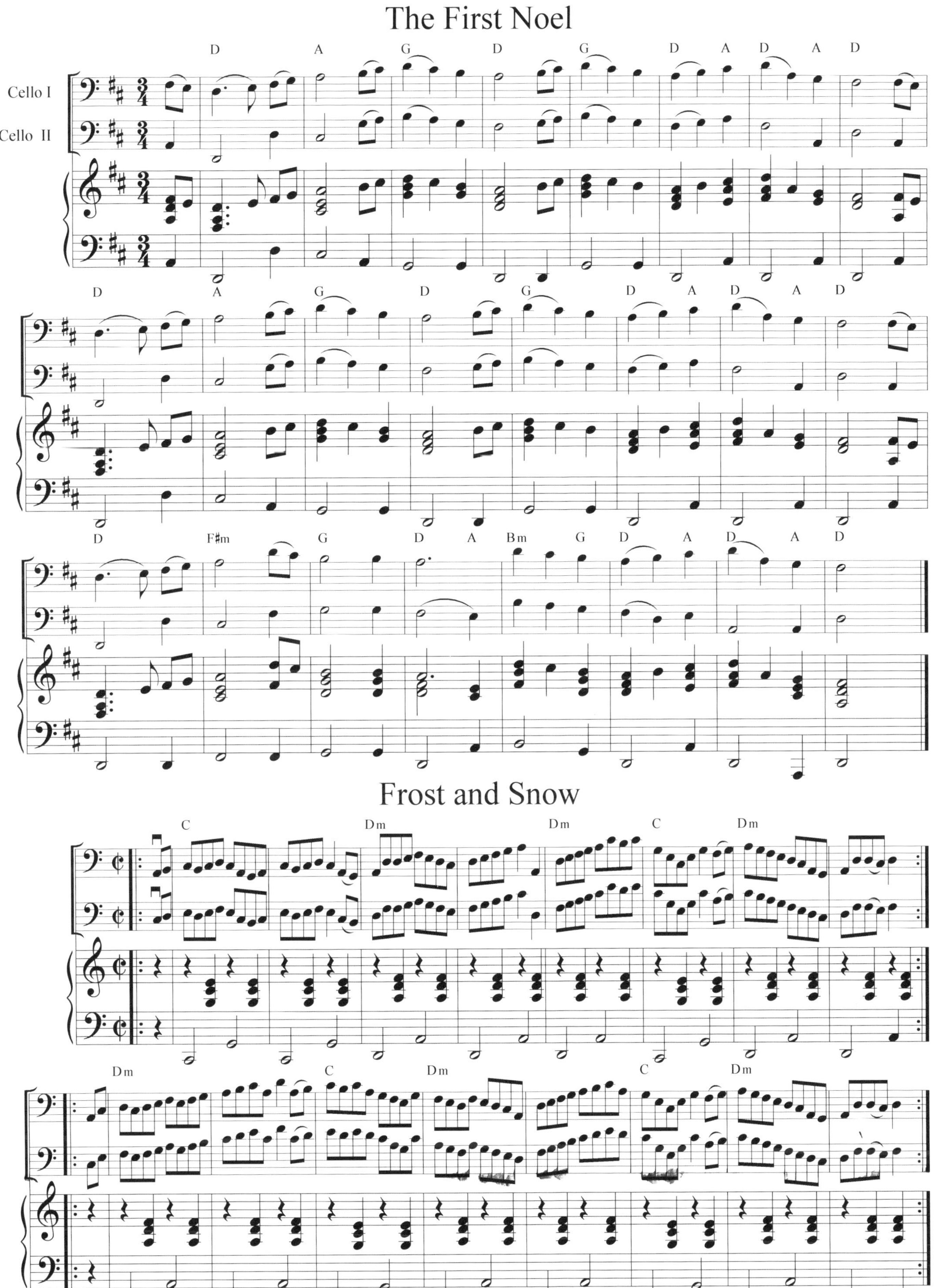

Frost and Snow

Go Tell It on the Mountain

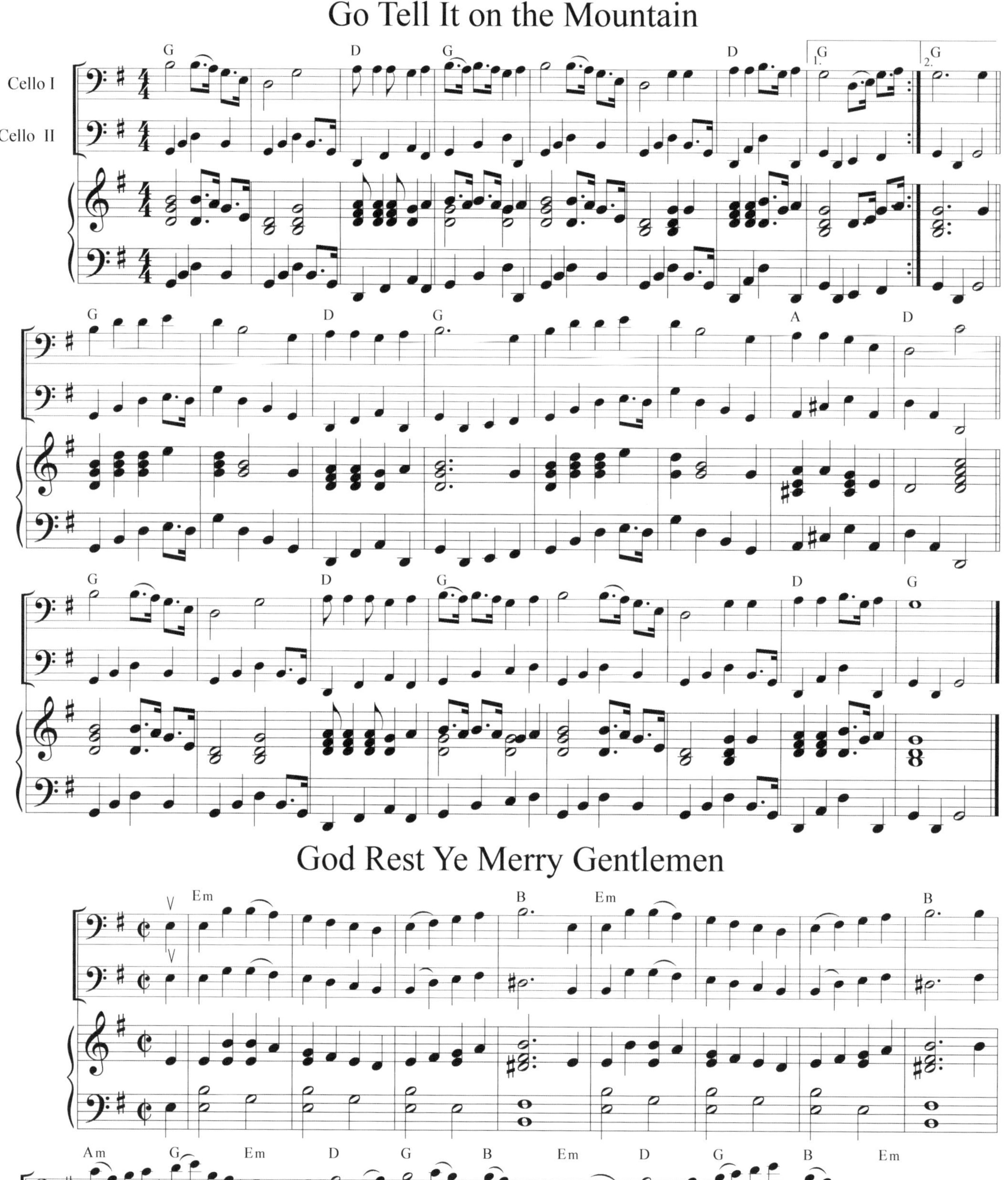

God Rest Ye Merry Gentlemen

The Golden Carol of the Wisemen

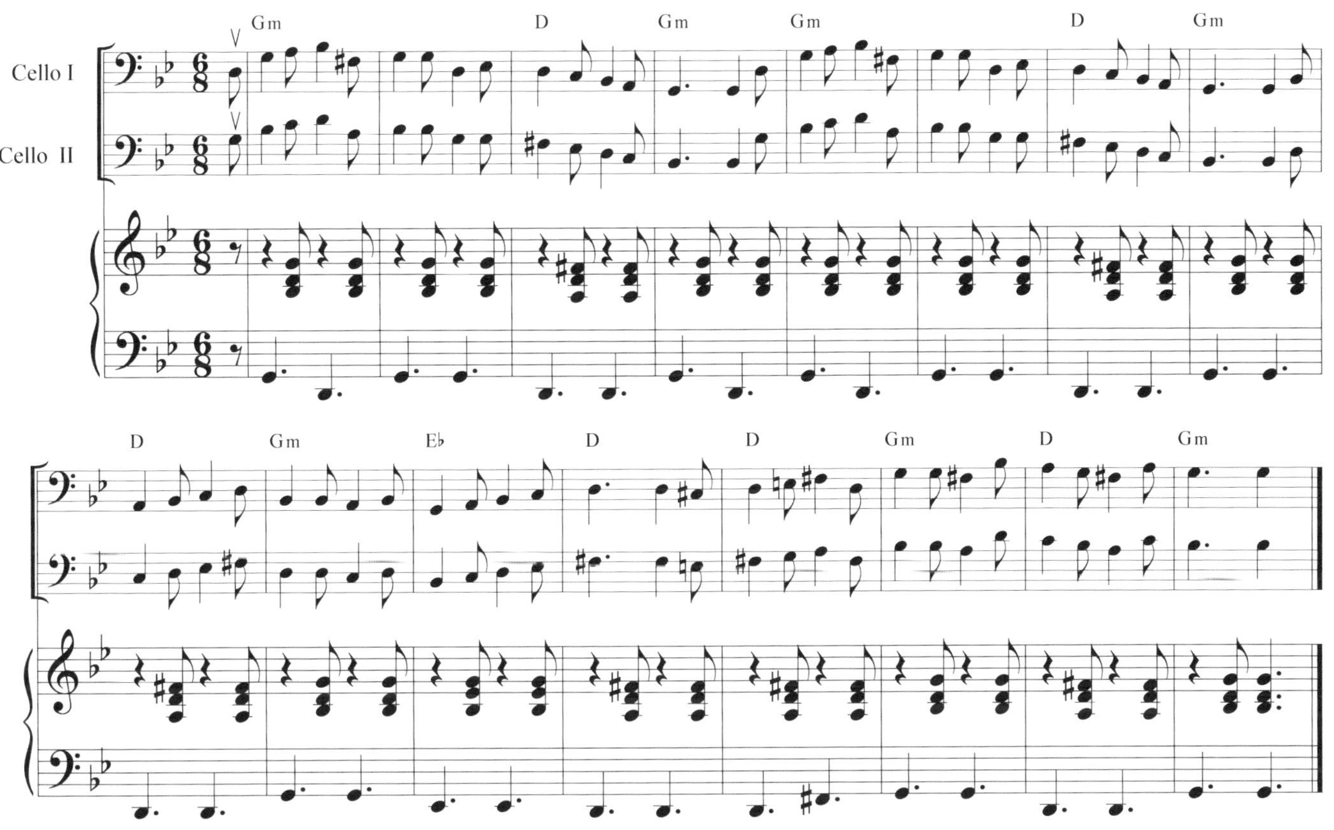

Good Christian Men Rejoice

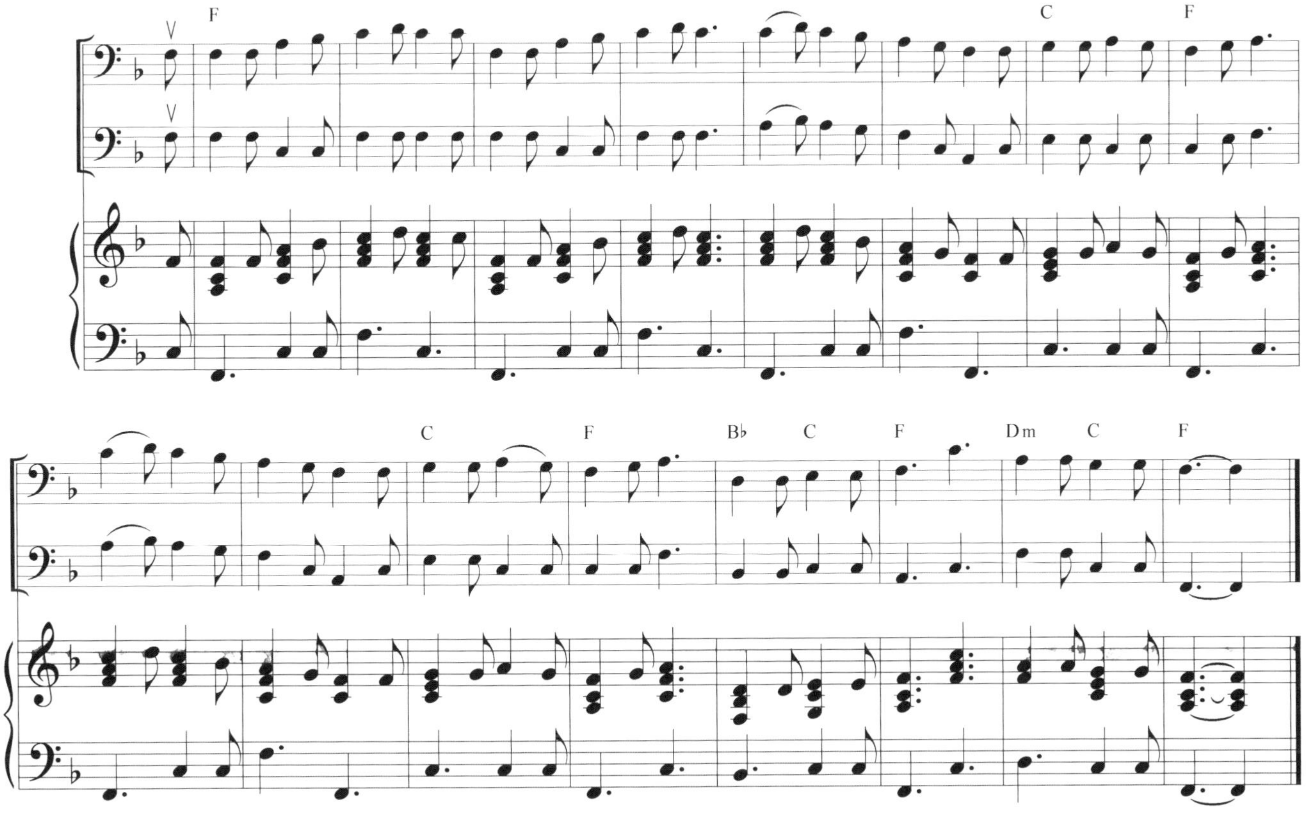

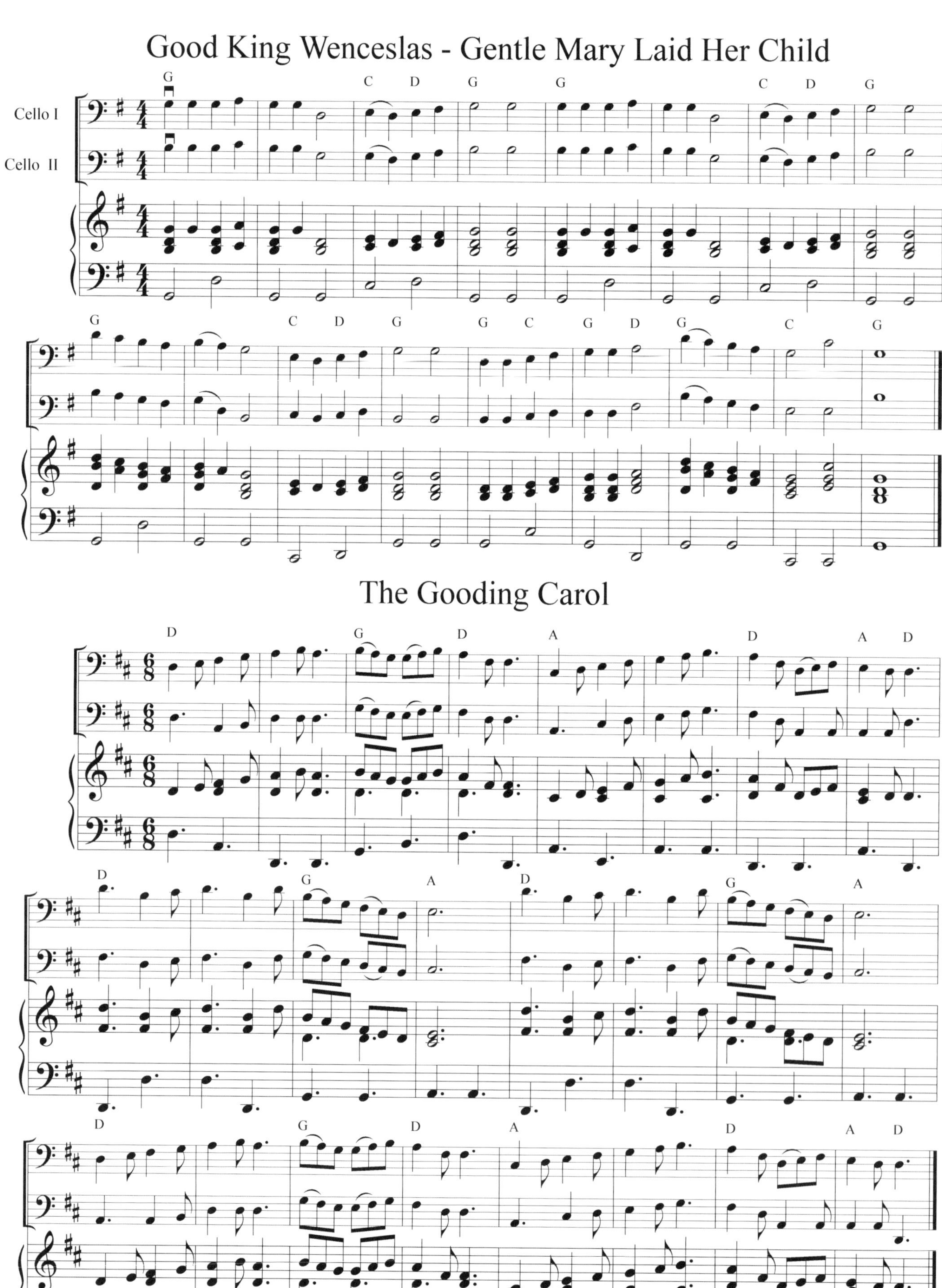
Good King Wenceslas - Gentle Mary Laid Her Child
Cello I
Cello II
G C D G G C D G
G C D G G C G D G C G
The Gooding Carol
D G D A D A D
D G A D G A
D G D A D A D

Hark! The Herald Angels Sing

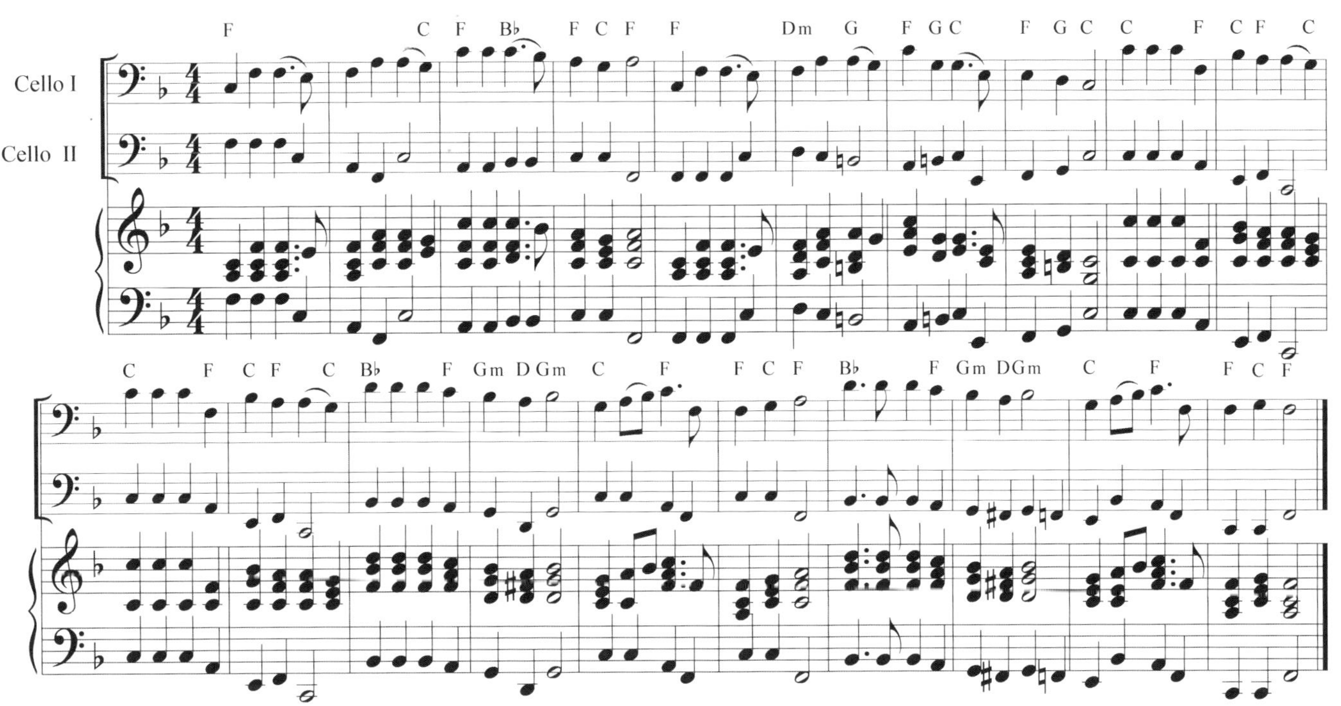

He is Born, the Divine Christ Child

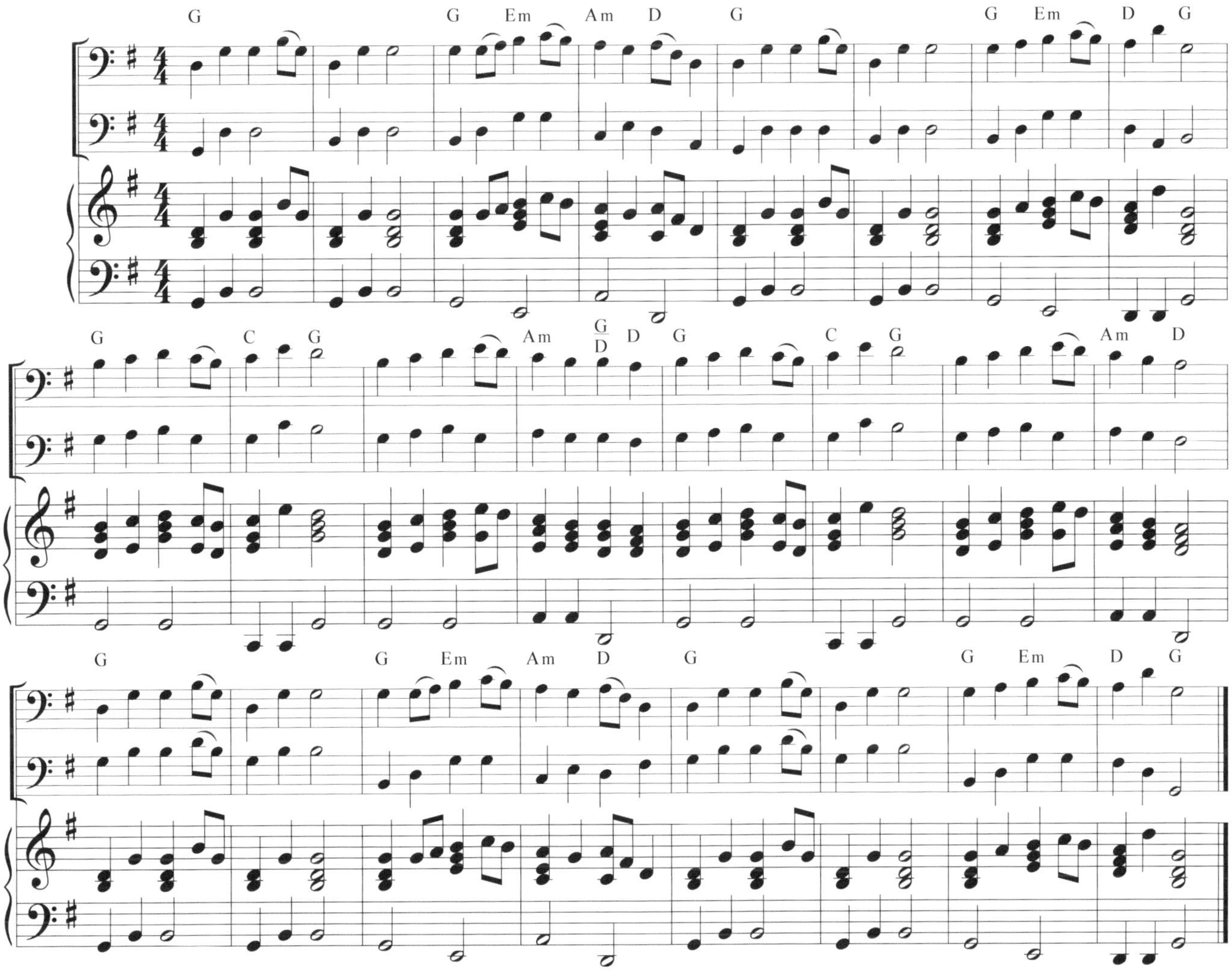

G G Em Am D G G Em D G

G C G Am G D D G C G Am D

G G Em Am D G G Em D G

The Holly and the Ivy

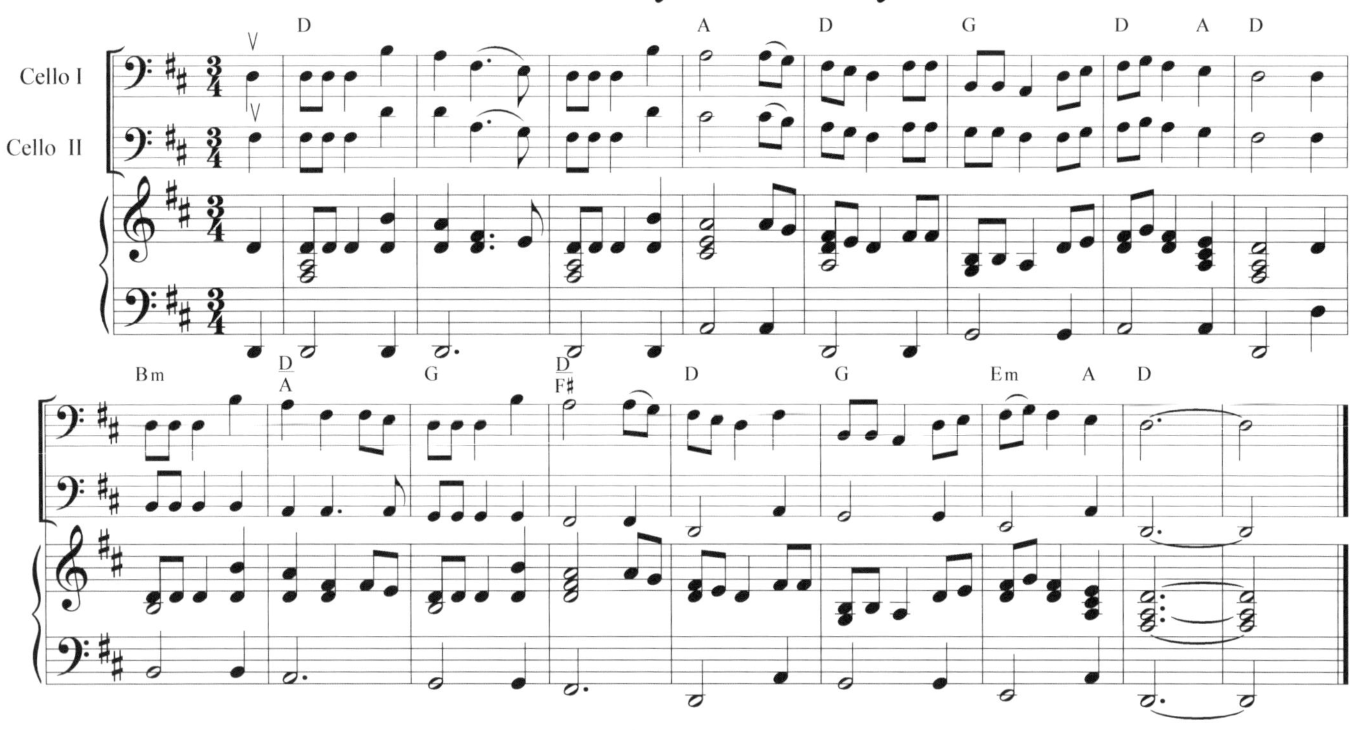

The Holly Bears a Berry - The Saint Day Carol

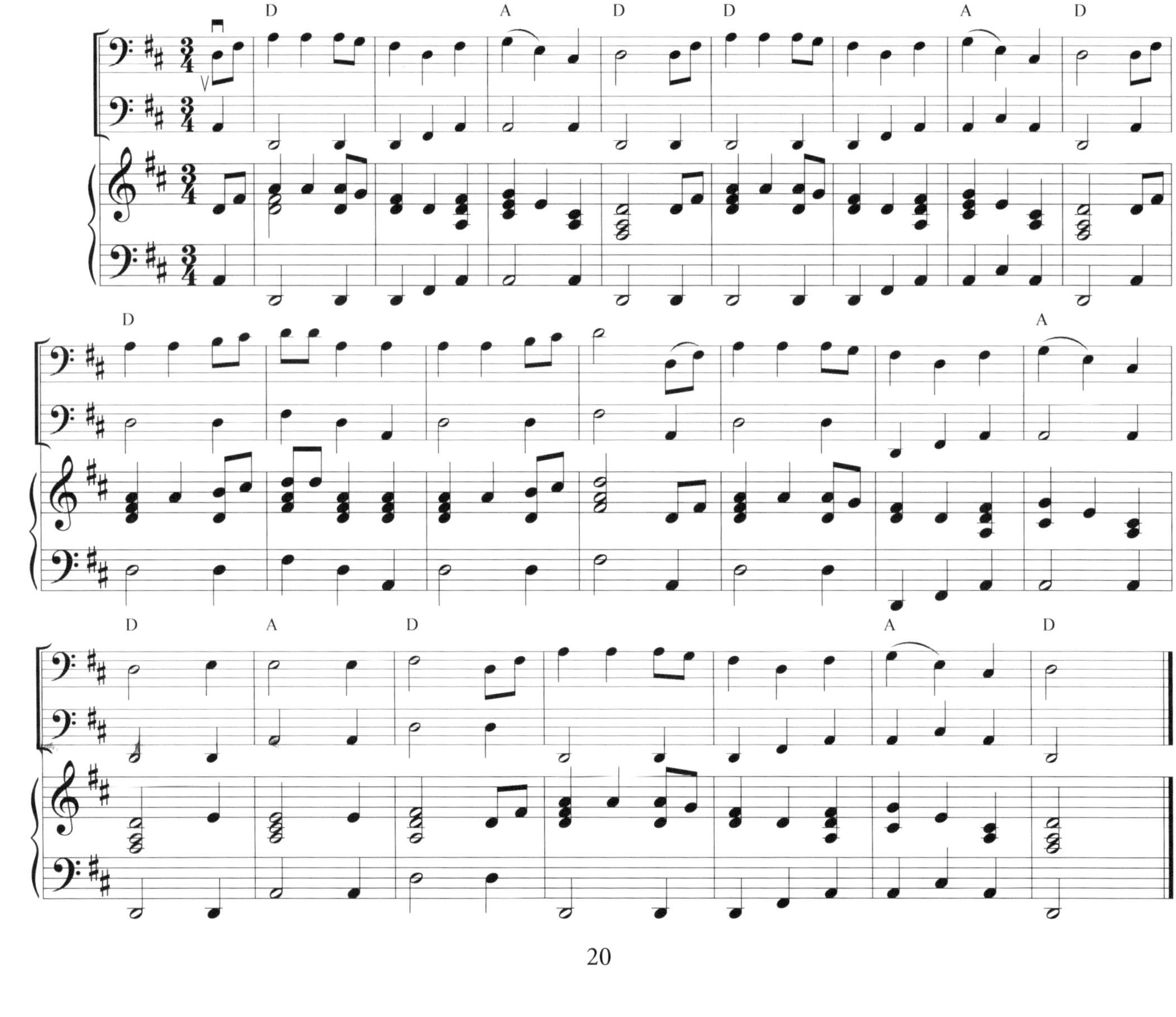

How Great Our Joy

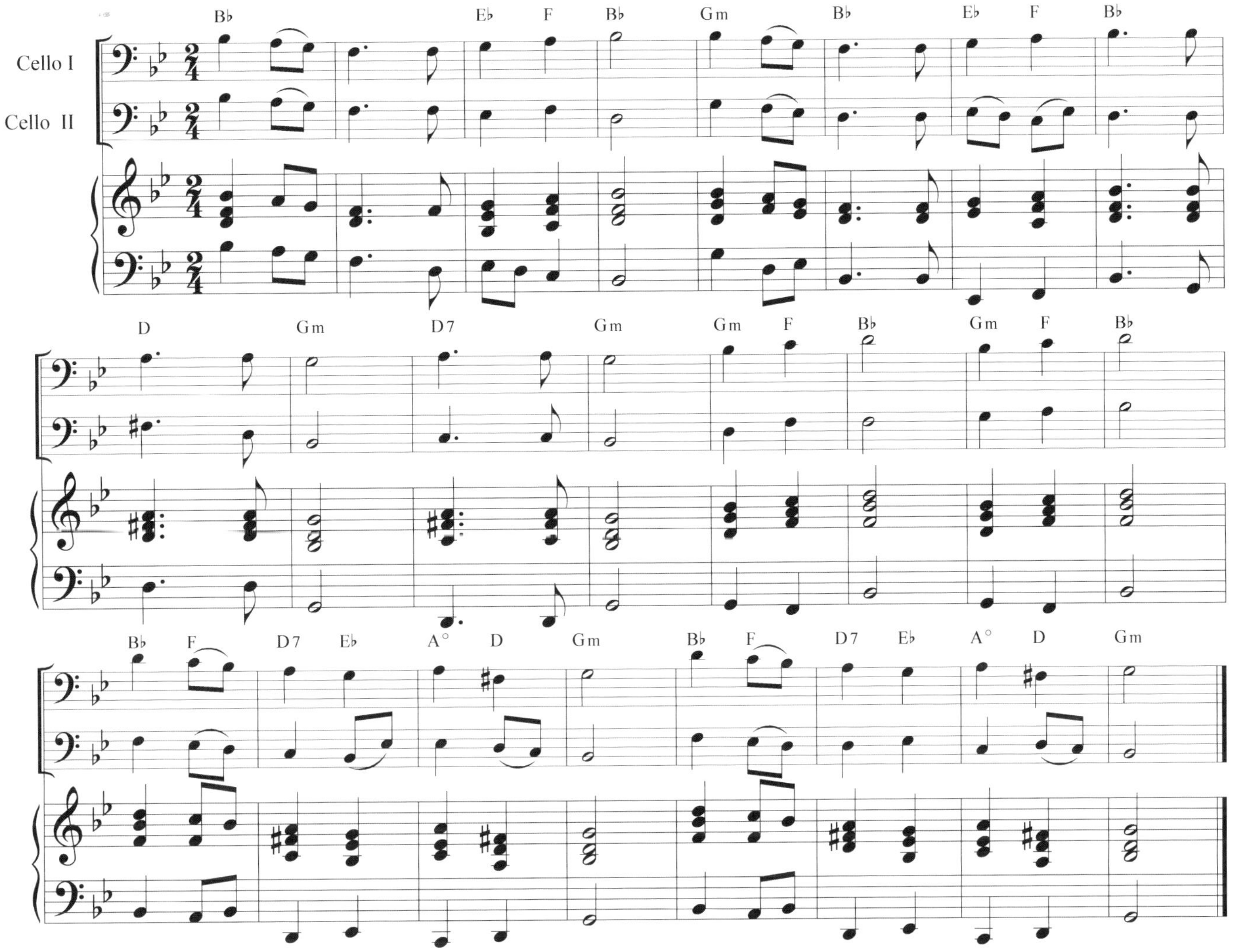

Cello I

Cello II

B♭ E♭ F B♭ Gm B♭ E♭ F B♭

D Gm D7 Gm Gm F B♭ Gm F B♭

B♭ F D7 E♭ A° D Gm B♭ F D7 E♭ A° D Gm

In the Bleak Midwinter

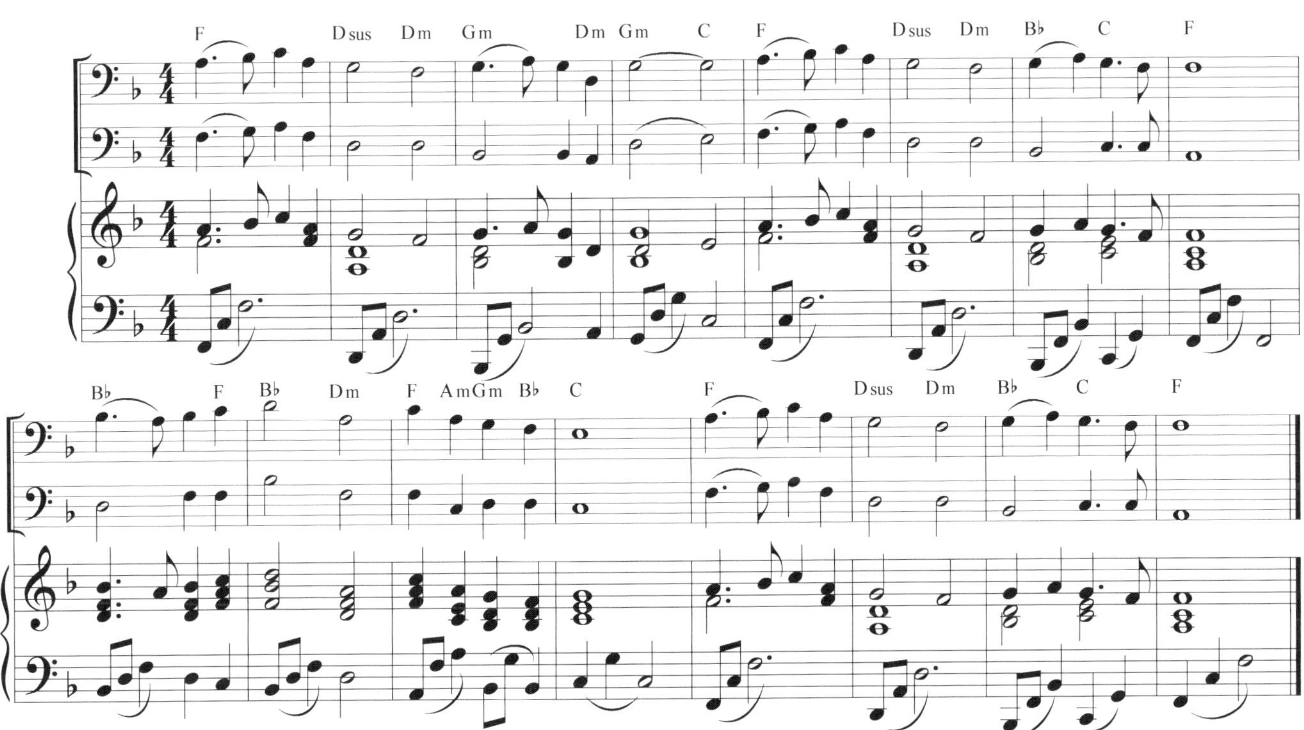

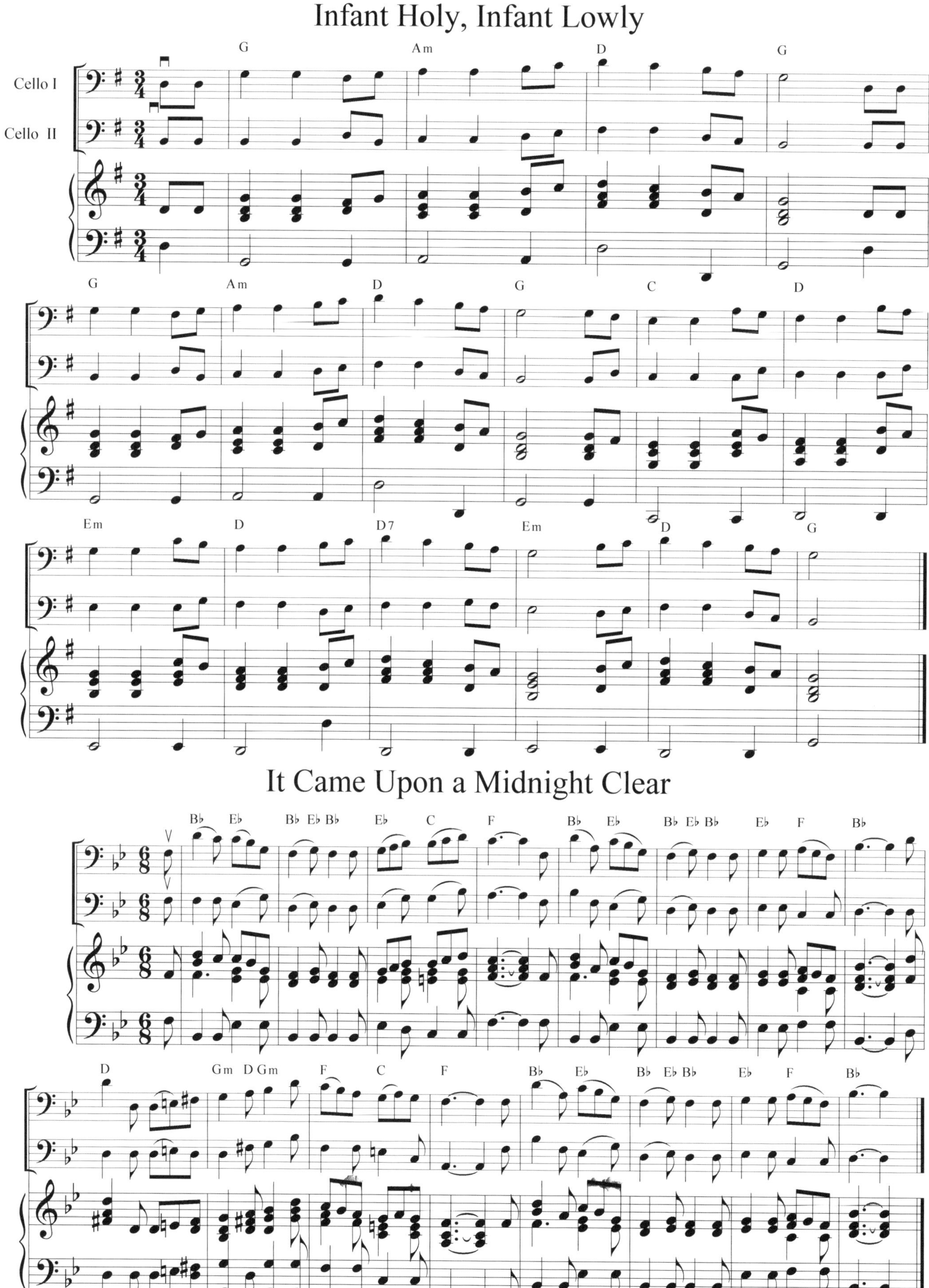
Infant Holy, Infant Lowly
Cello I
Cello II
G Am D G
G Am D G C D
Em D D7 Em D G
It Came Upon a Midnight Clear
B♭ E♭ B♭ E♭ B♭ E♭ C F B♭ E♭ B♭ E♭ B♭ E♭ F B♭
D Gm D Gm F C F B♭ E♭ B♭ E♭ B♭ E♭ F B♭

Jingle Bells

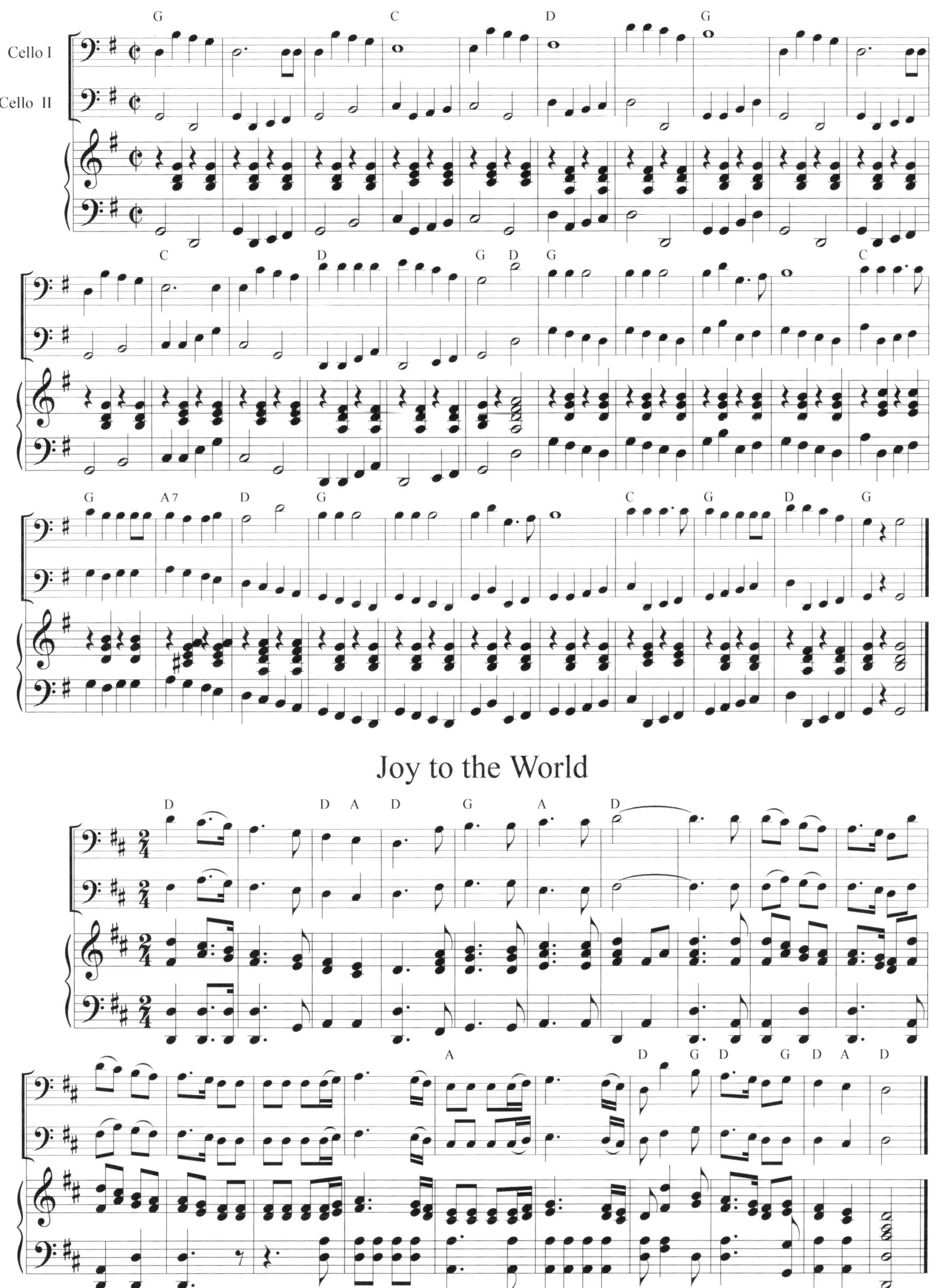

Joseph Dearest, Joseph Mine

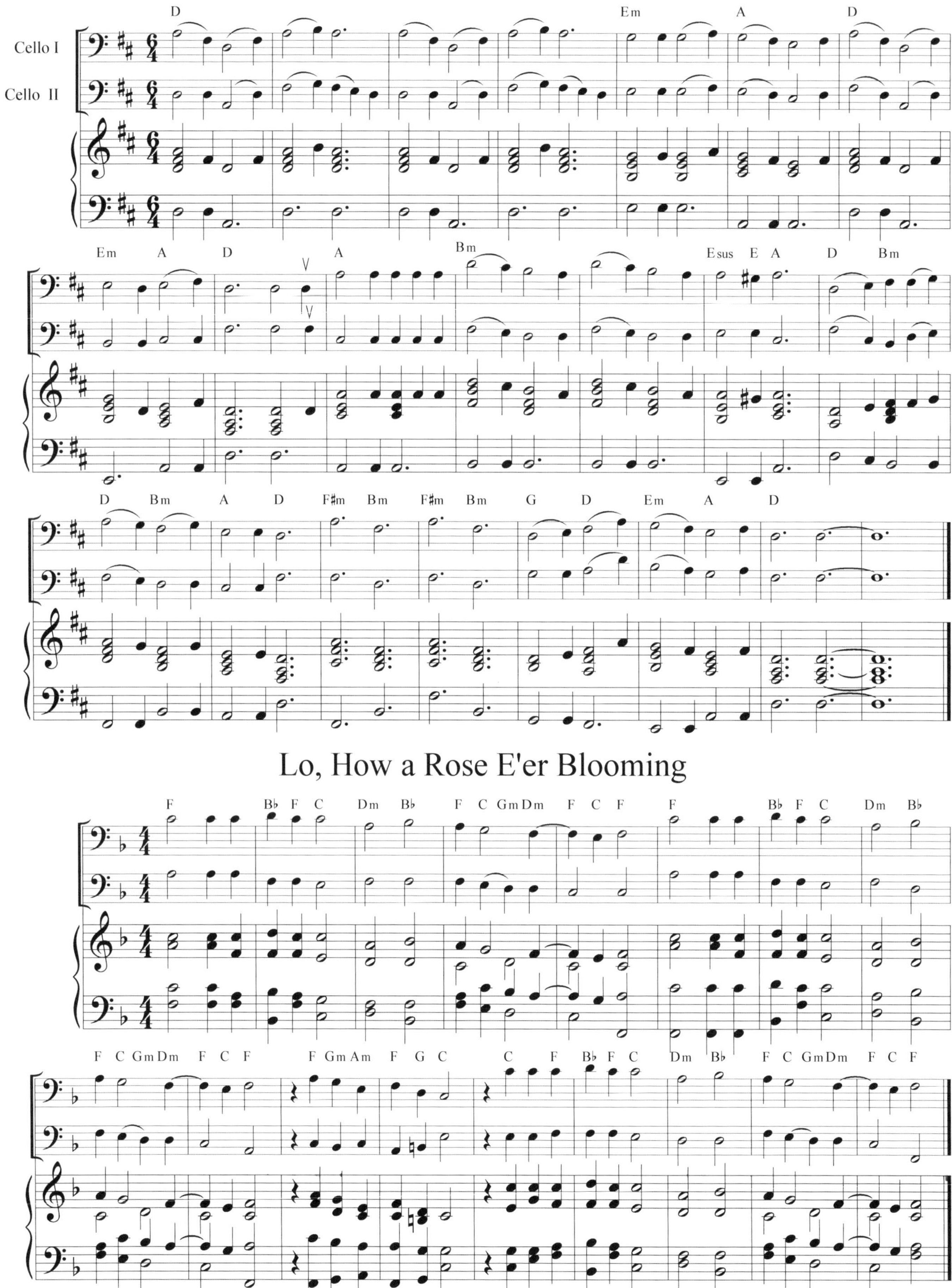

Lo, How a Rose E'er Blooming

Masters in This Hall

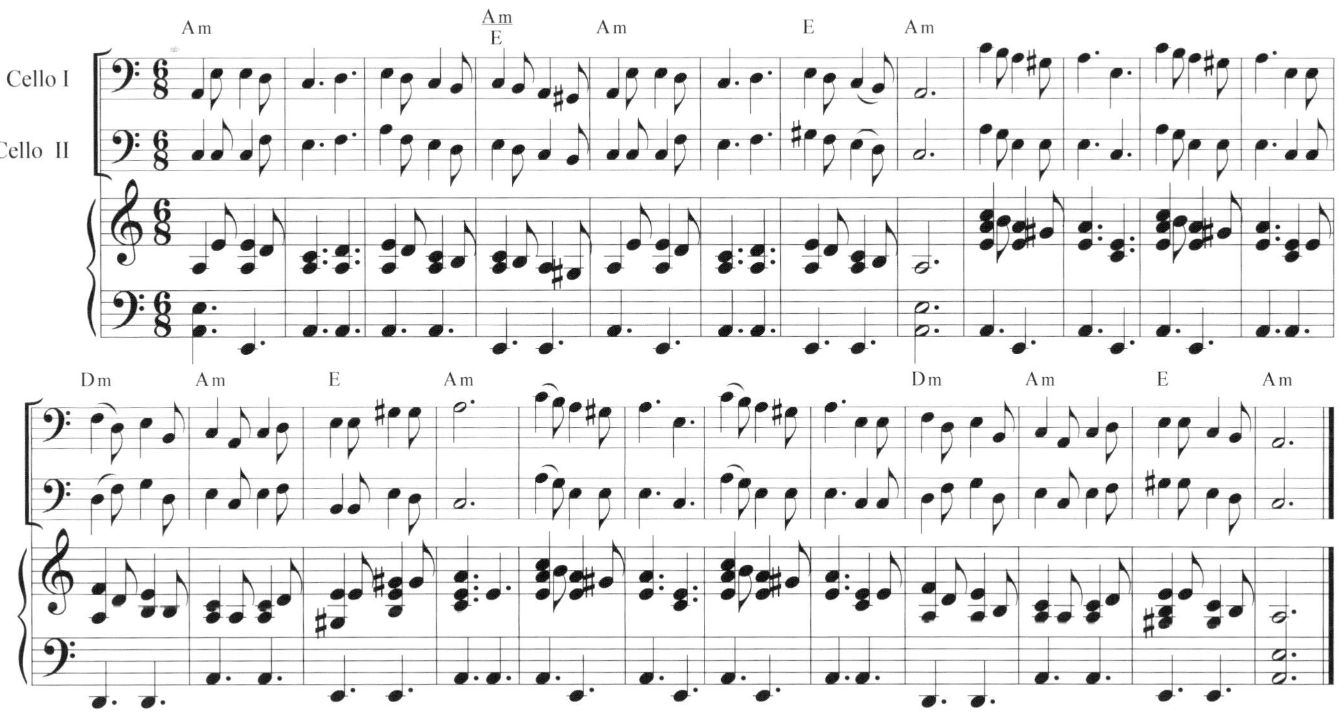

O Come, All Ye Faithful

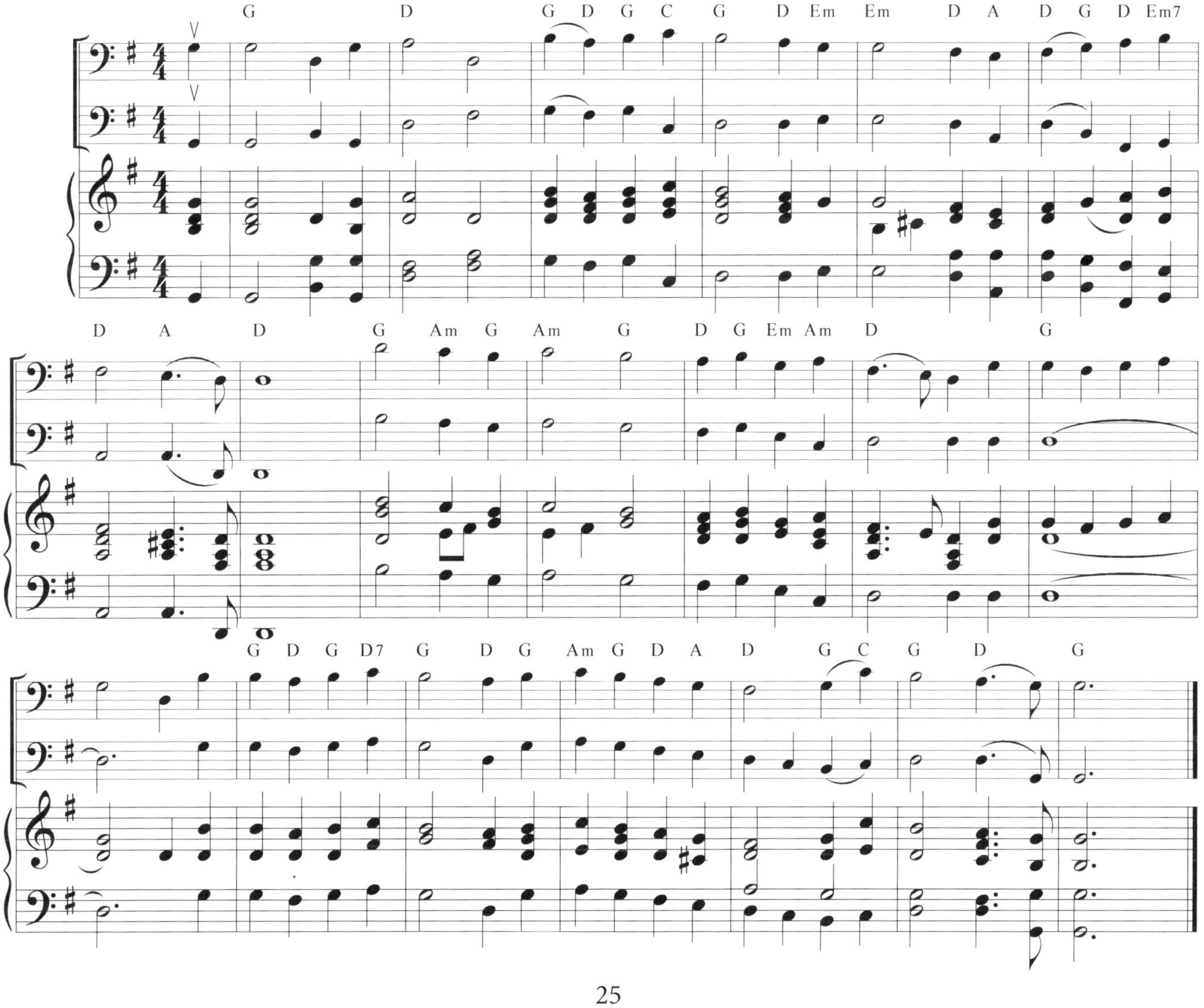

G D G D G C G D Em Em D A D G D Em7

D A D G Am G Am G D G Em Am D G

G D G D7 G D G Am G D A D G C G D G

O Come, O Come Emmanuel

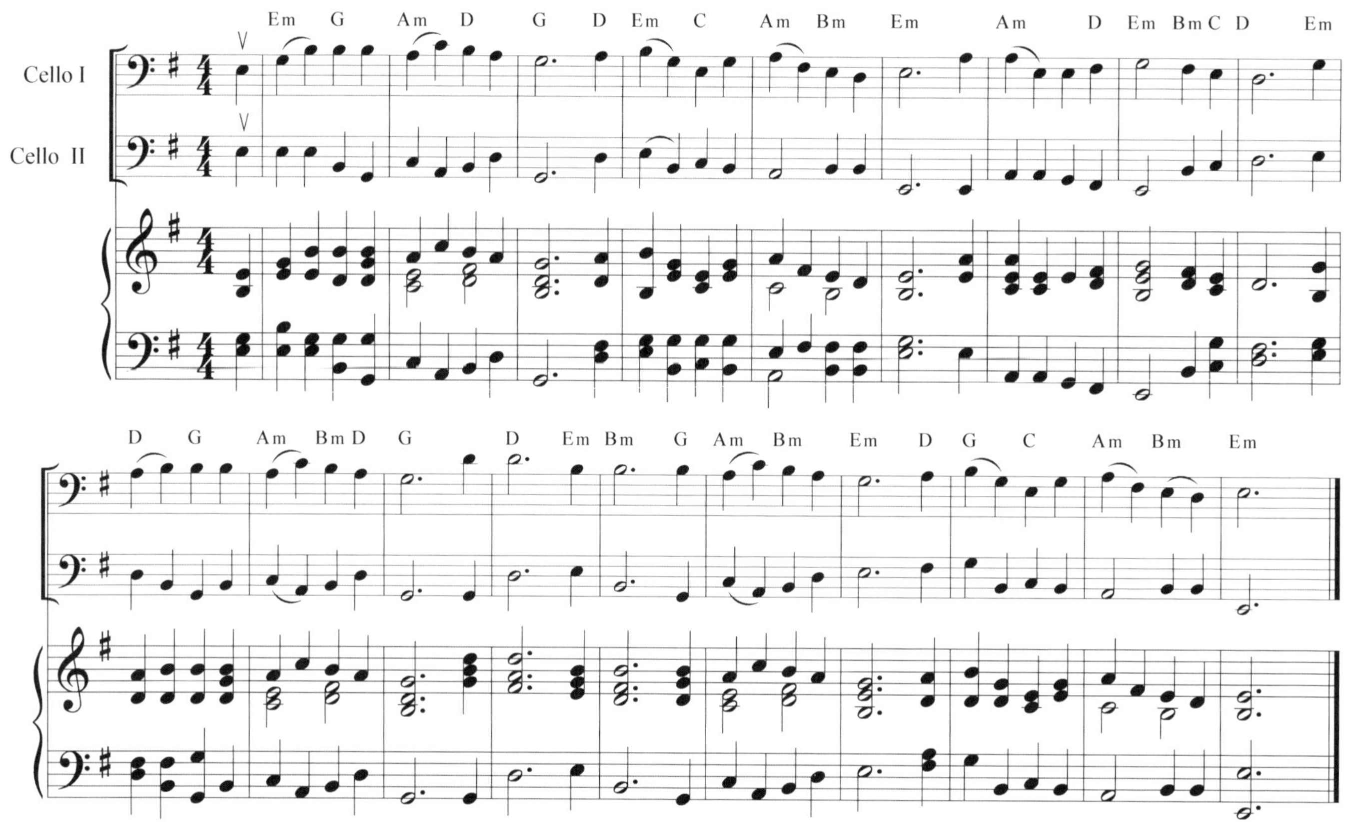

O Little Town of Bethlehem

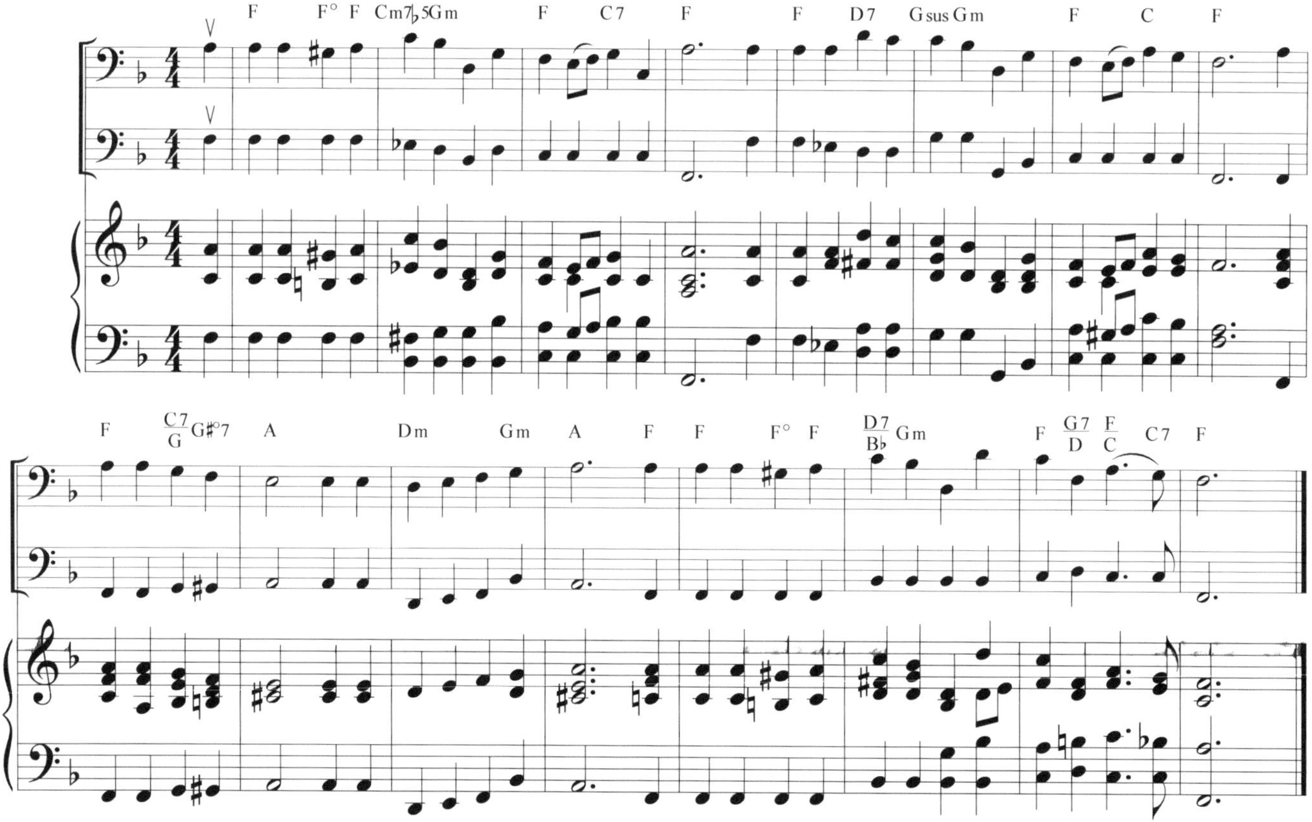

O Holy Night - Cantique de Noël

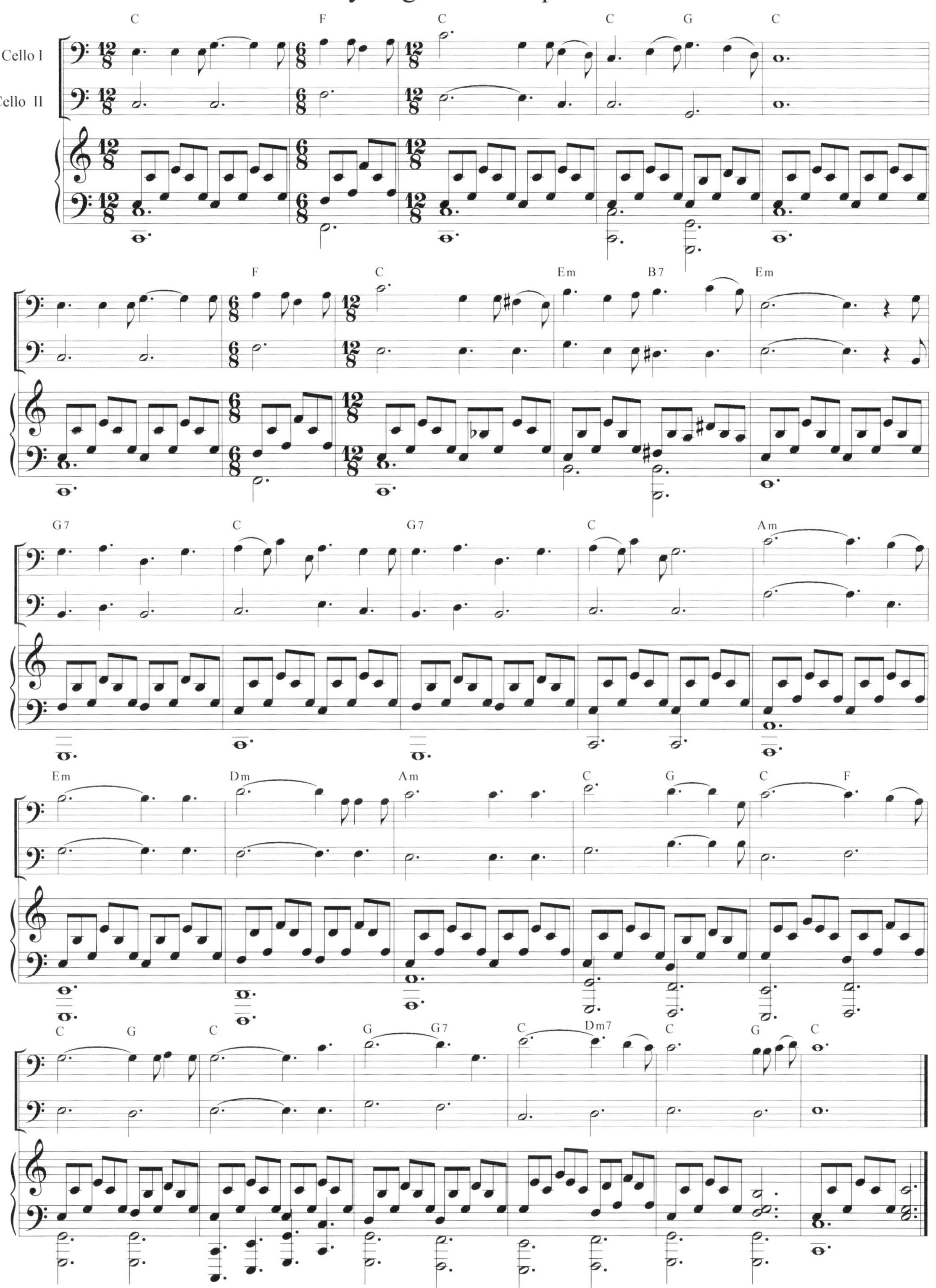

Of the Father's Love Begotten

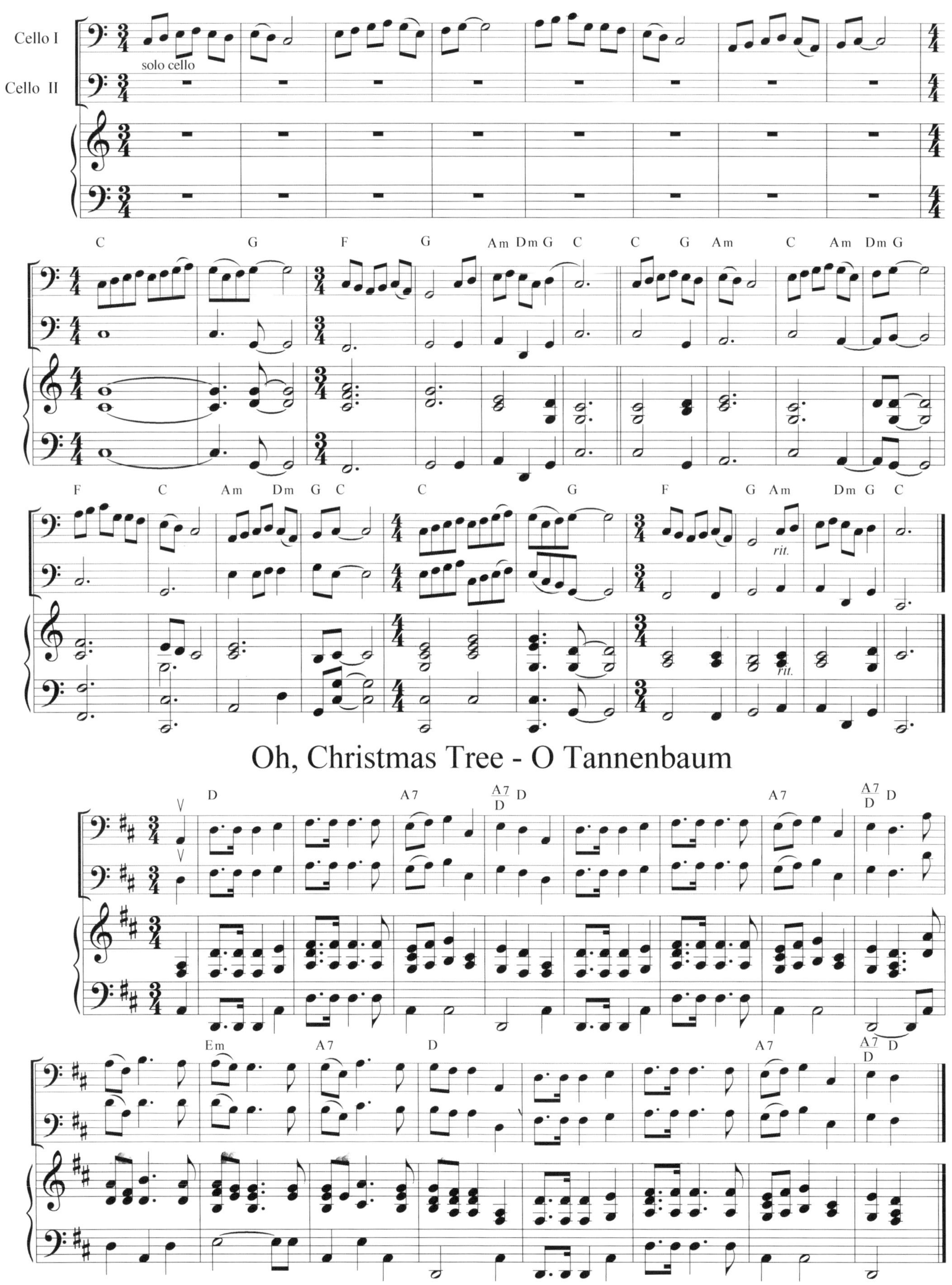

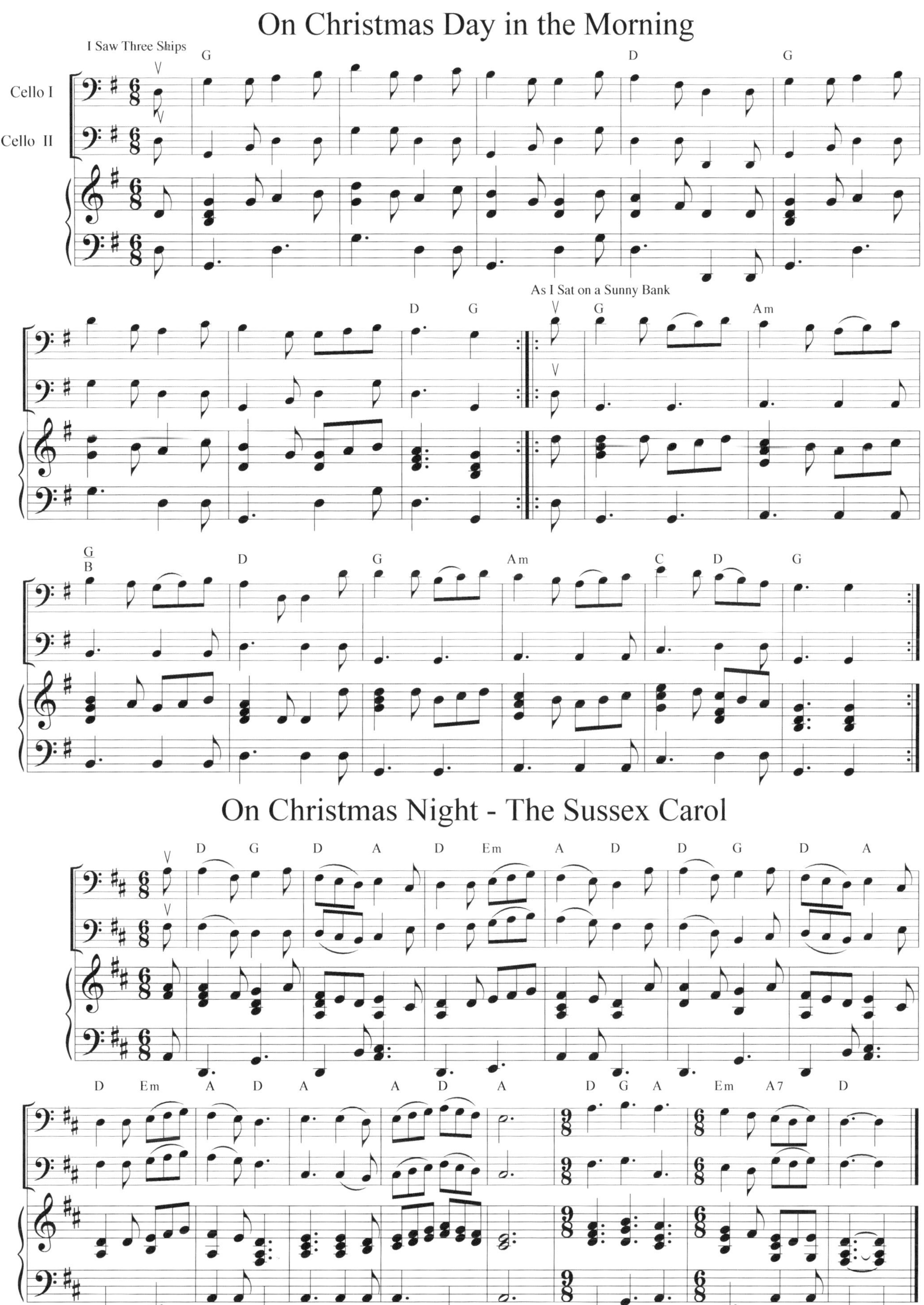
On Christmas Day in the Morning
I Saw Three Ships
Cello I
Cello II
G D G
D G
As I Sat on a Sunny Bank
G Am
G/B D G Am C D G
On Christmas Night - The Sussex Carol
D G D A D Em A D D G D A
D Em A D A A D A D G A Em A7 D

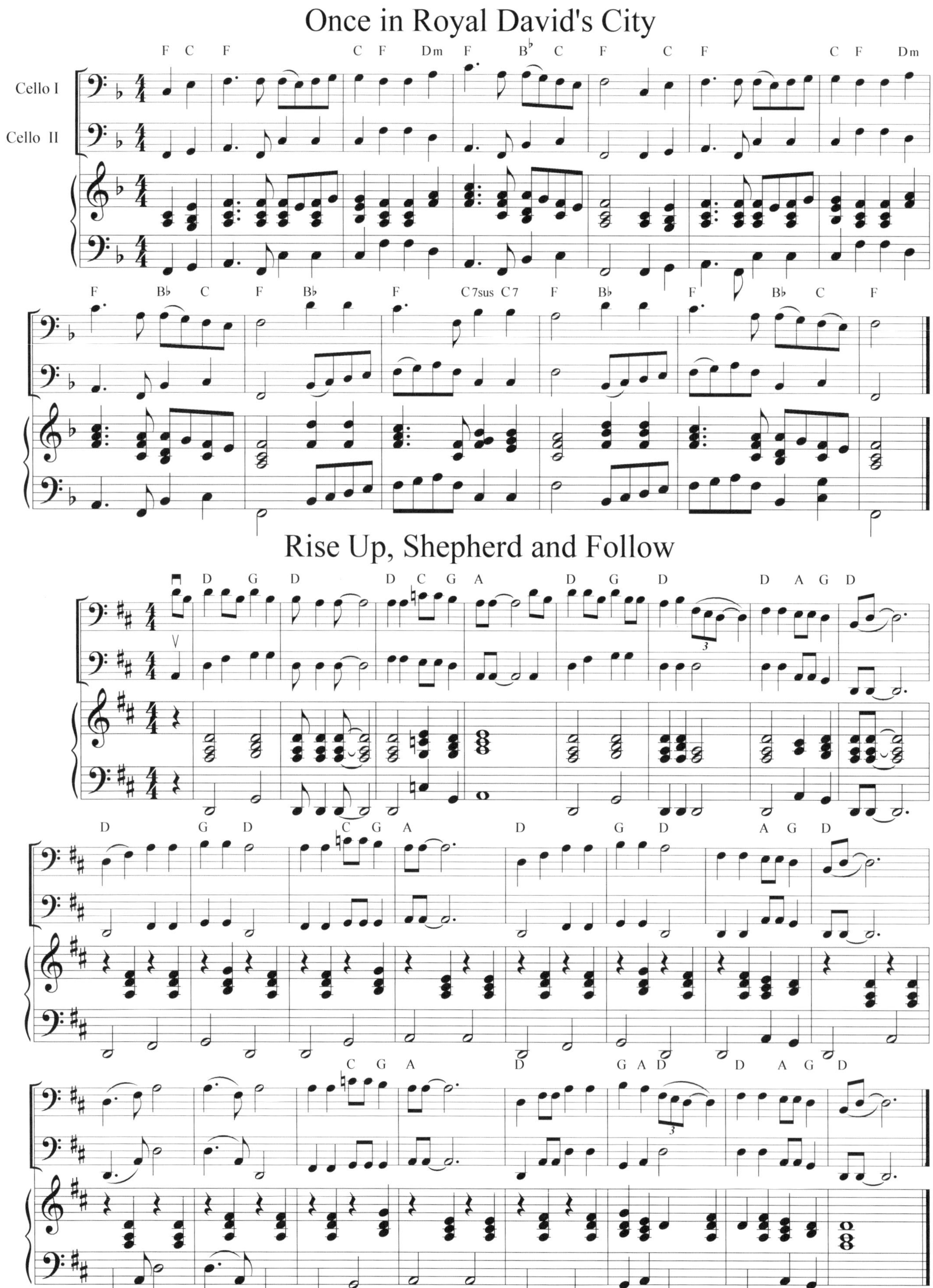
Once in Royal David's City
Cello I
Cello II
F C F C F Dm F B♭ C F C F C F Dm
F B♭ C F B♭ F C7sus C7 F B♭ F B♭ C F
Rise Up, Shepherd and Follow
D G D D C G A D G D D A G D
D G D C G A D G D A G D
C G A D G A D D A G D

Silent Night

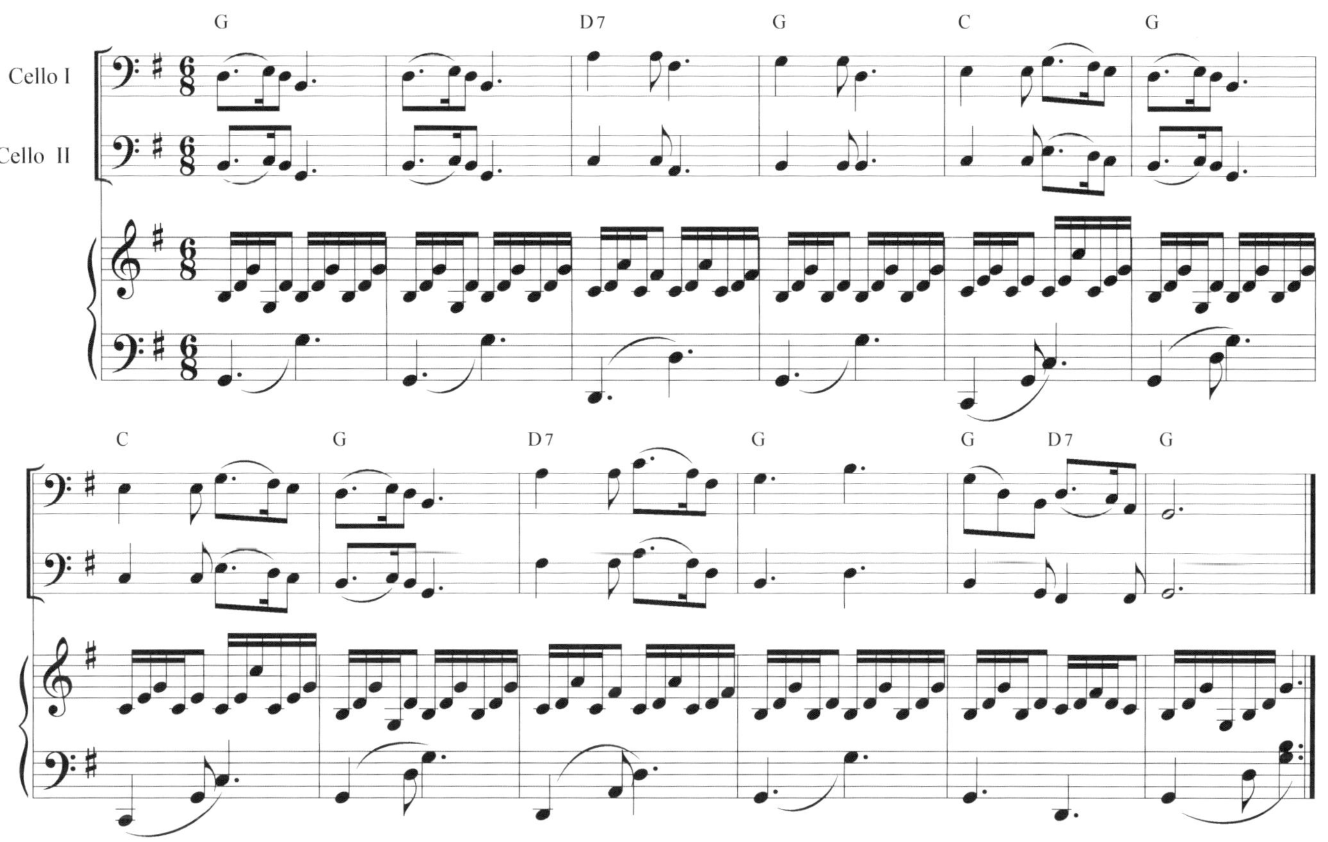

Sing We Now of Christmas

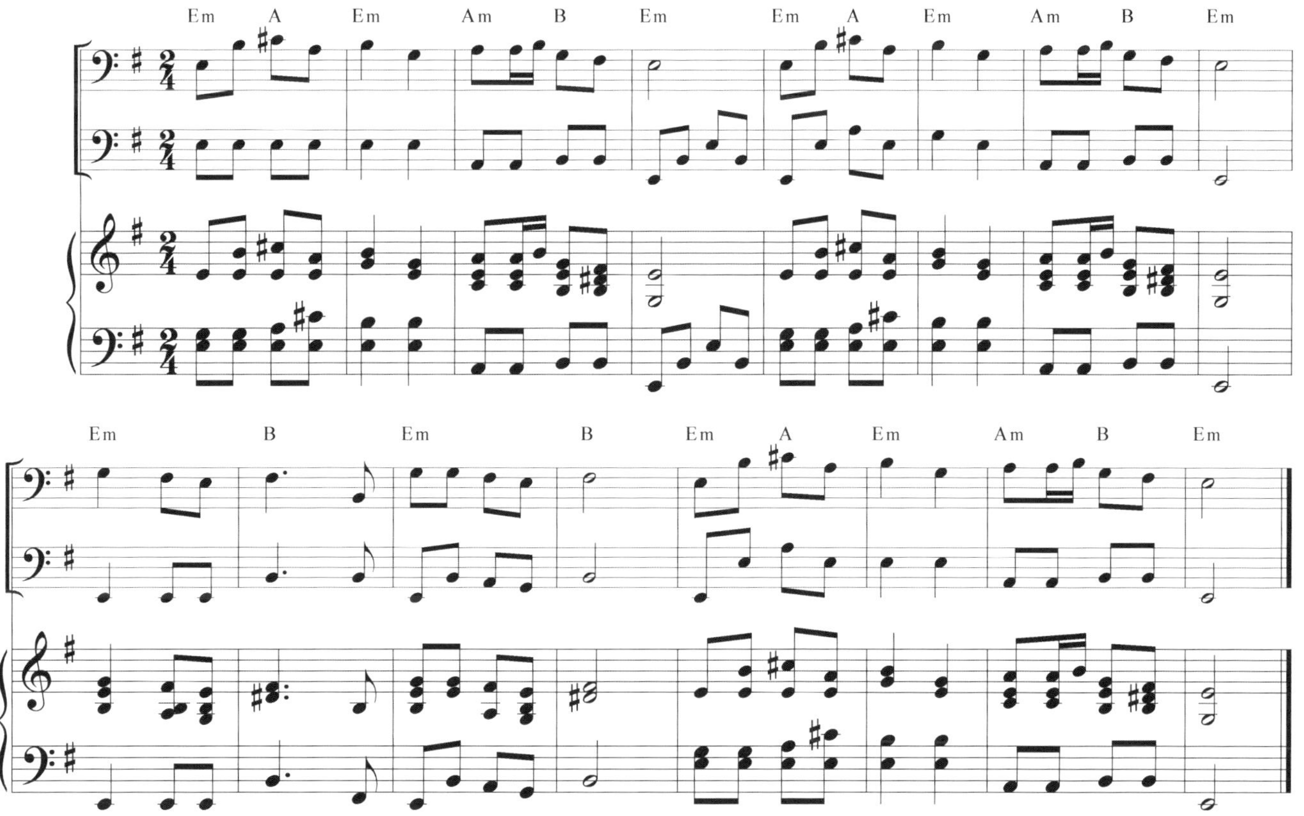

The Snow Lay on the Ground

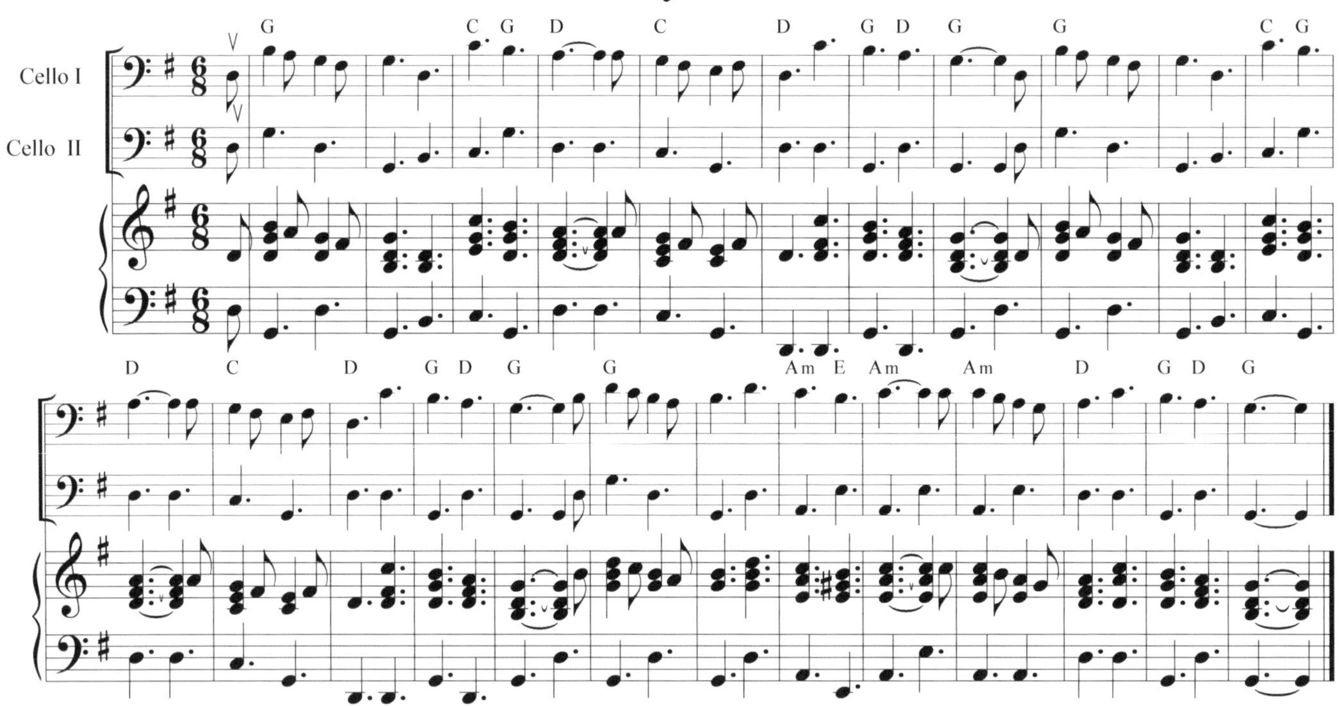

Star in the East - Brightest and Best - Hail the Blest Morn

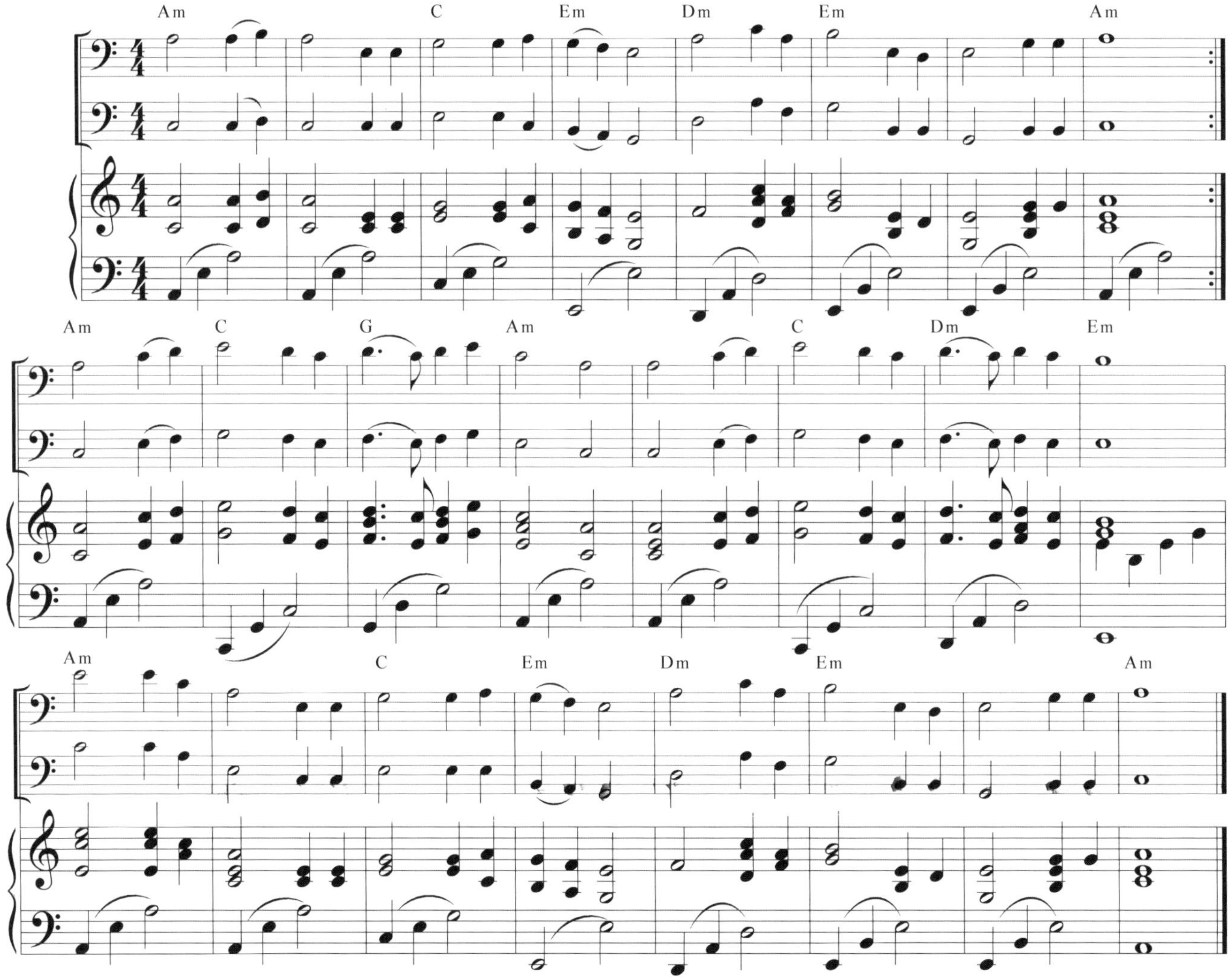

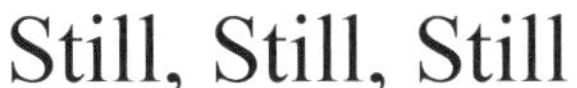

C Em/B Am Am/G F G C C Em/B Am Am/G F G C

Cello I

Cello II

G C G C G C Em/B Am Am/G F G C

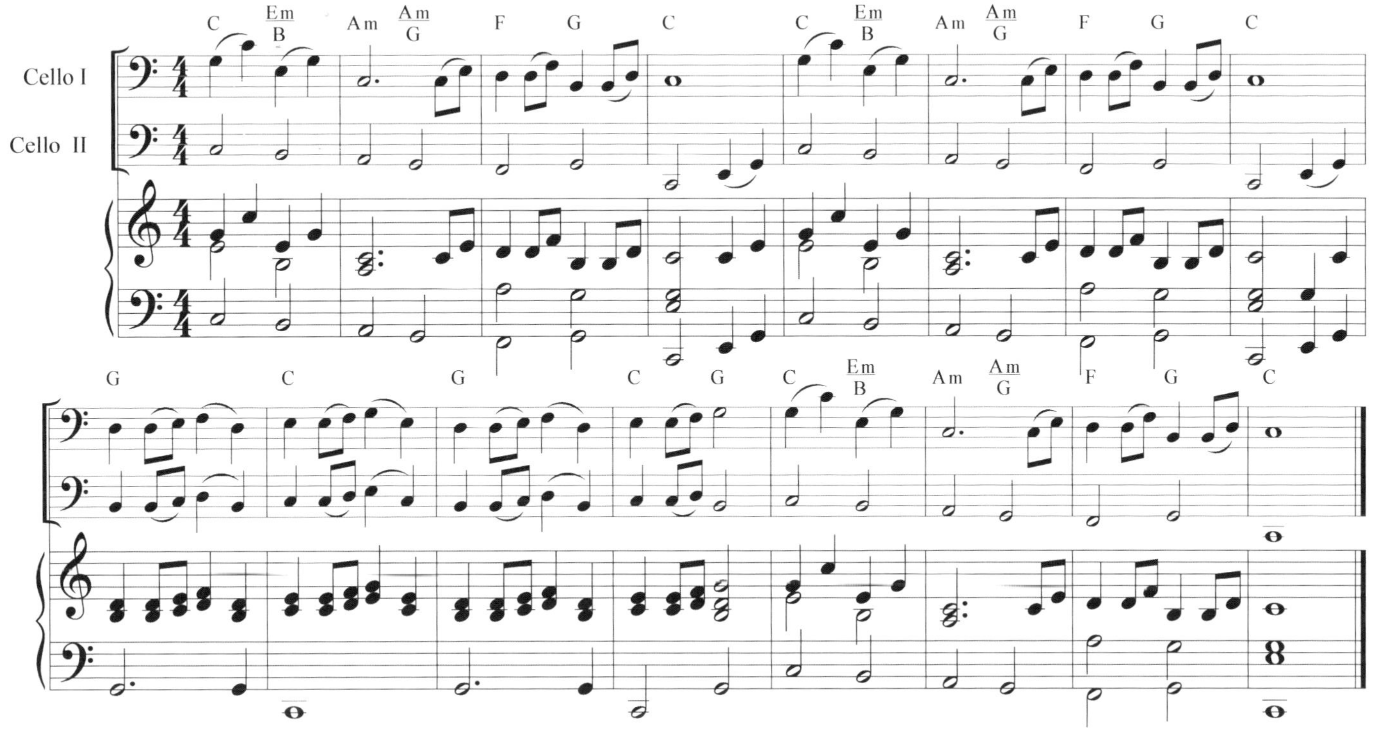

Tomorrow Shall Be My Dancing Day

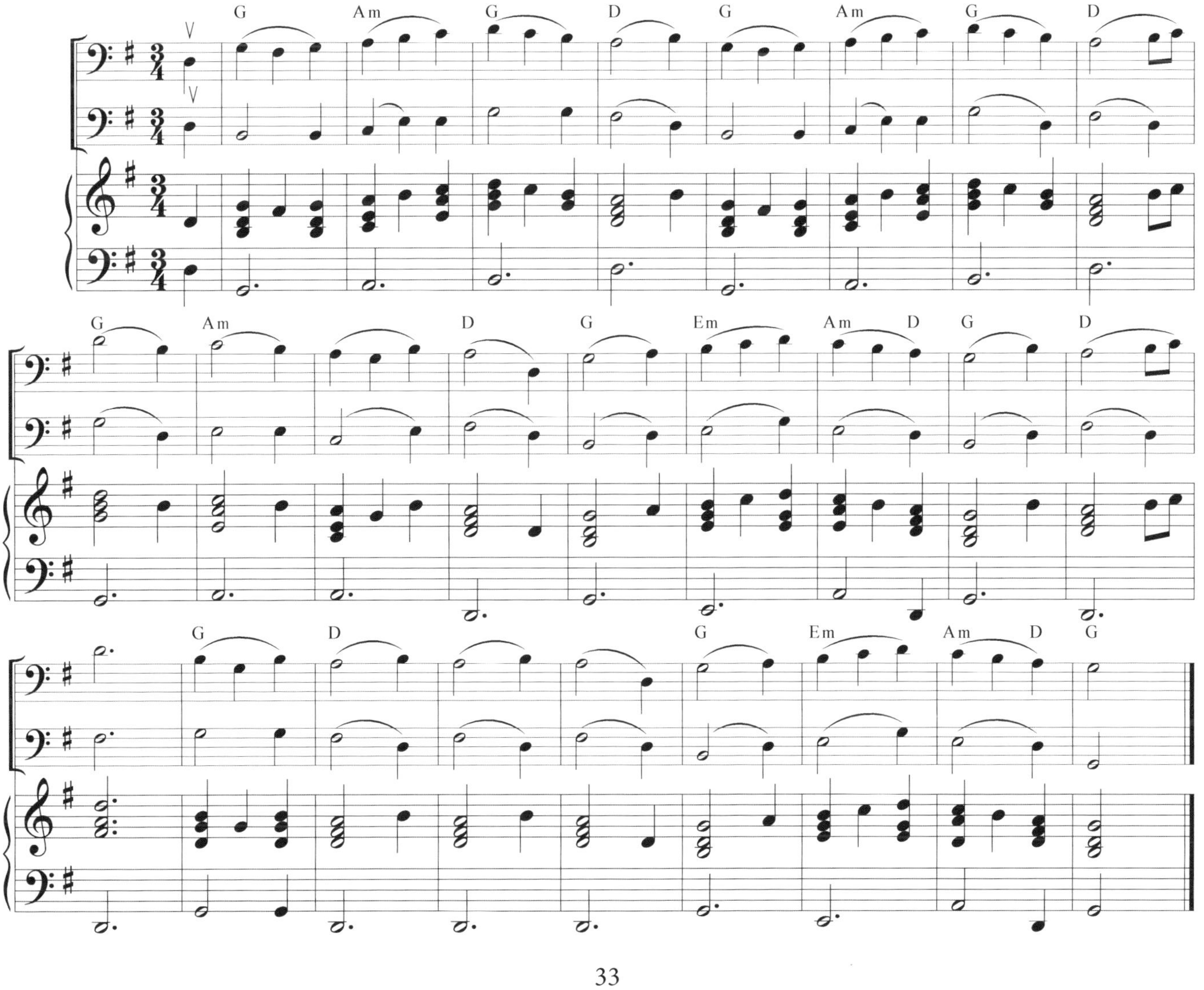

G Am G D G Am G D

G Am D G Em Am D G D

G D G Em Am D G

Wassail Song - Here We Come A-Wassailing

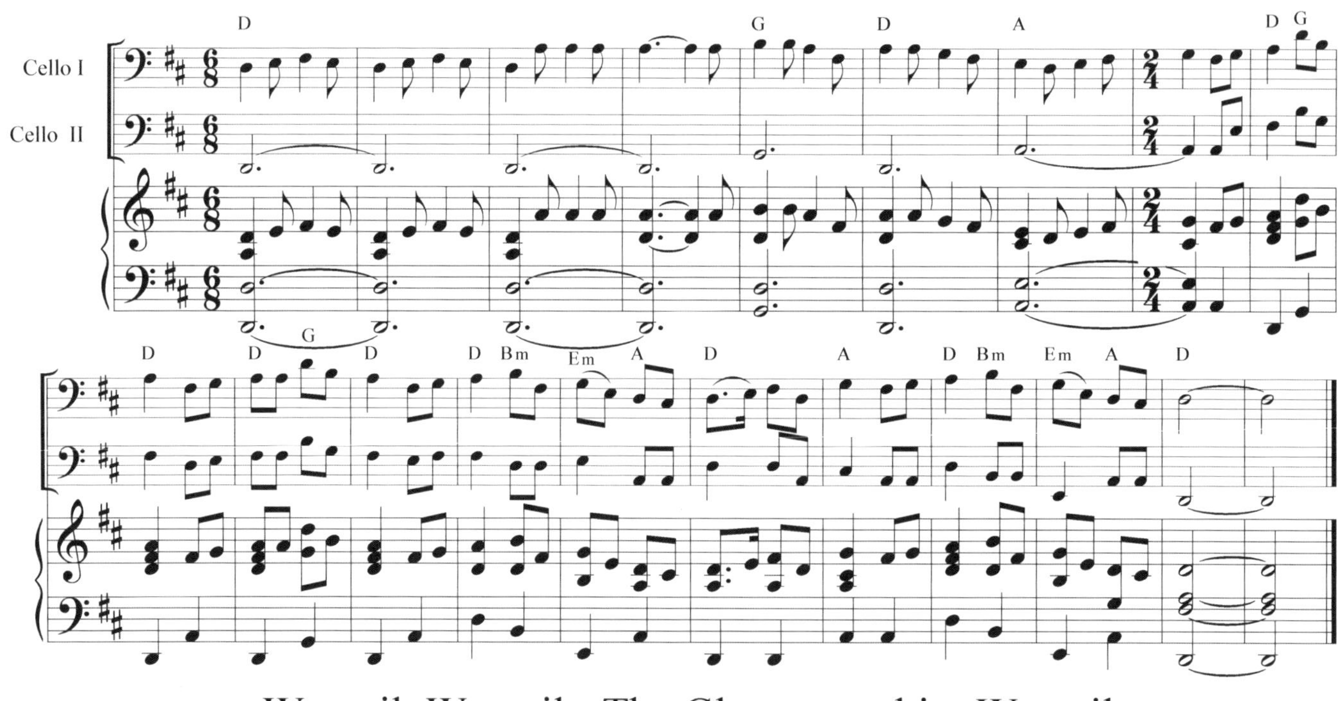

Wassail, Wassail - The Gloucestershire Wassail

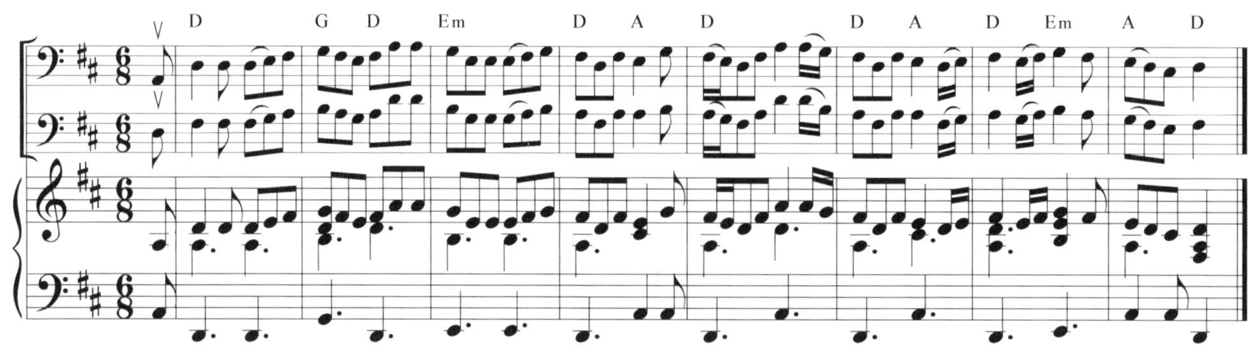

A Wassail, a Wassail Throughout the Town

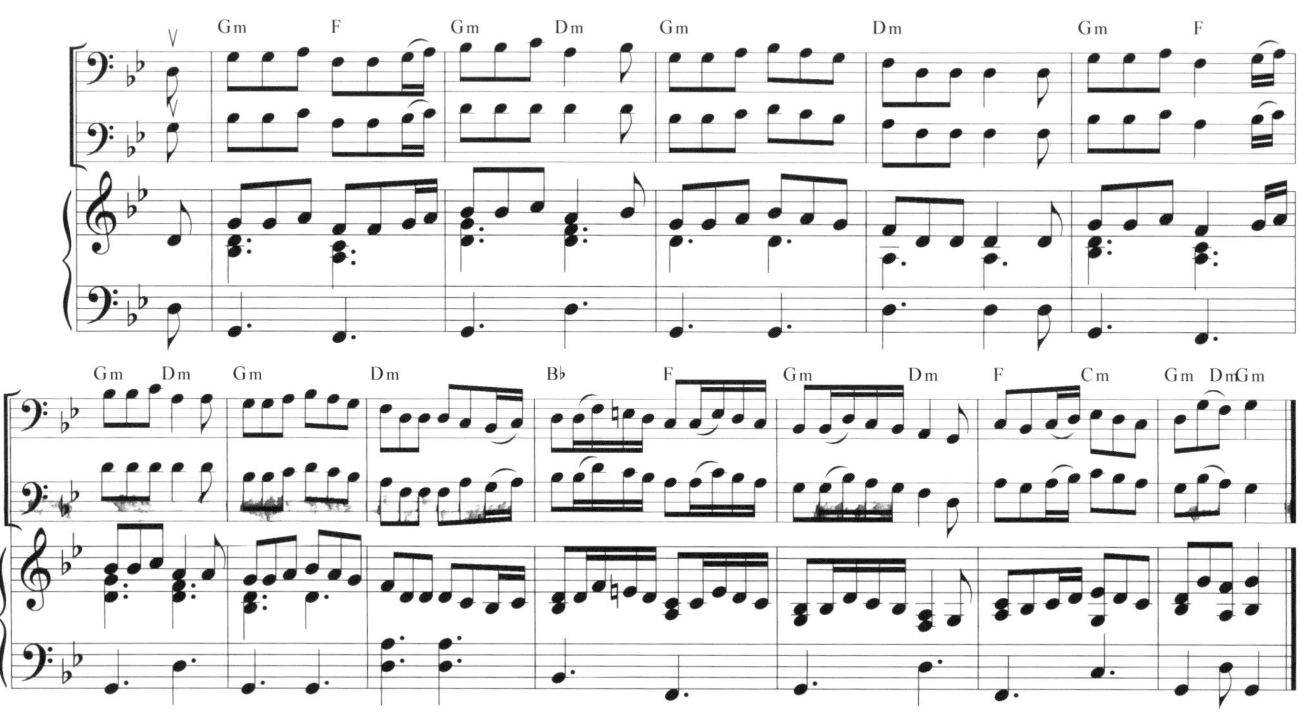

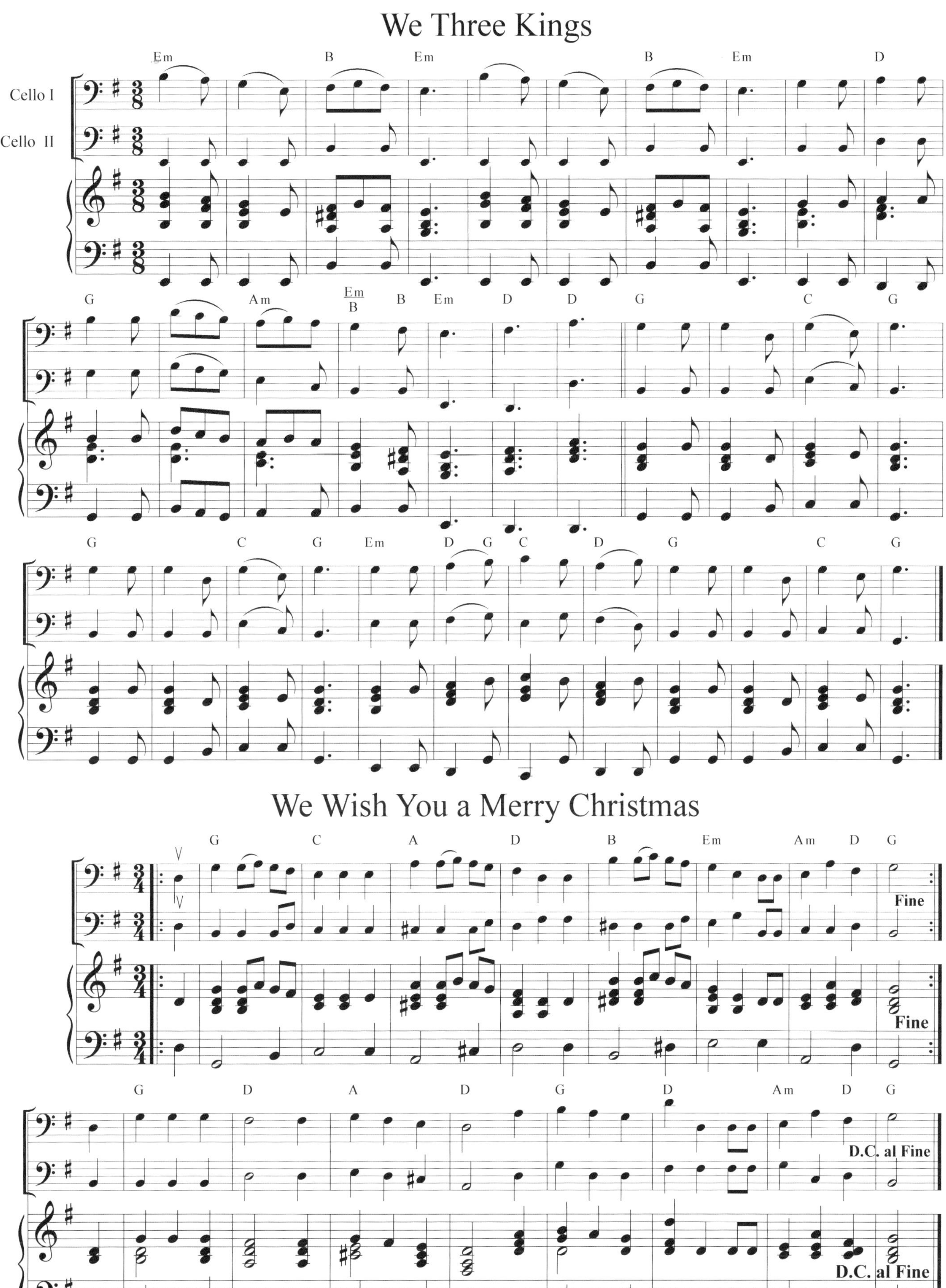
We Three Kings
Cello I
Cello II
We Wish You a Merry Christmas
Fine
D.C. al Fine

What Child Is This

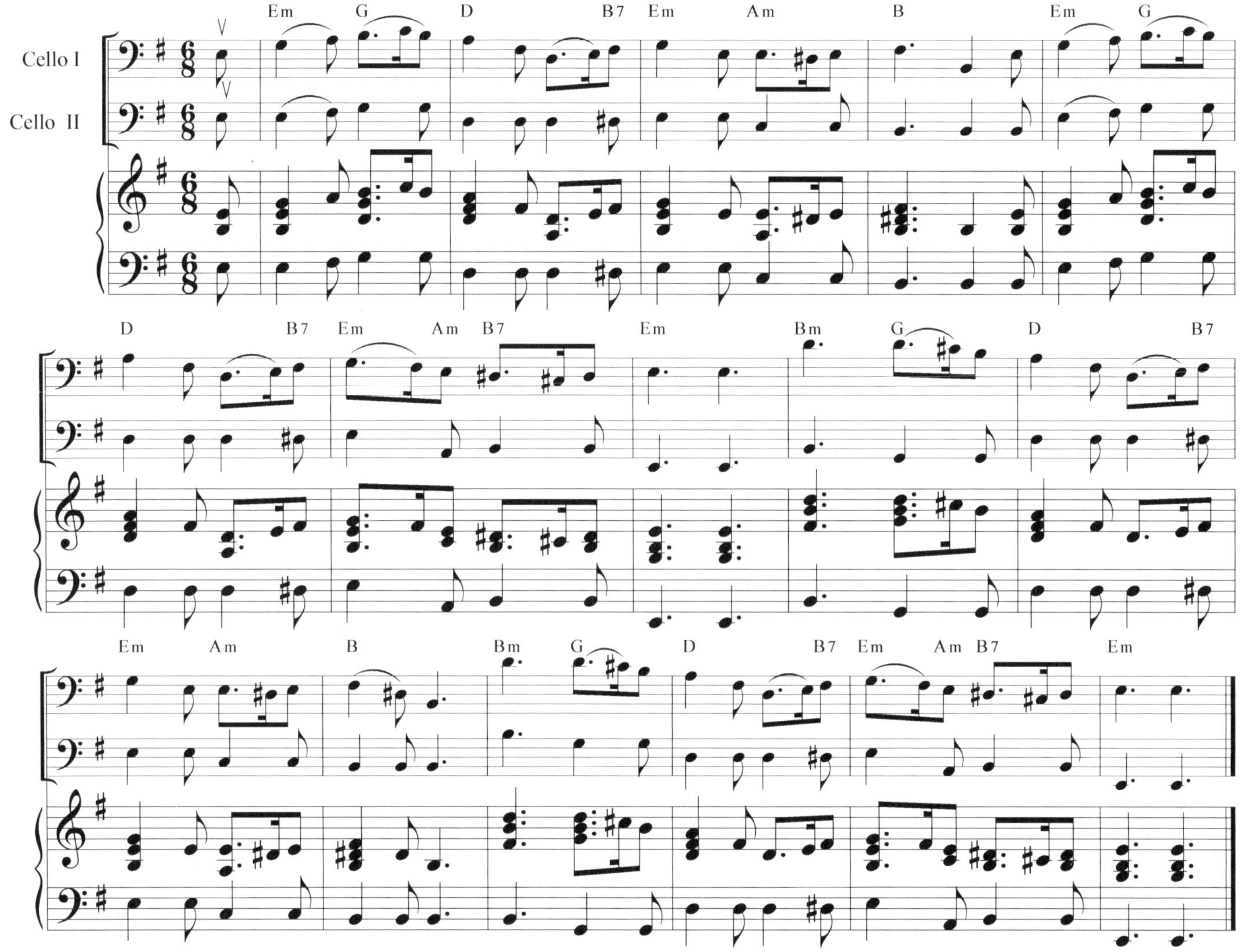

Cello I
Cello II

Em G D B7 Em Am B Em G

D B7 Em Am B7 Em Bm G D B7

Em Am B Bm G D B7 Em Am B7 Em

While Shepherds Watched Their Flocks

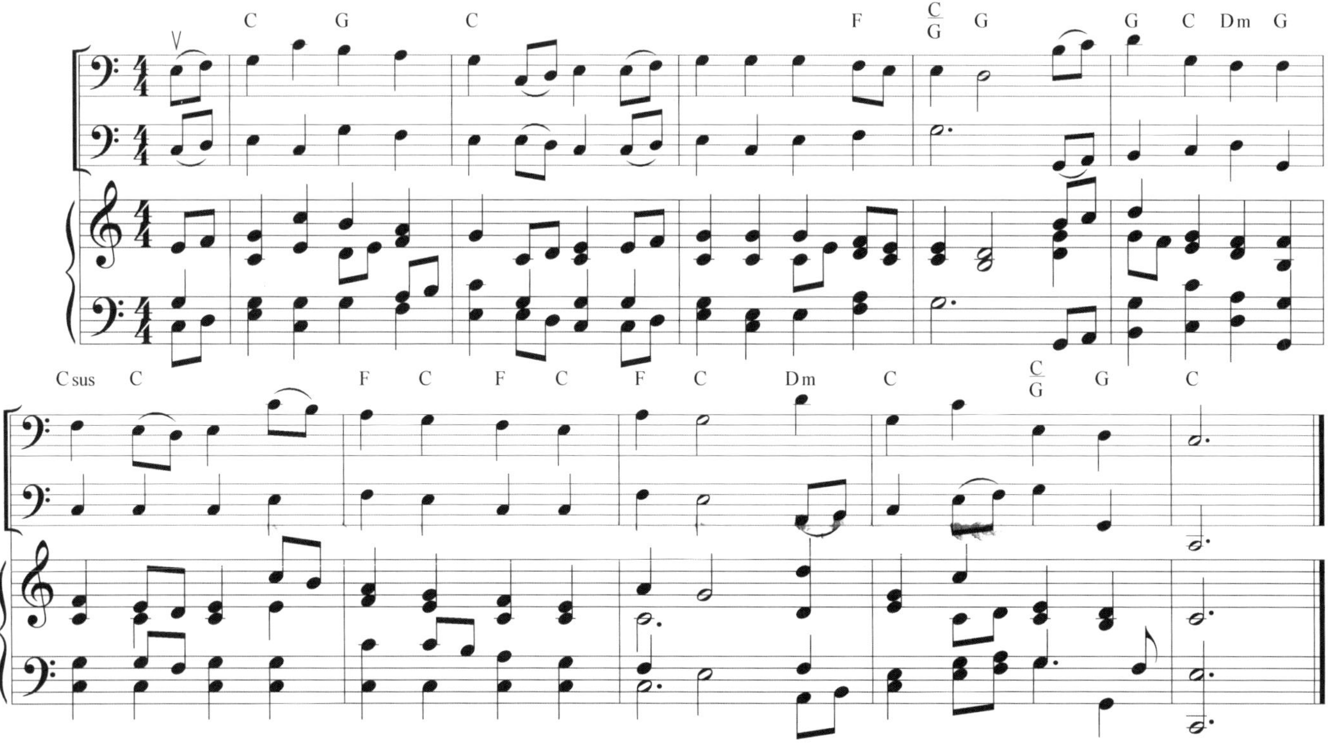

How Great Our Joy

This traditional German melody has been traced to 1623 and the text has been traced to around 1500. Hugo R. Jüngst arranged the text with the melody around 1890, giving us this carol.

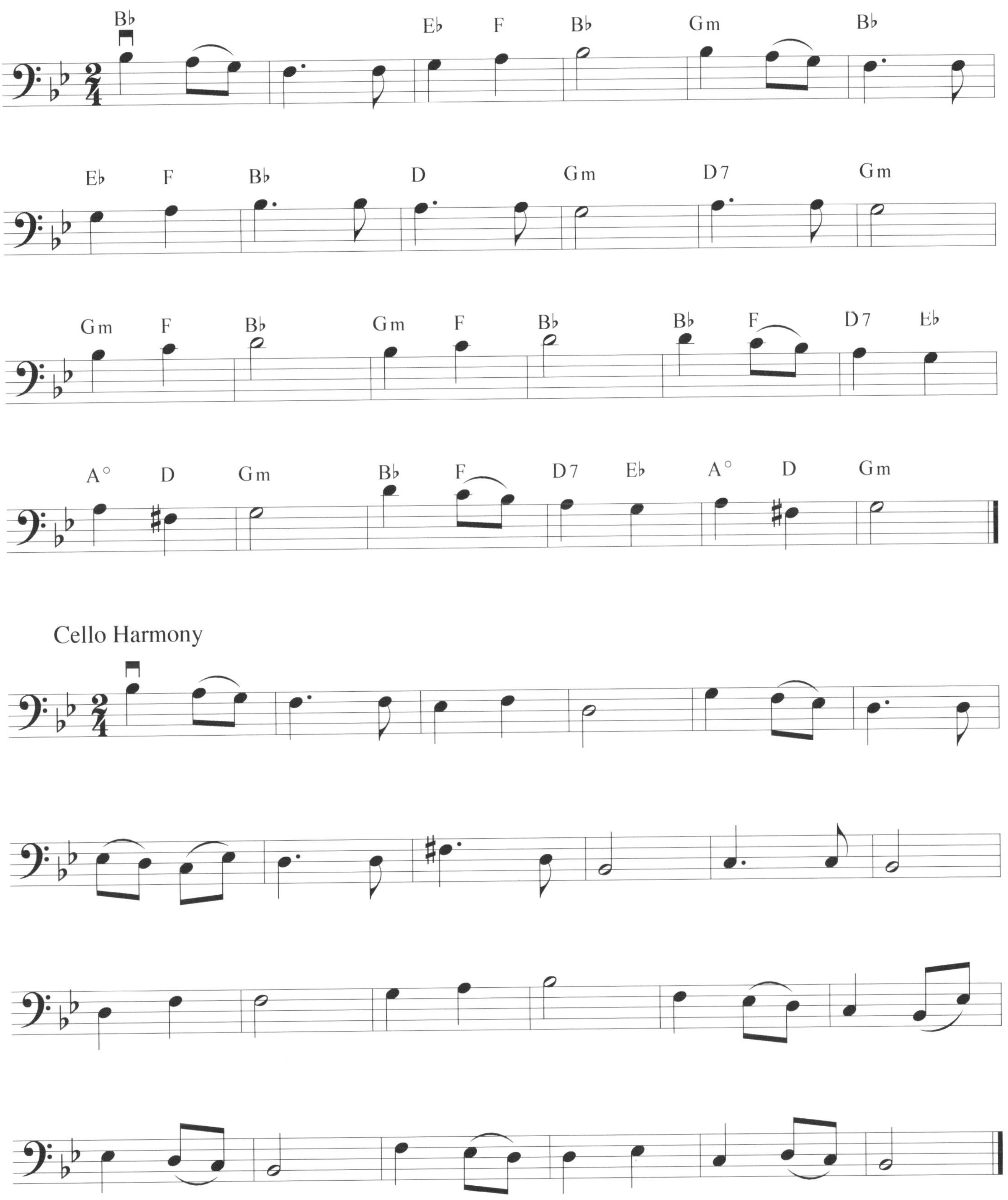

In the Bleak Midwinter

This English carol was first published in 1906 in *The English Hymnal*. Gustav Holst wrote this melody and Christina Rossetti wrote the poem that became the lyric.

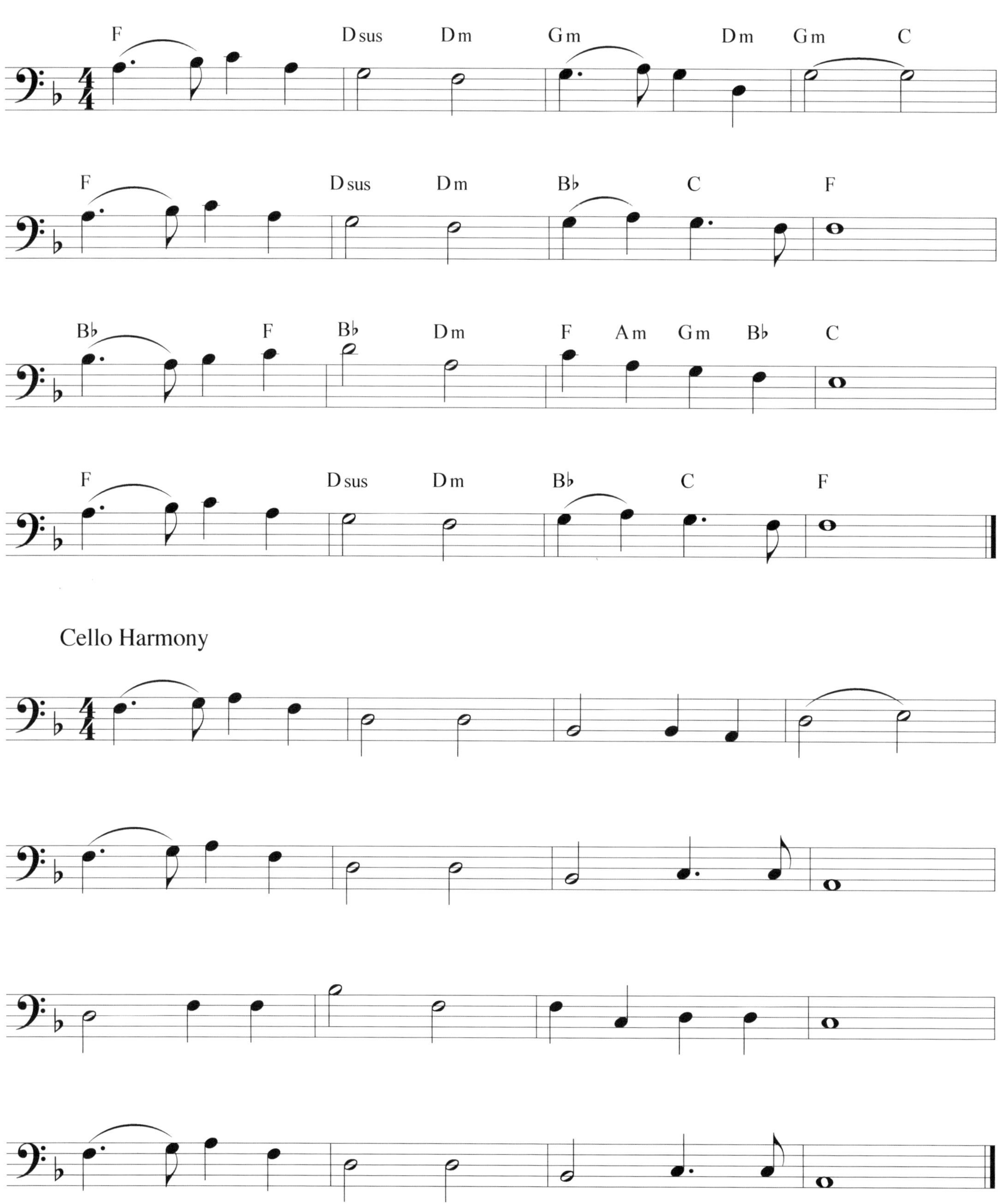

Infant Holy, Infant Lowly

Edith Reed translated and published this Polish carol in 1921 in the journal *Music and Youth.* The last two measures of the tune are a repeat of the previous two measures and are omitted in some versions.

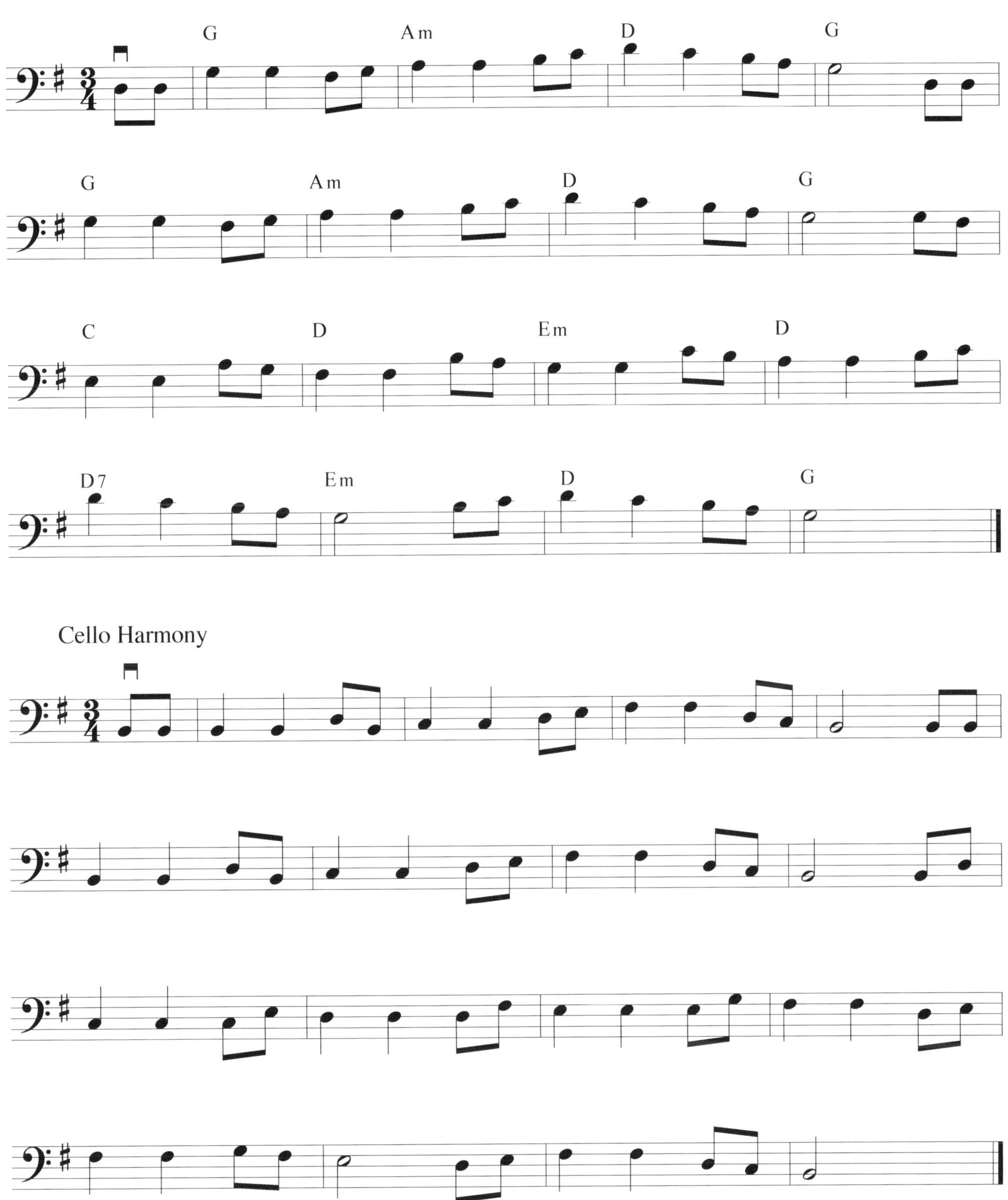

It Came Upon a Midnight Clear

Unitarian minister Edmund H. Sears of Massachusetts wrote the lyric to this carol in 1849. The tune was arranged by Uzziah Christopher Burnap from an organ study by Richard Storrs Willis.

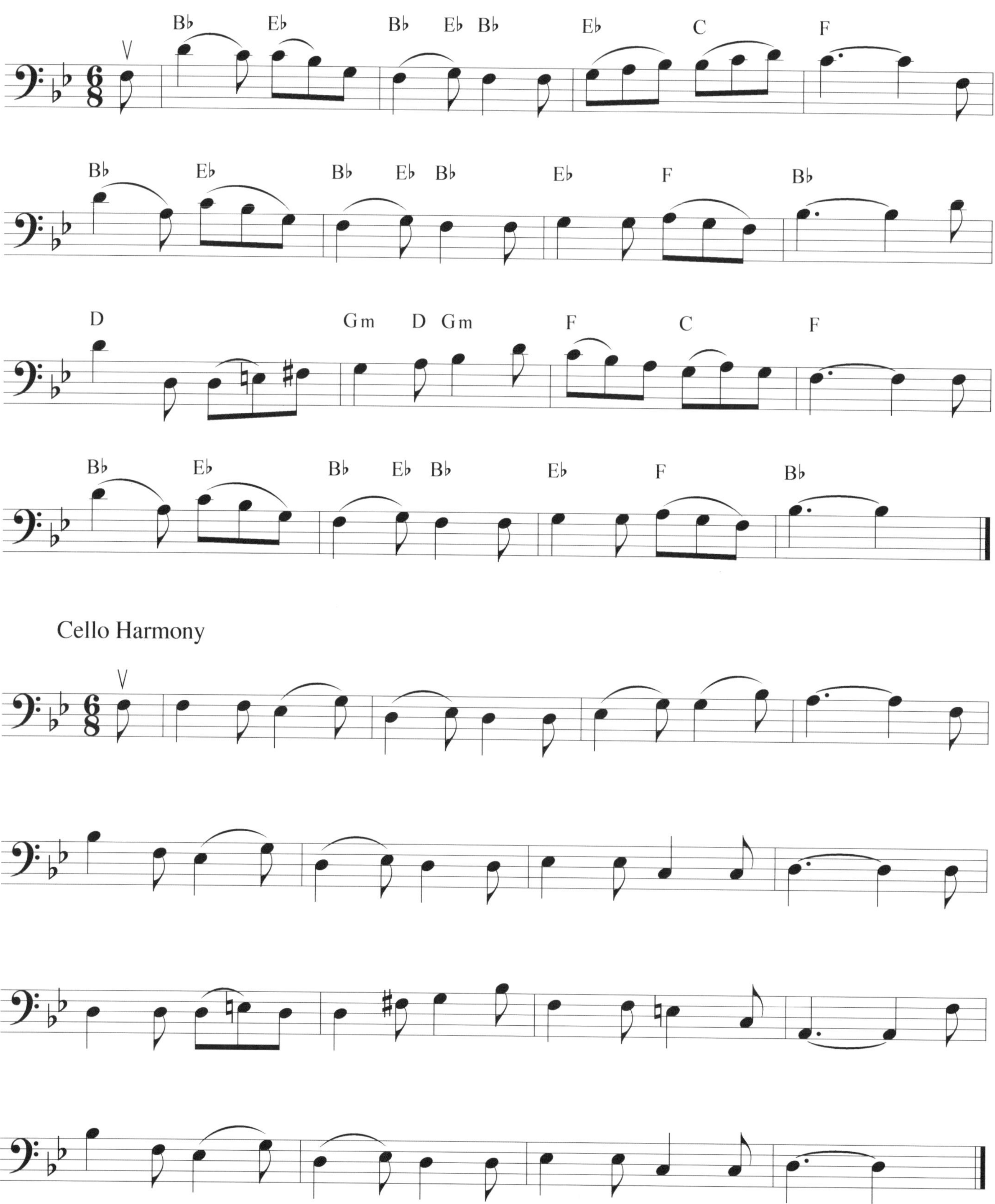

Jingle Bells

James L. Pierpont published this song in 1857 as "One Horse Open Sleigh". After achieving some popularity as a Christmas song, it was published again in 1859 with the name "Jingle Bells". The cello harmony part in this arrangement is a fun bass line and can be played arco or pizzicato.

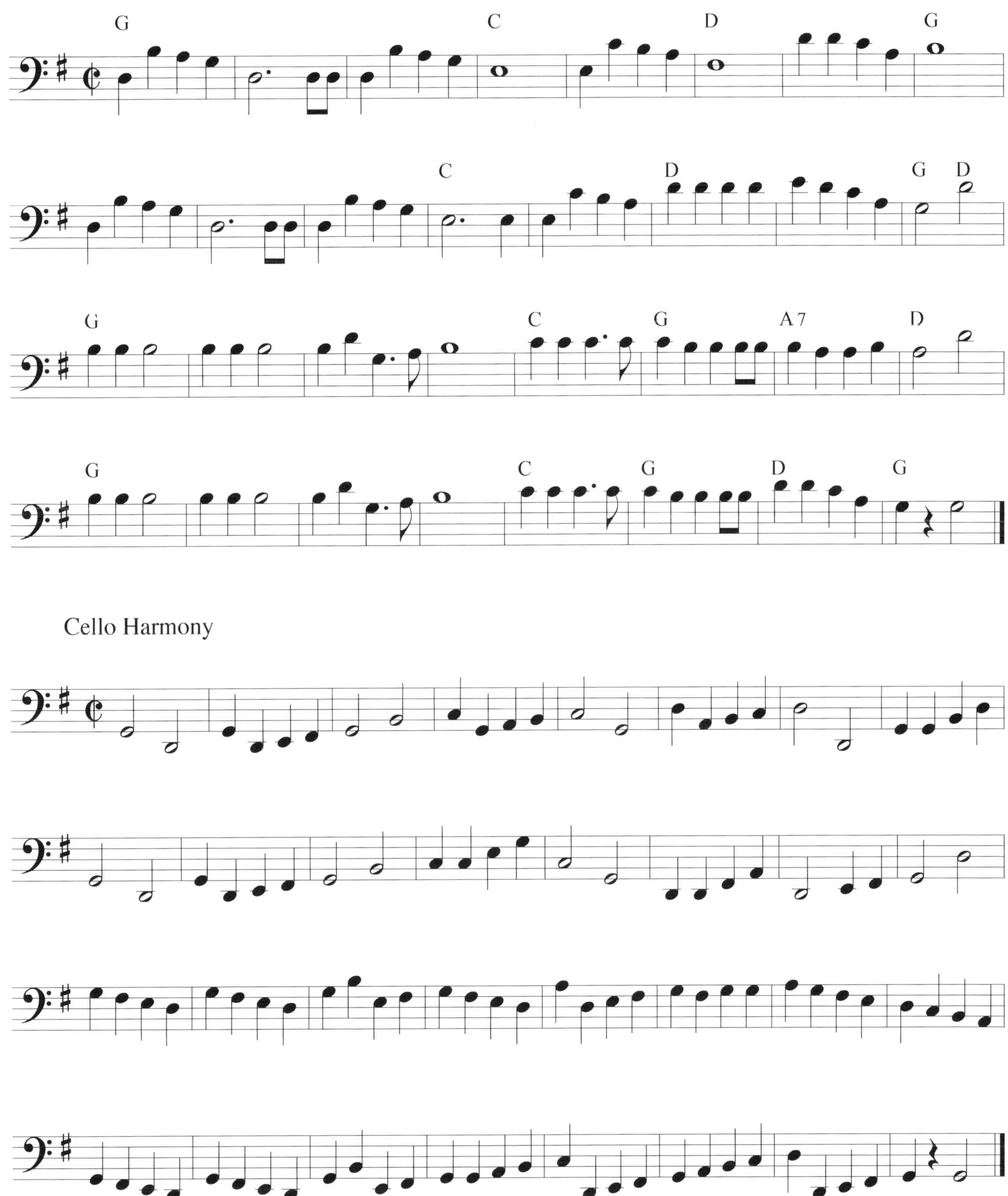

Joy to the World

Lowell Mason published Isaac Watts's text, "Joy to the World", in 1836. Although Mason credited Handel with writing the tune, there are several other sources listed in *The New Oxford Book of Carols* suggesting a different origin.

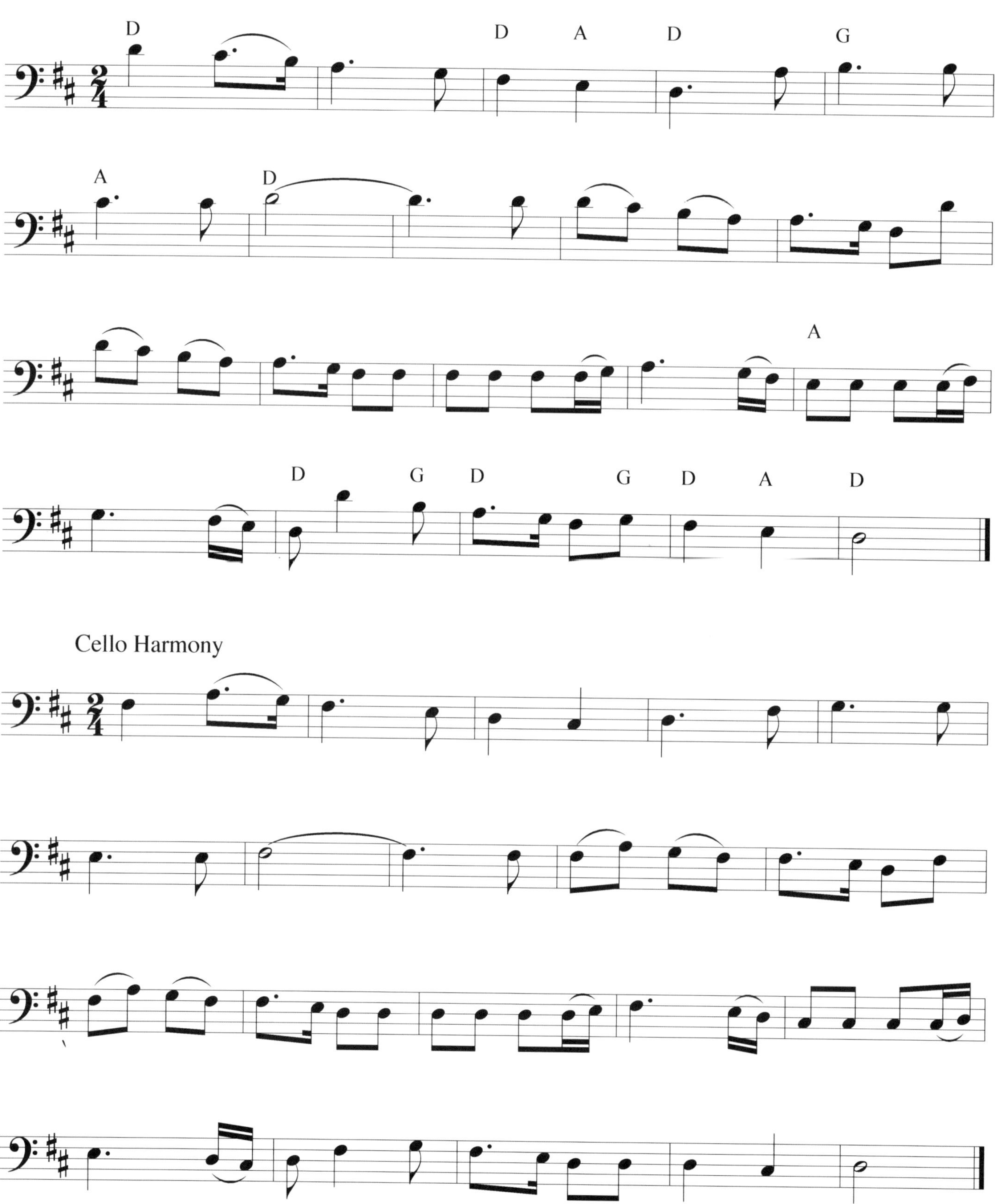

Joseph Dearest, Joseph Mine

The text of this carol was first recorded in a Leipzig University manuscript around 1400. It is one of the most popular carols sung in Germany. The first nine measures also state the melody of "Christ Was Born On Christmas Day".

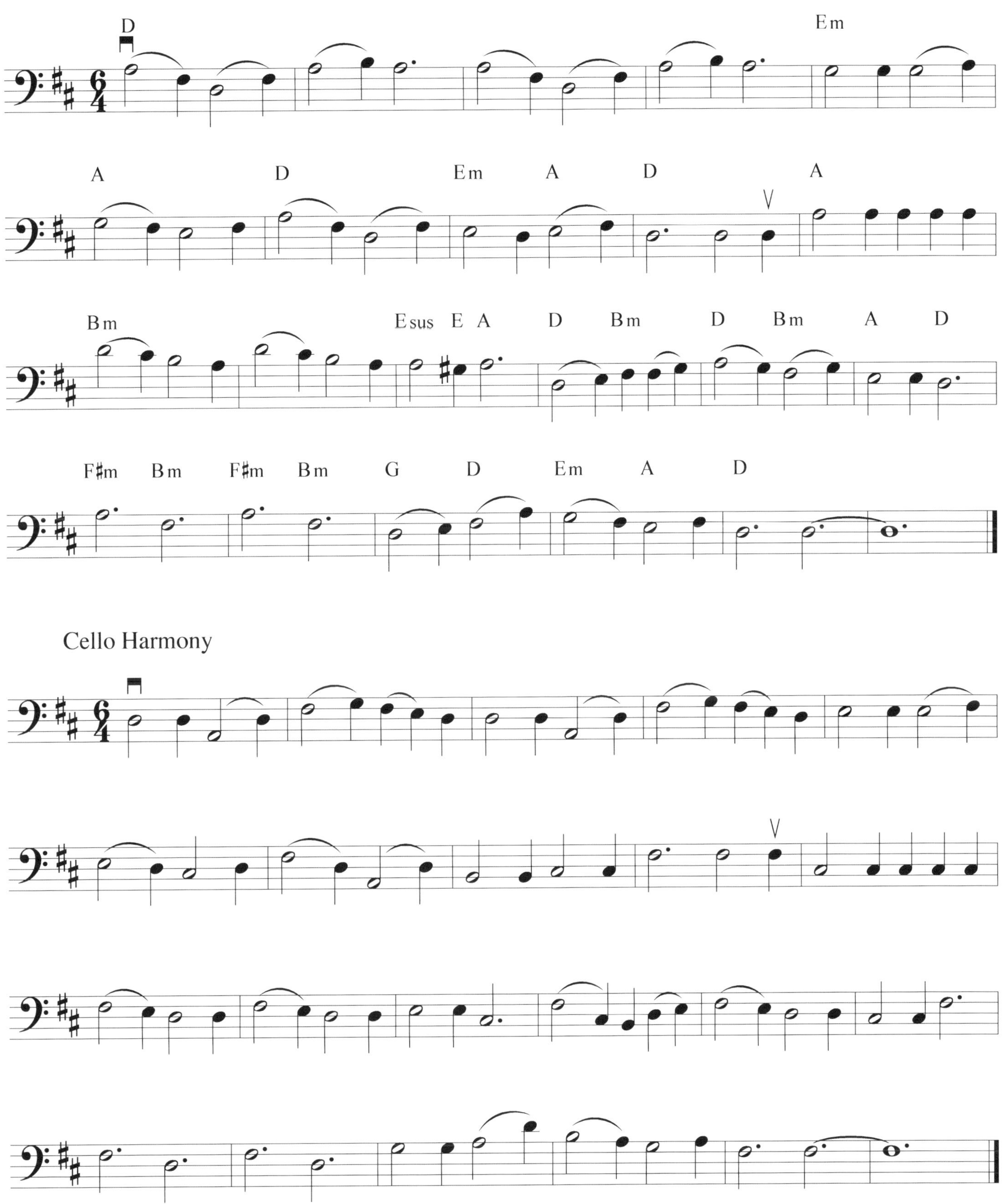

Lo, How a Rose E'er Blooming

This is believed to have originated in the fifteenth or early sixteenth century as a Twelfth Night carol. The most popular setting is by Michael Praetorius. He is often given credit for writing the tune.

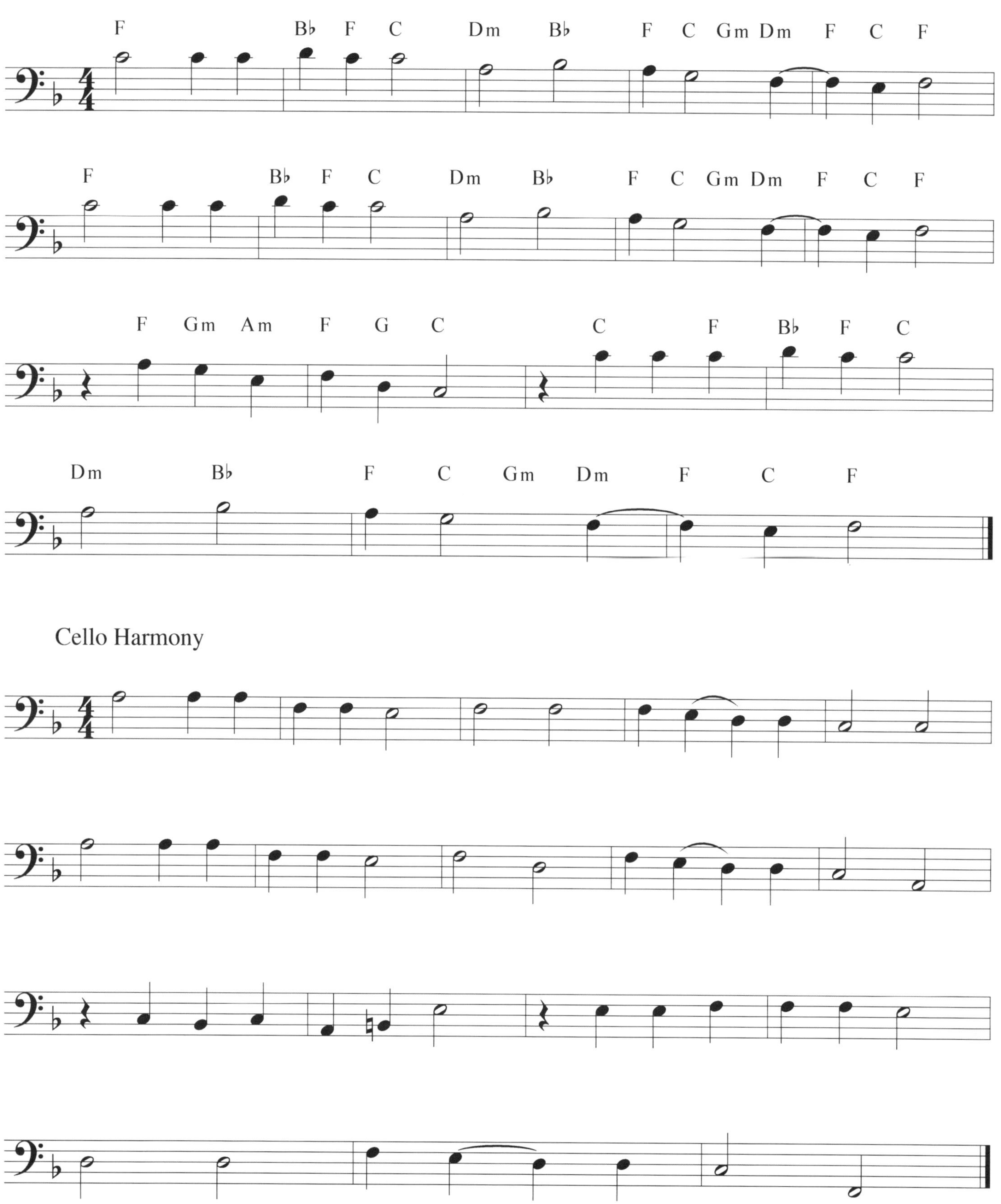

Masters in This Hall

This traditional English carol should be played with the energy of an Irish fiddle jig. A harmony part is included, but performing the tune in unison is also very stylistic.

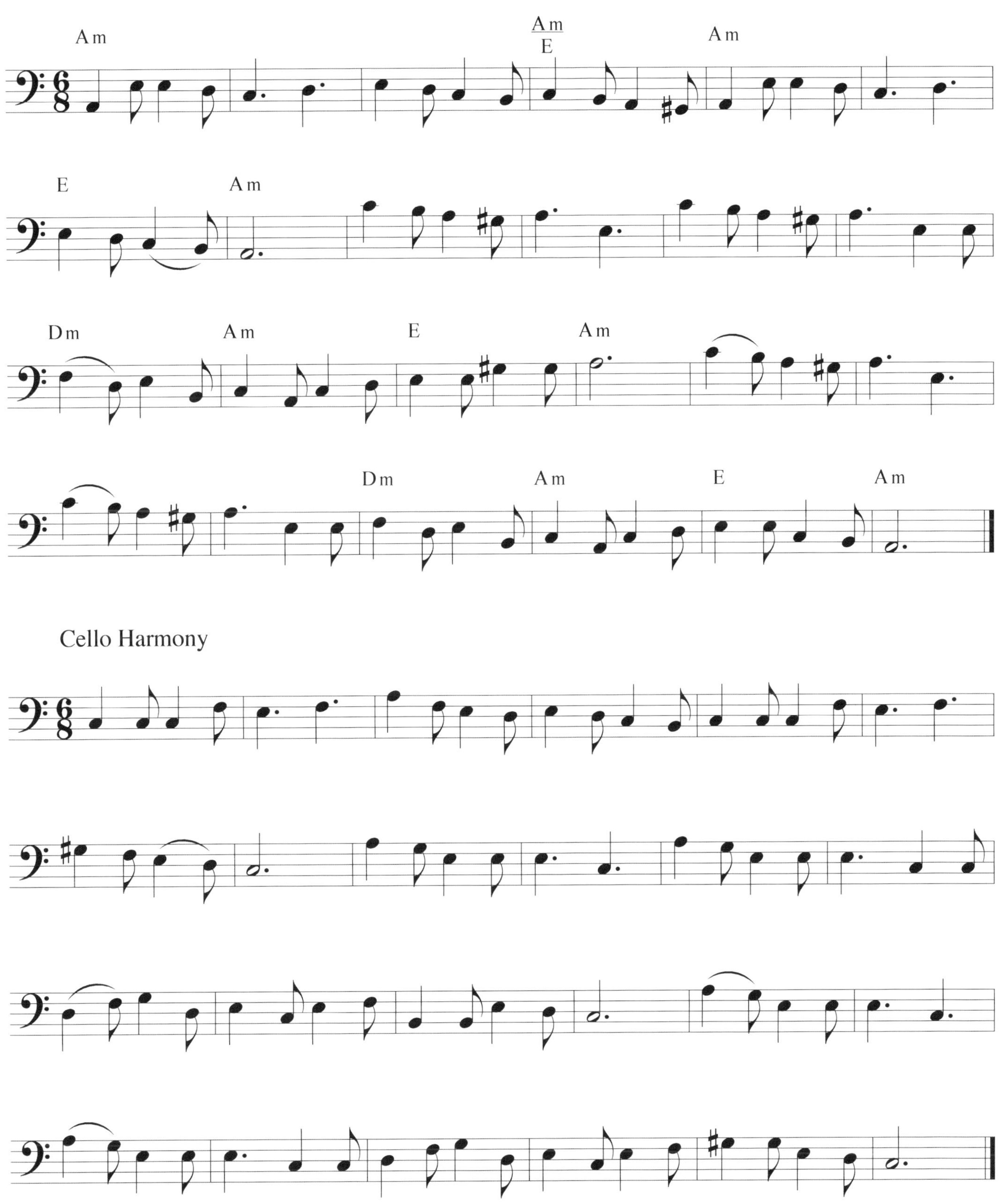

O Come, All Ye Faithful

"Adeste, fideles" is the Latin title of this carol. It has been traced to the writing of English scribe, John Francis Wade, who lived from 1711-1786. It is not known if he wrote or collected the carol.

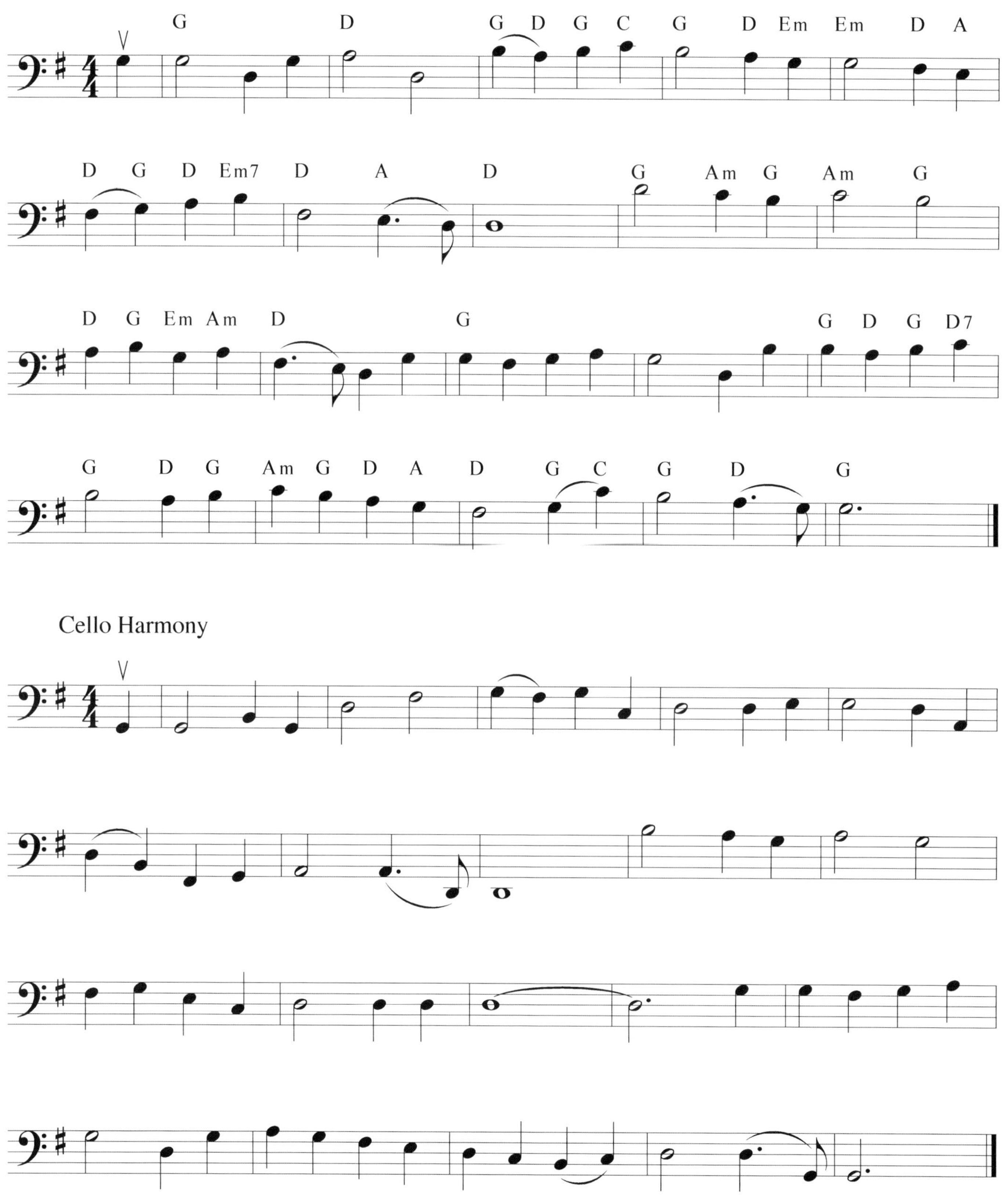

O Come, O Come, Emmanuel

This fifteenth century French plainsong melody was a part of a Franciscan processional. The text can be traced back to the reign of Charlemagne, 771-814. The Latin text was translated into English in the nineteenth century. The tune title is "Veni Emmanuel".

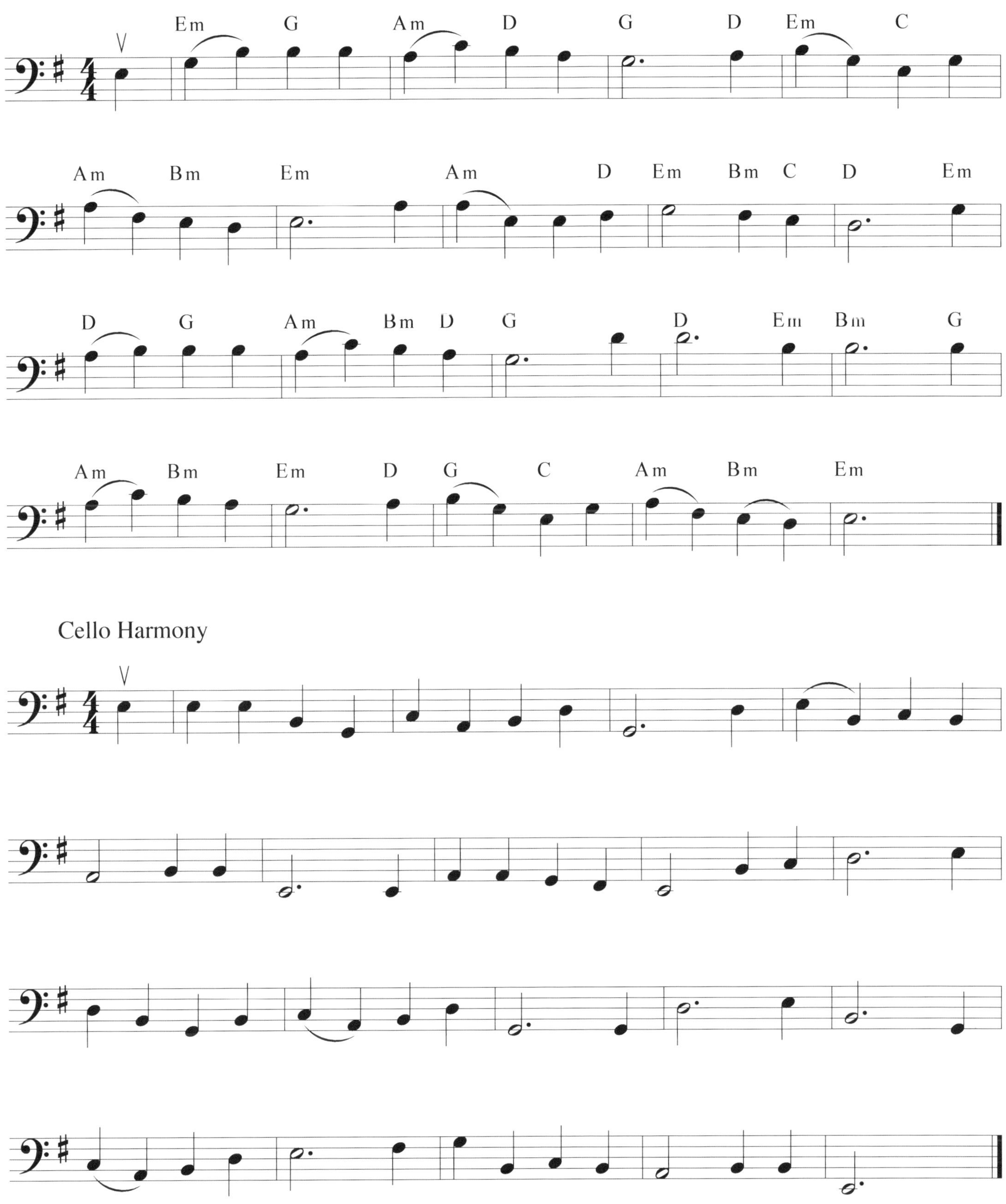

O Holy Night

Cantique de Noël

Adolphe Adam composed "O Holy Night" in 1847 to go with the French poem *Minuit, chrétiens* by Placide Cappeau. John Sullivan Dwight translated it into English 1855. The carol is also known as "Cantique de Noël".

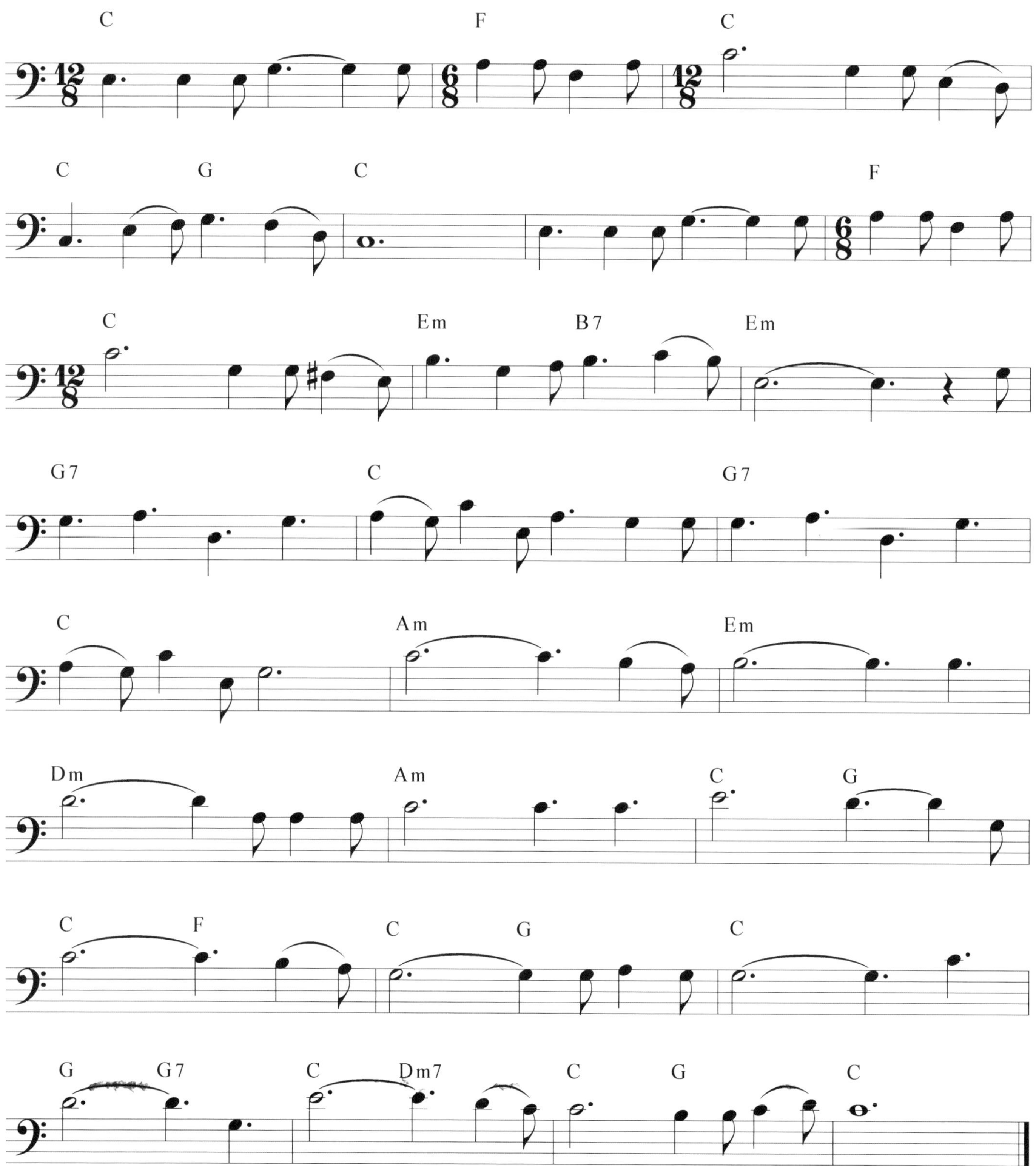

O Holy Night

Cello Harmony

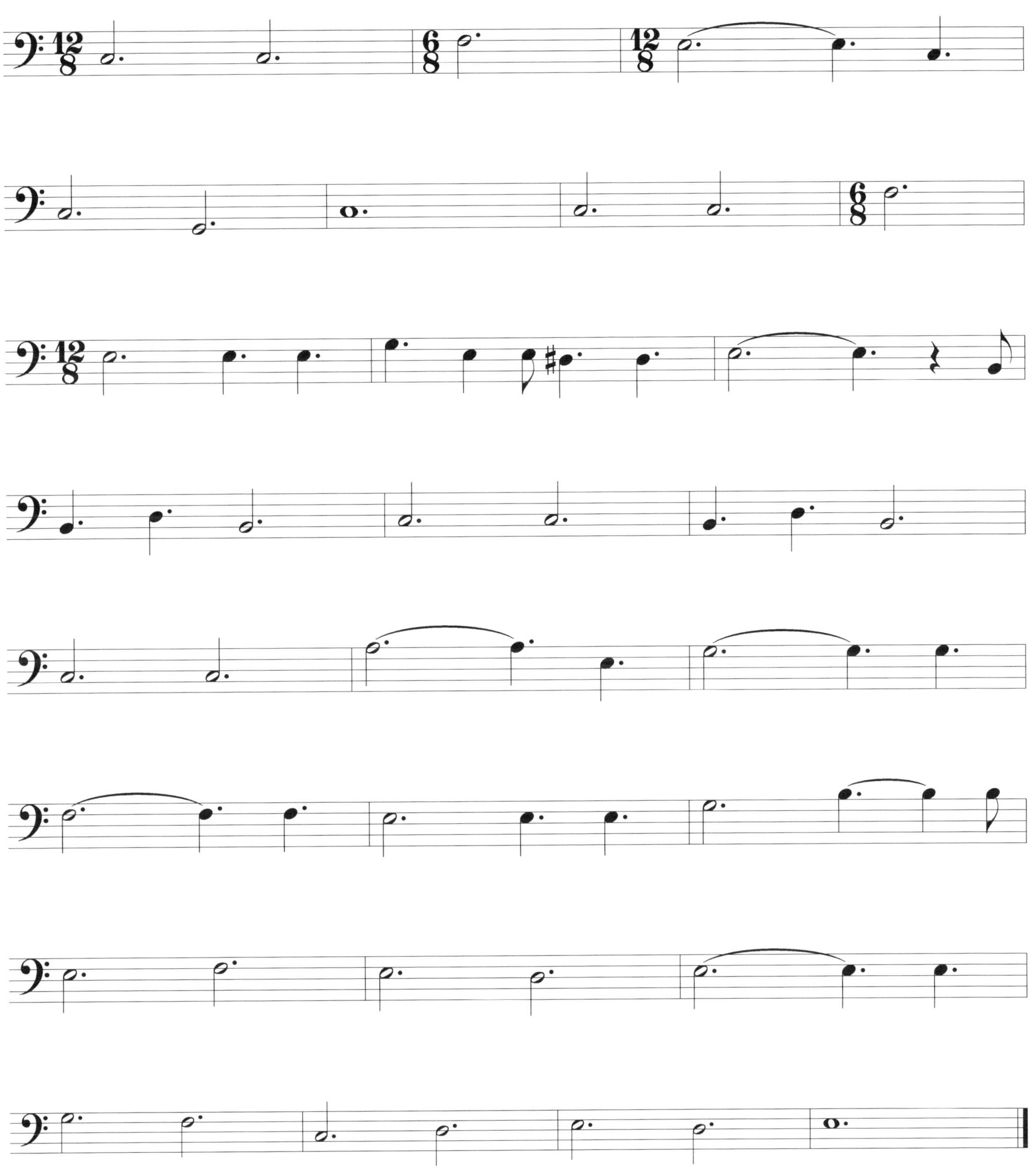

O Little Town of Bethlehem

The text of this carol was written by Phillips Brooks after a visit to the Holy Land in 1865. Lewis Redner wrote the music on Christmas Day, 1868.

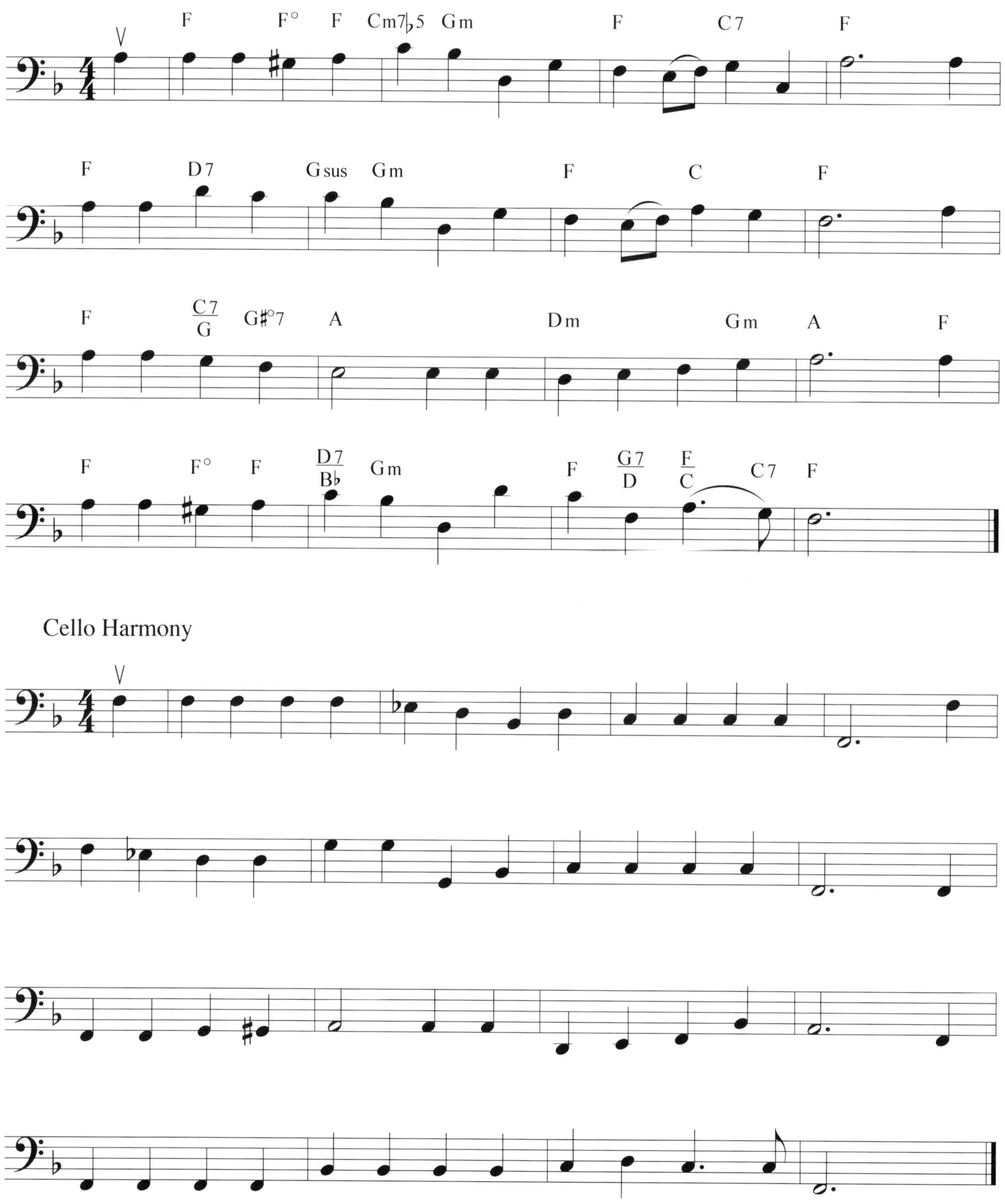

Of the Father's Love Begotten

The Latin name for this tenth century plainchant melody is "Divinum mysterium". The first print version is in the 1582 Finnish song book *Piae Cantiones*. In 1851 Thomas Helmore published the Latin poem *Corde natus* with the melody giving us this carol.

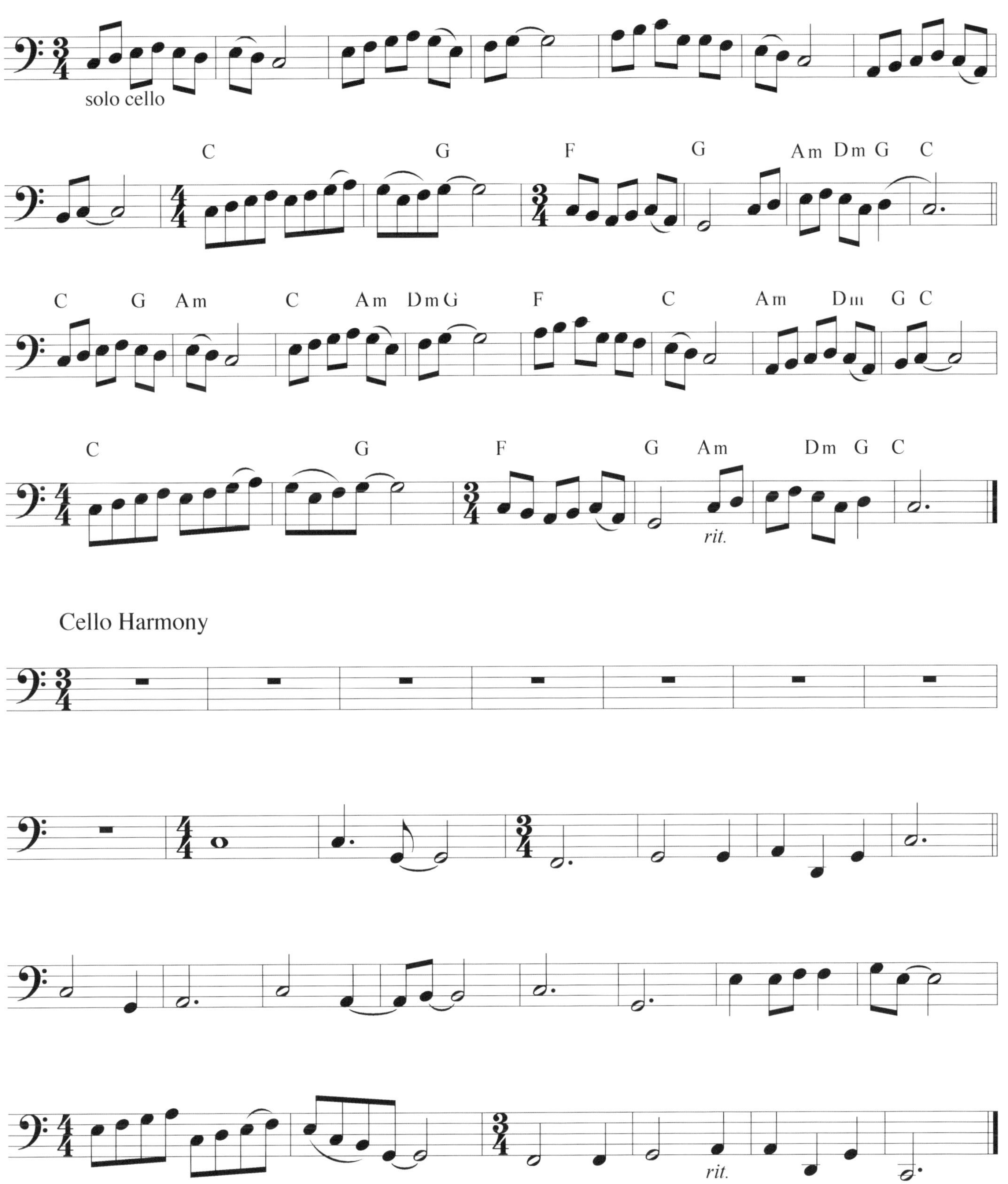

Oh, Christmas Tree

O Tannenbaum

This carol was written as "O Tannenbaum" in Leipzig, Germany in 1824 by Ernst Anschütz. In addition to being a carol, Delaware, Maryland, and Missouri have all used the melody for a state song.

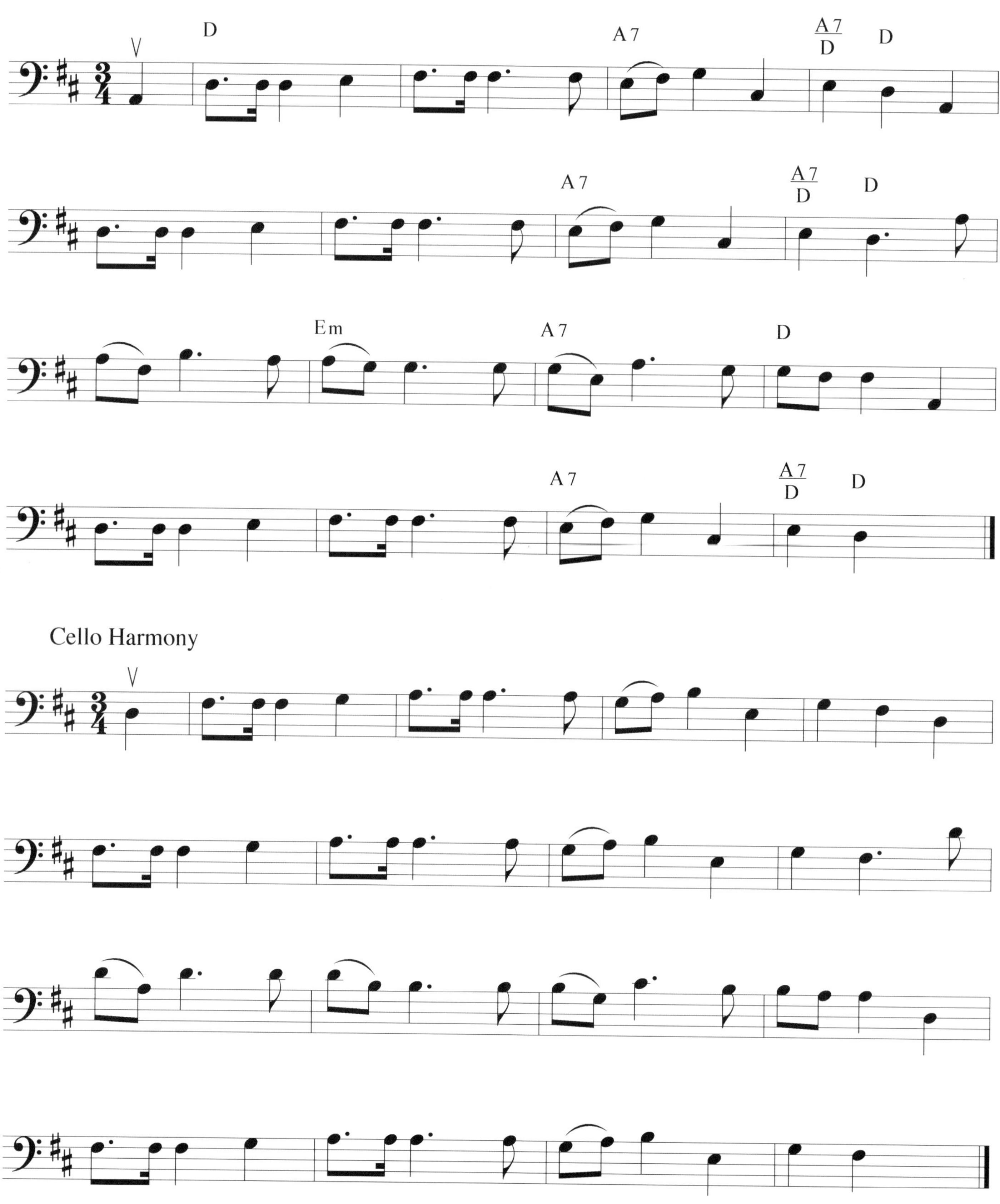

On Christmas Day in the Morning

"I Saw Three Ships" and "As I Sat on a Sunny Bank" are both English carols with similar texts that end with "on Christmas day in the morning." The two eight-measure melodies are combined here to create a very effective "jig" medley. Both carols are found in the *New Oxford Book of Carols*.

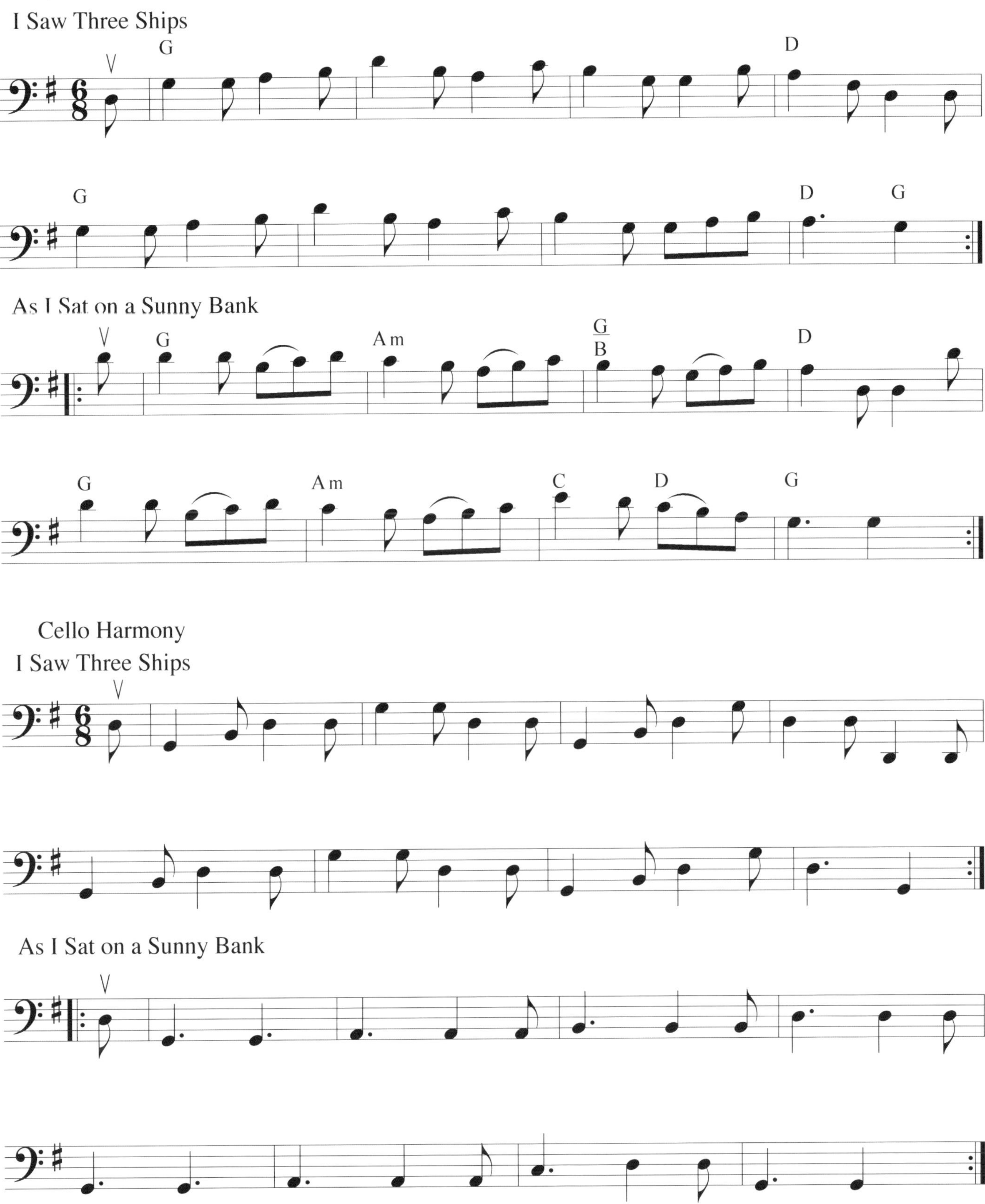

On Christmas Night
The Sussex Carol

Ralph Vaughan Williams collected this carol from a Mrs. Verrall near Horsham, Sussex in 1904. Although the tune was not published until 1904, the text dates from 1686.

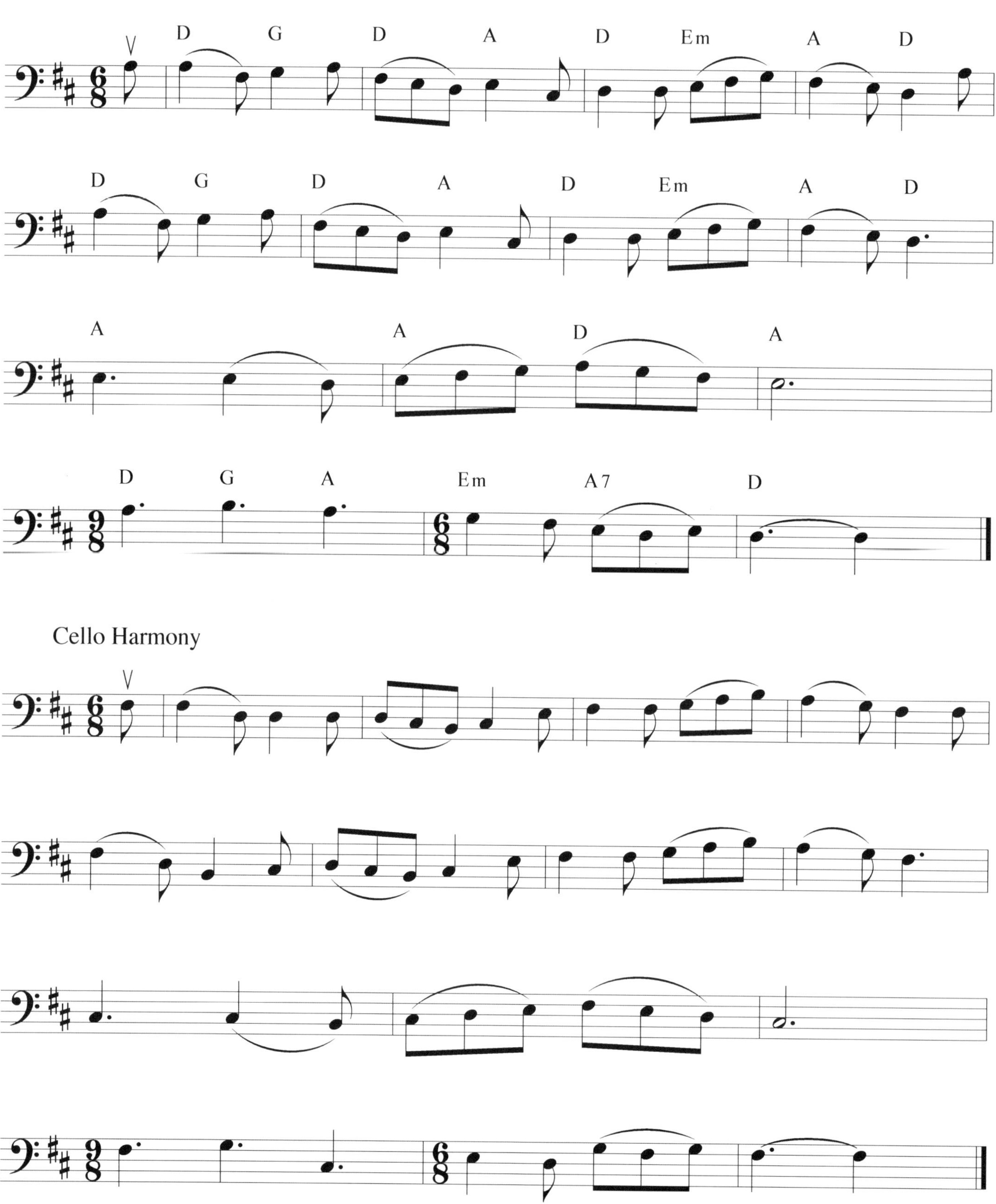

Once in Royal David's City

Mrs. Cecil Frances Alexander wrote the lyric to this carol and Henry John Gauntlett set it to music in 1848. It was written to be a children's tune, but has since become one of the well-known hymns of Christmas.

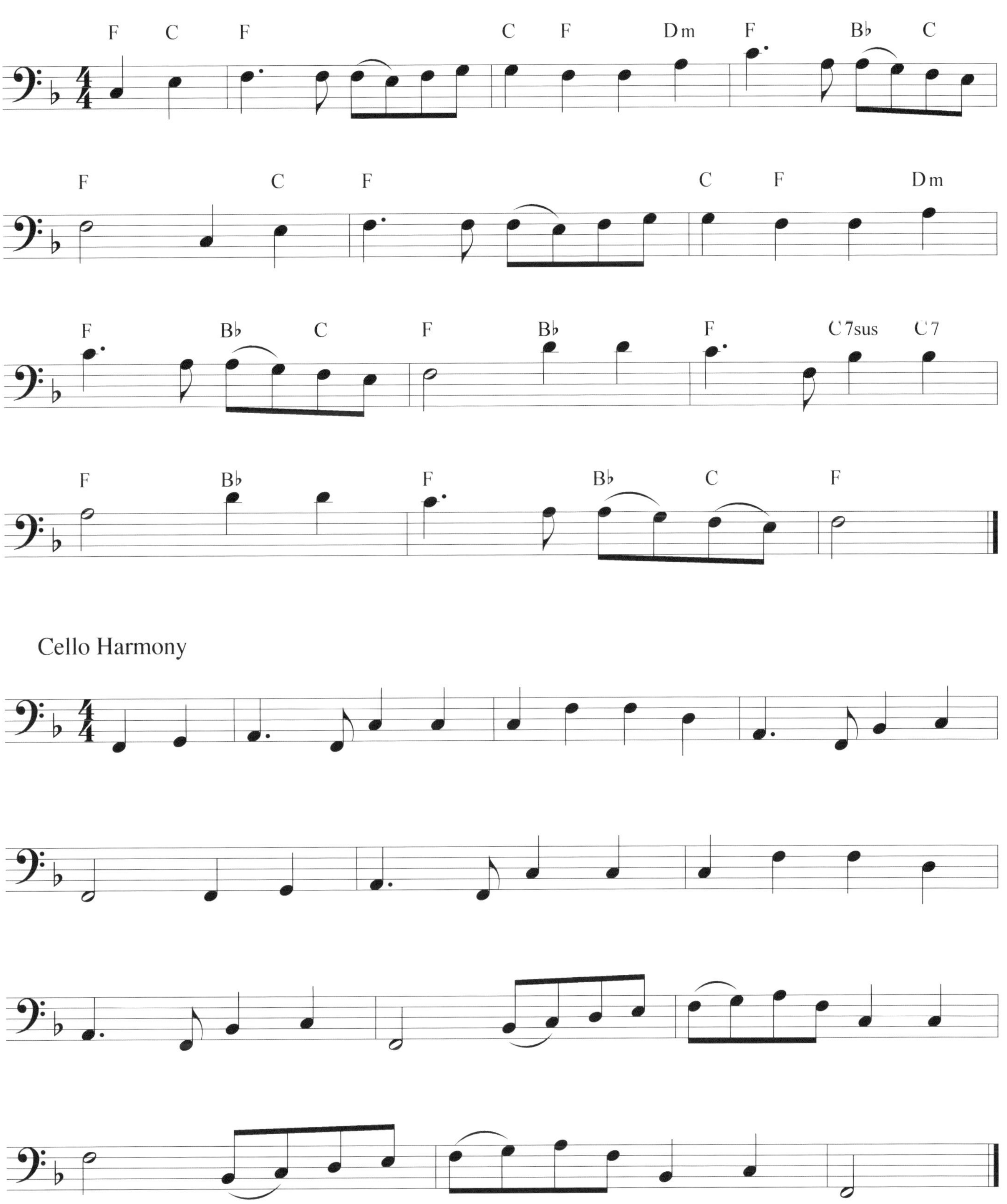

Rise Up, Shepherd and Follow

This American Spiritual first appeared in print in 1867 as "A Christmas Plantation Song". It most likely came from the coastal regions of Georgia and North and South Carolina.

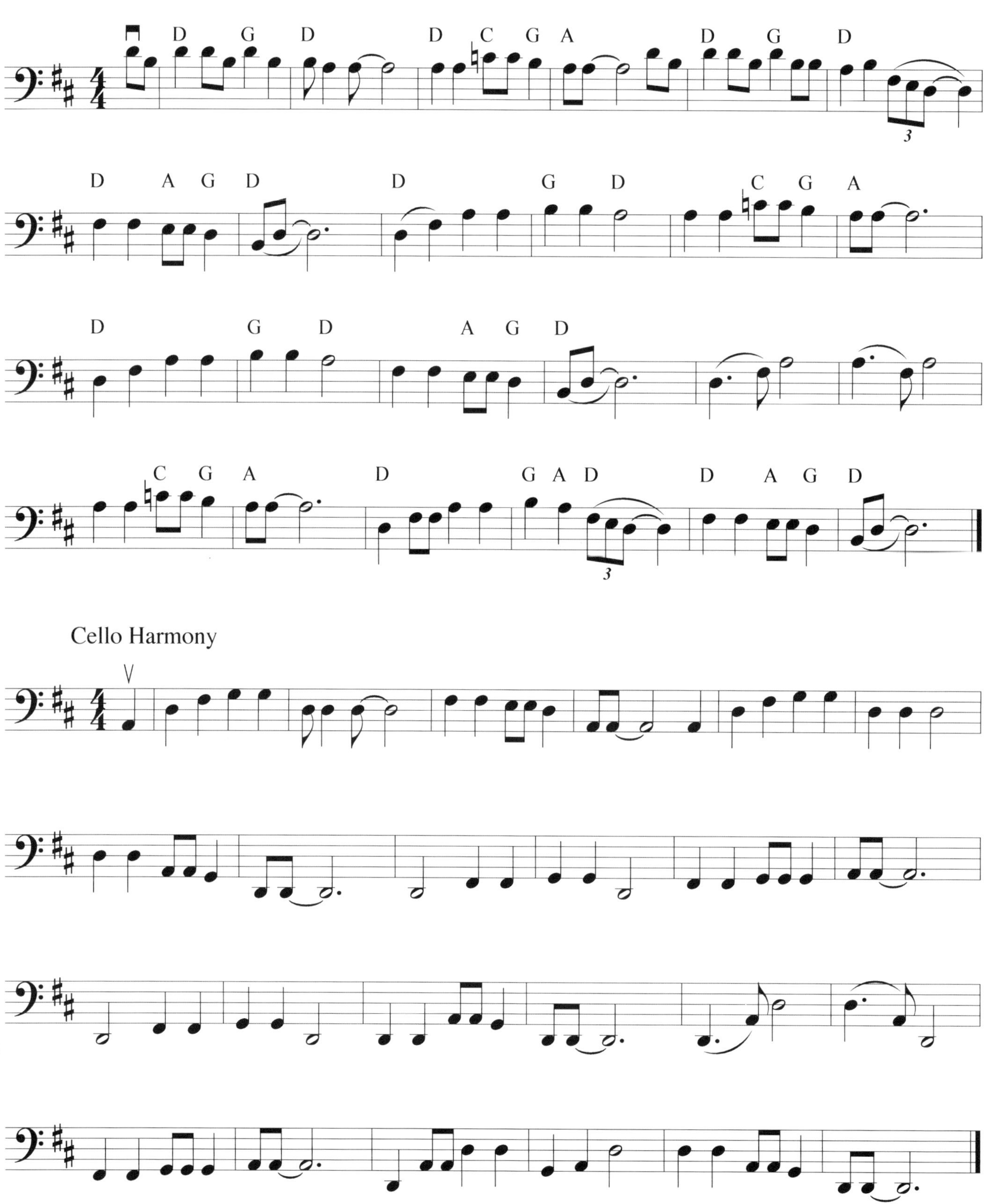

Silent Night

Franz Gruber wrote one of the most popular of all carols in 1818 for the Christmas Eve midnight mass at Oberdorf. It was originally written for voice with guitar accompaniment.

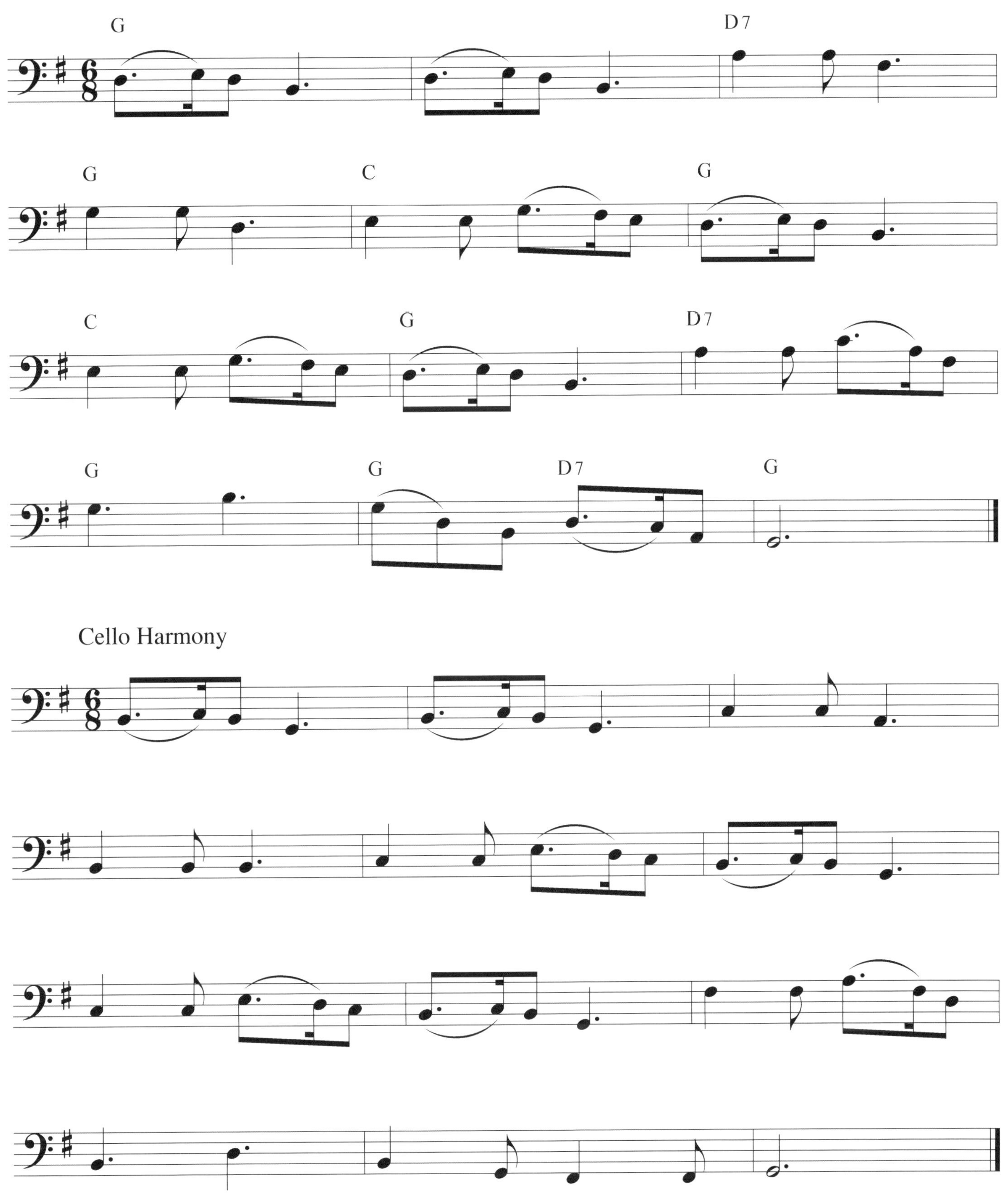

Sing We Now of Christmas

This traditional French carol from the late-fifteenth century is also known as "Noël Nouvelet". It was translated into English in the seventeenth or eighteenth century.

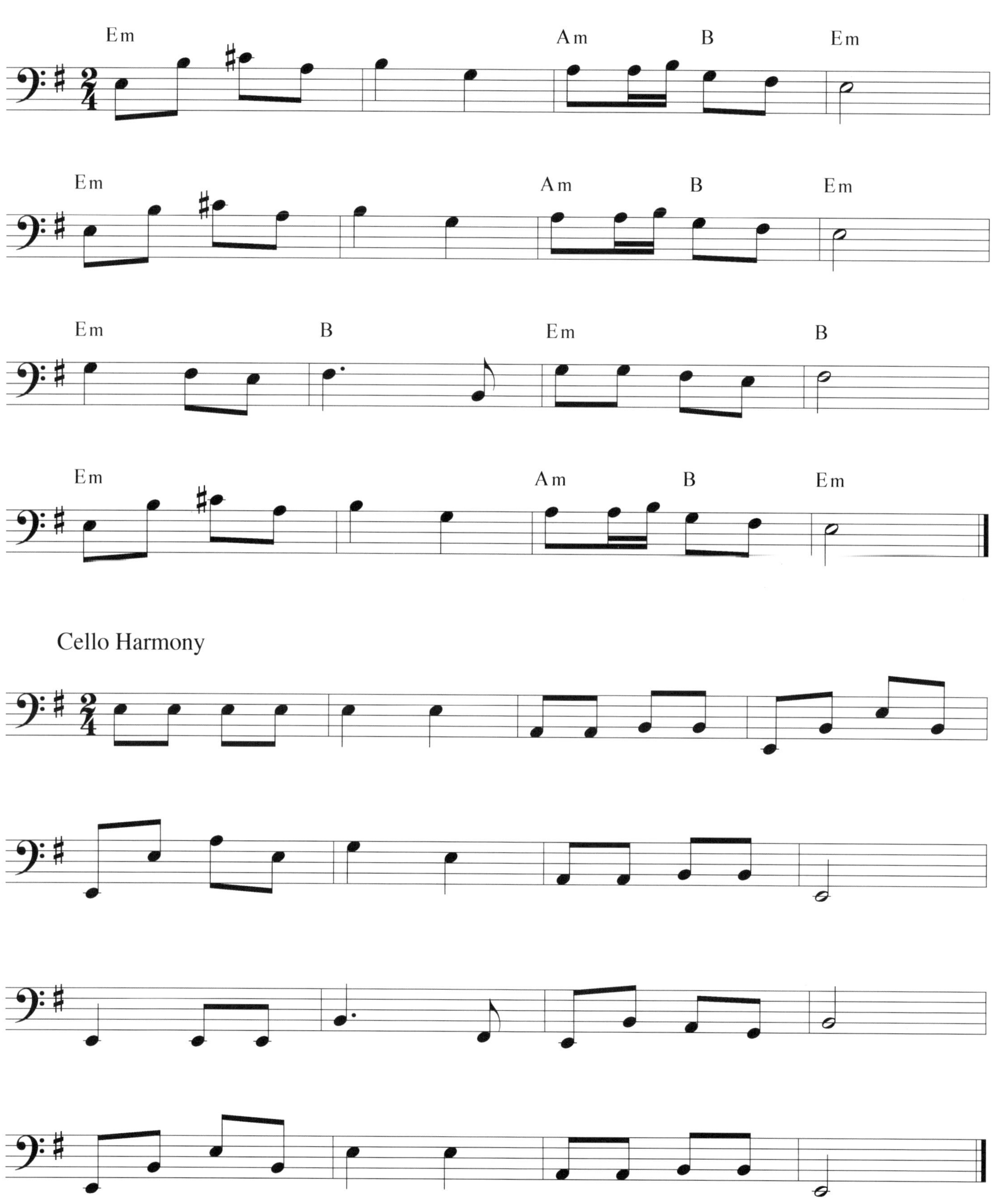

The Snow Lay on the Ground

"Venite Adoremus" is the Latin name for this traditional English carol from the mid-nineteenth century.

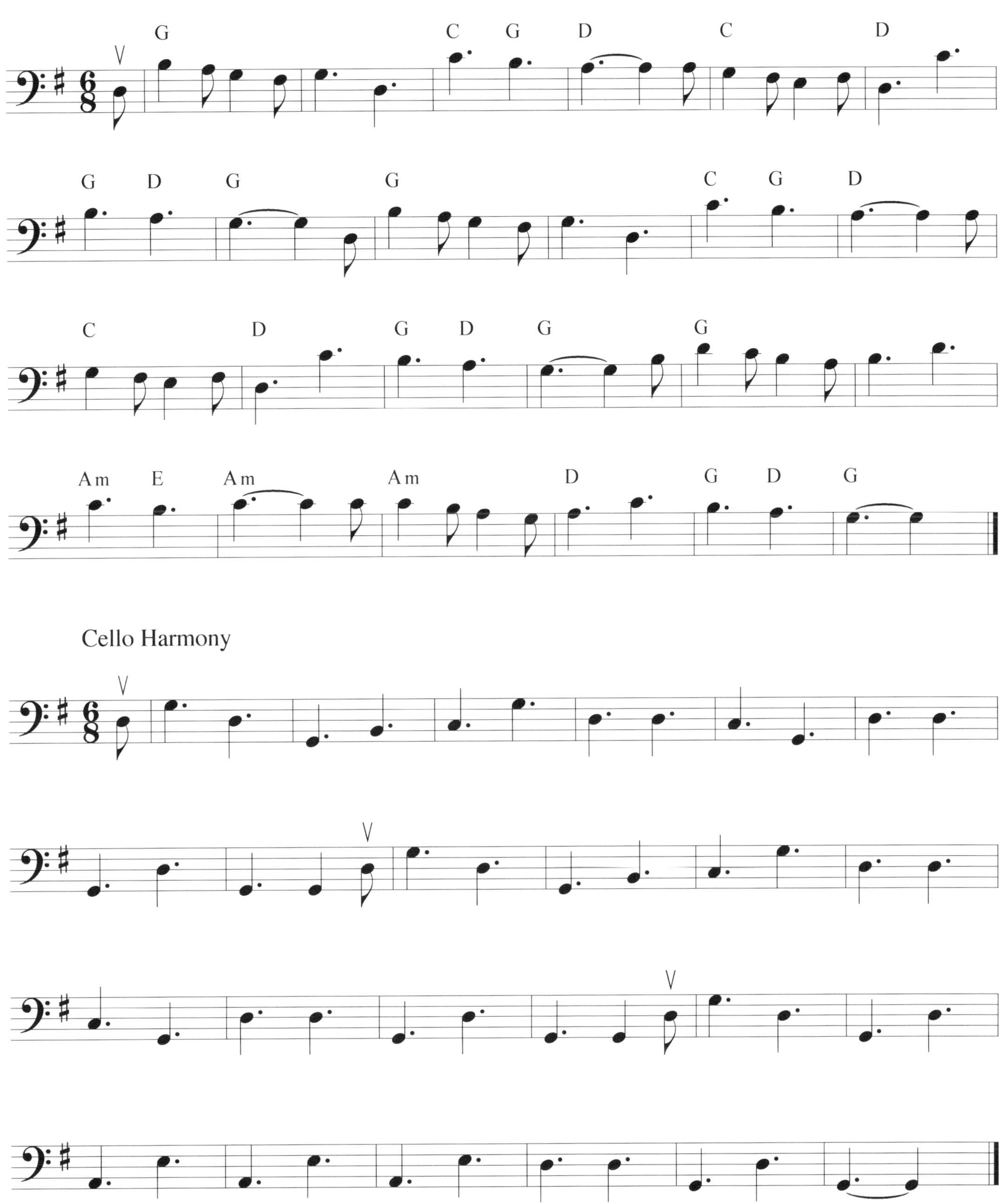

Star in the East

Brightest and Best/Hail the Blest Morn

William Walker published "Star in the East" in 1835 in *The Southern Harmony*. The text has been traced to the writings of Bishop Reginald Heber of England. "Hail the Blest Morn" and "Brightest and Best" are additional titles for the carol.

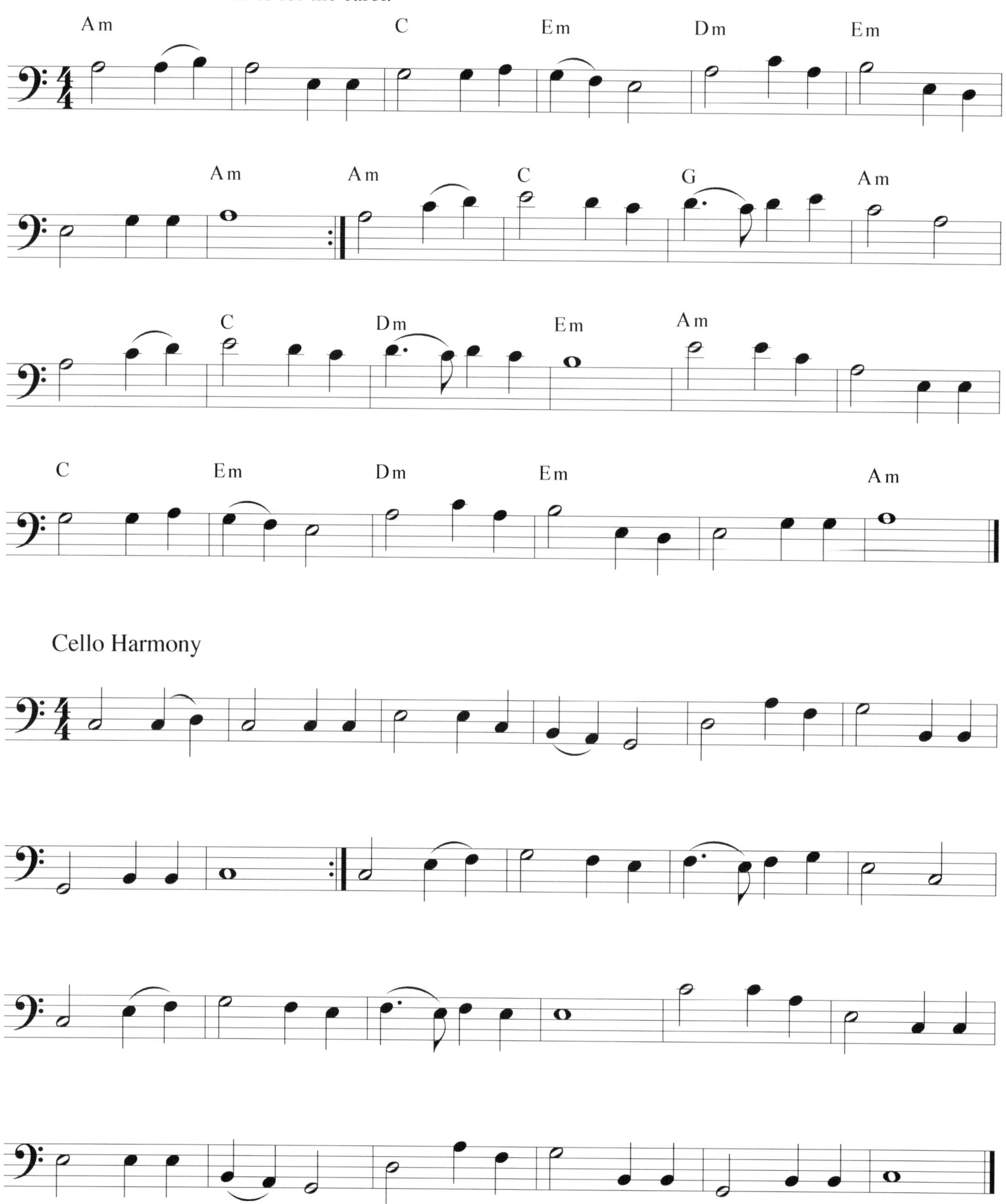

Still, Still, Still

This Christmas lullaby is a traditional Austrian melody from the early-nineteenth century. The modern version of the song is attributed to Georg Götsch (1895-1956).

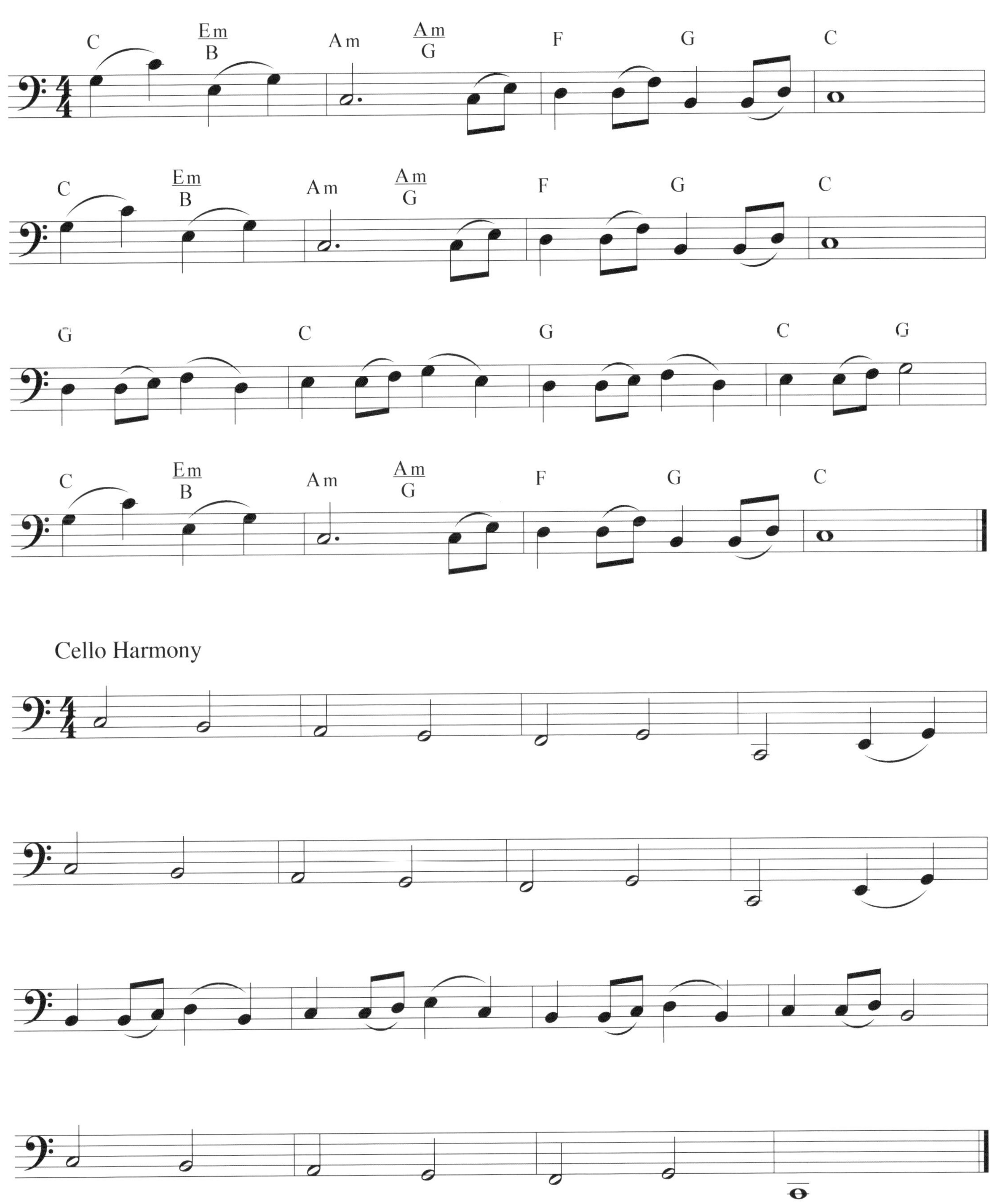

Tomorrow Shall Be My Dancing Day

Also known as "Dancing Day" and "My Dancing Day", this carol was published in *Christmas Carols, Ancient and Modern* by William Sandys in 1833. The text includes eleven verses tracing the life of Christ. It should be performed briskly at a playful dance tempo.

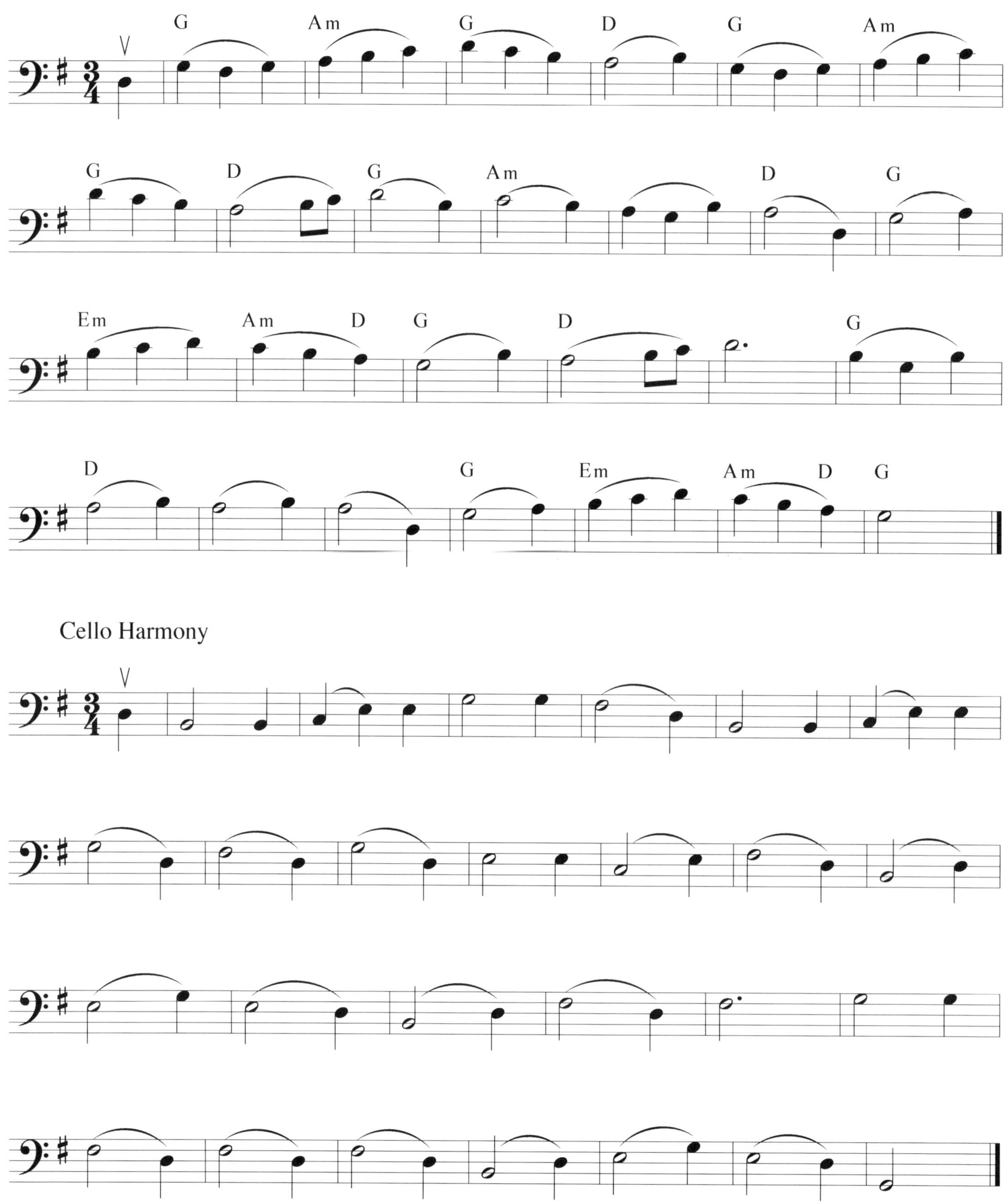

Wassail Song

Here We Come A-Wassailing

This carol comes from Yorkshire and was first printed in 1871 in *Christmas Carols New and Old*. It is one of the best known "wassail" songs in the United States.

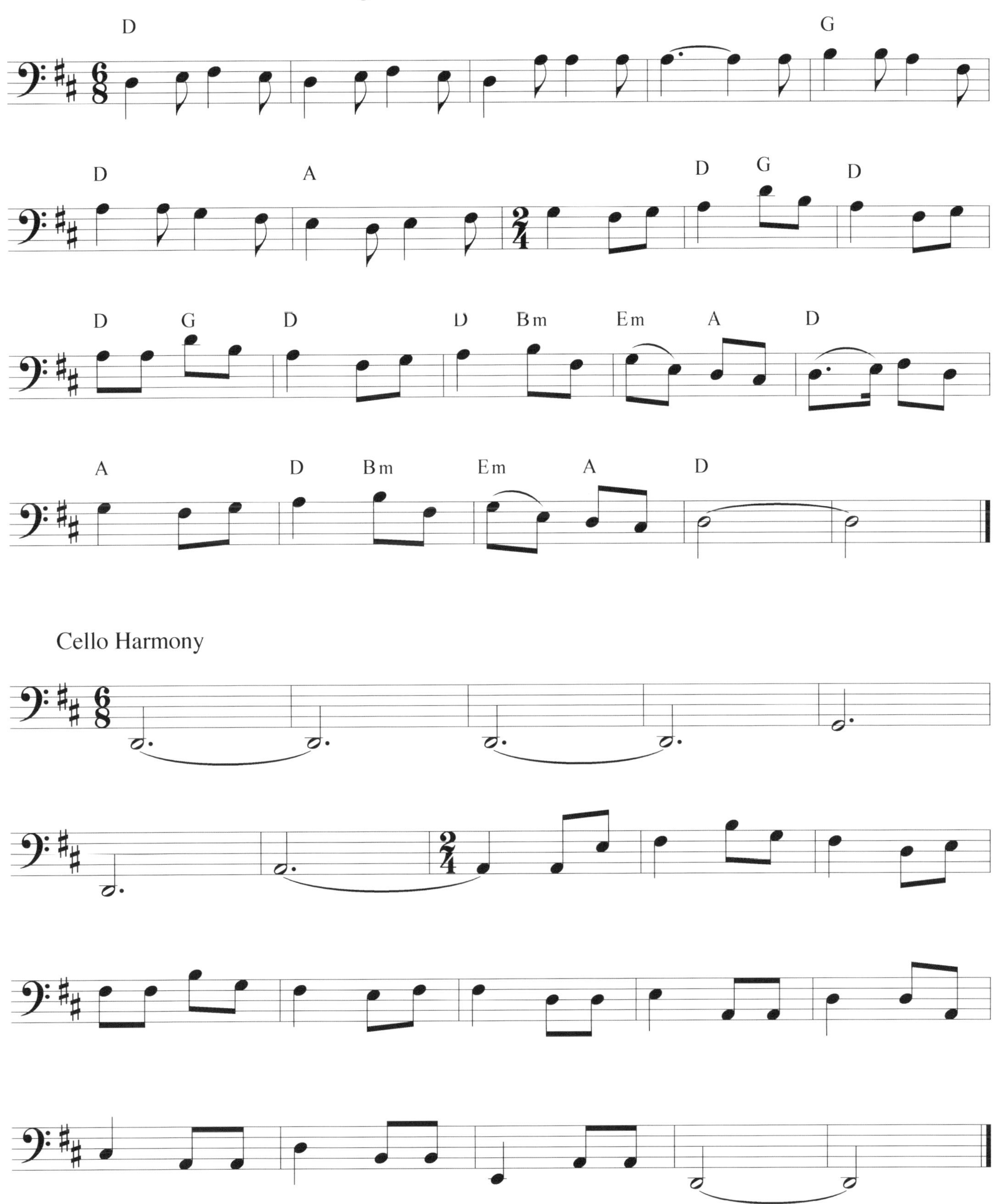

Wassail, Wassail

The Gloucestershire Wassail

Gloucestershire wassailers sang this tune as early as the eighteenth century, carrying a decorated bowl from door to door.

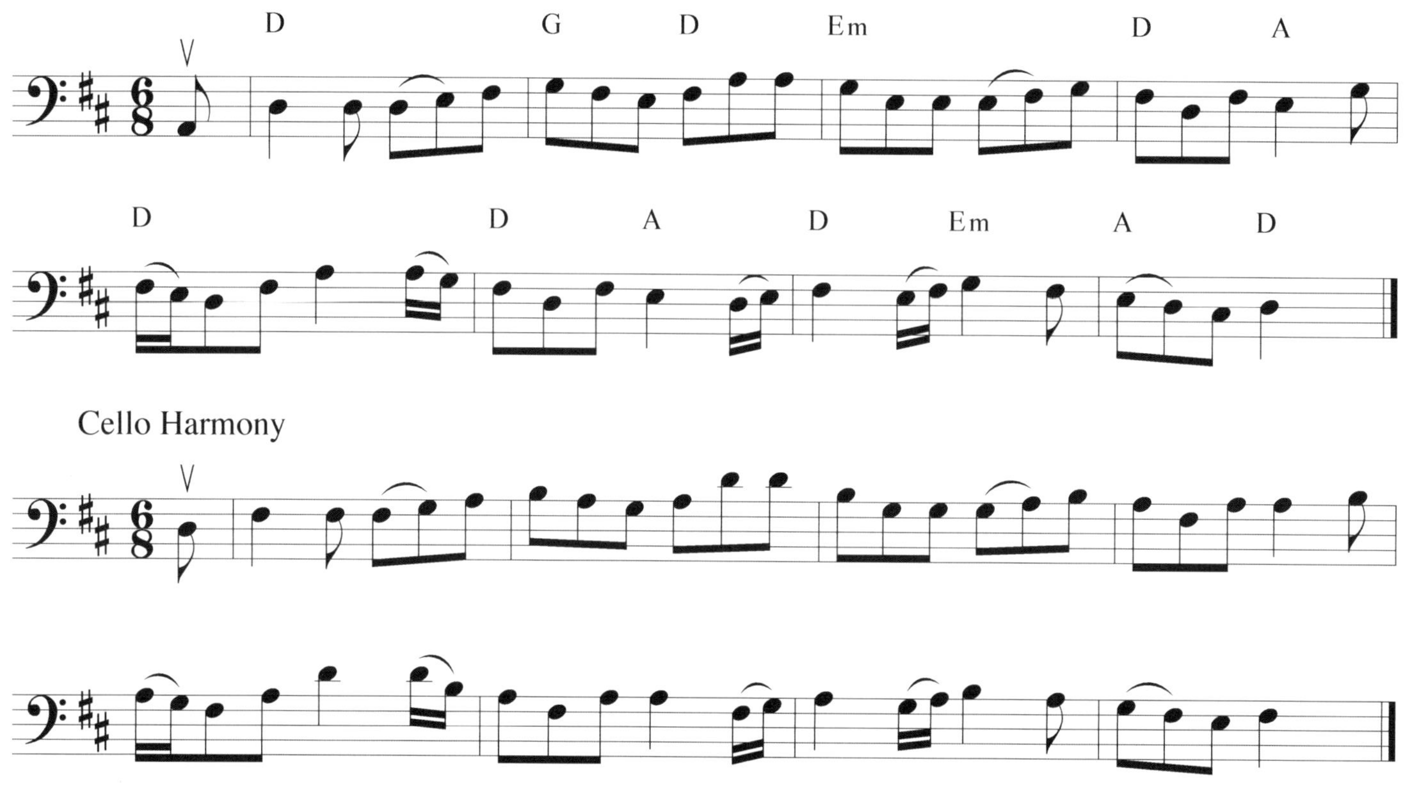

A Wassail, a Wassail Throughout the Town

This tune was collected from Phil Tanner of Wales in the early-nineteenth century, but the origin is unknown.

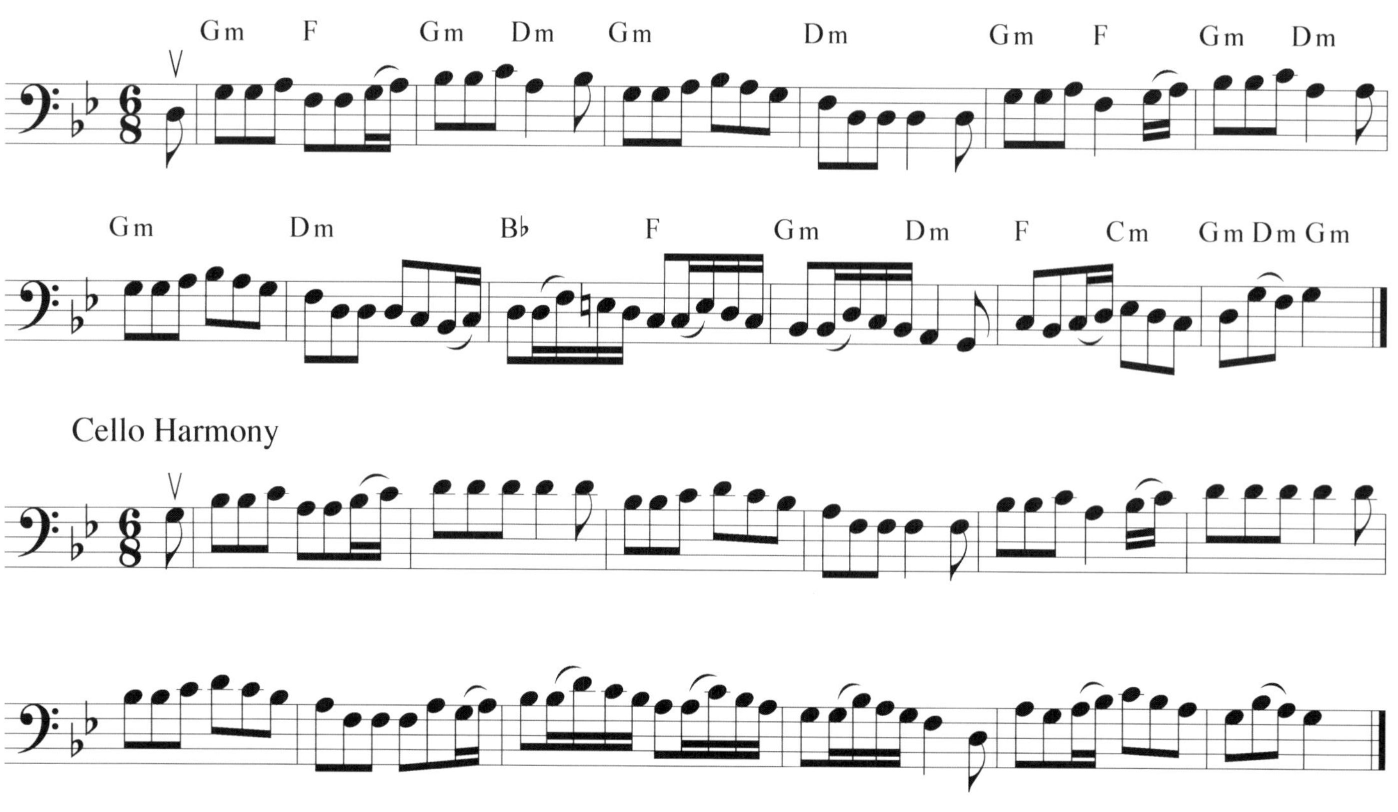

We Three Kings

John Henry Hopkins of Pennsylvania wrote and published this carol in *Carols, Hymns and Songs* in 1865. In this arrangement, measures 16-17 are presented as two measures, so the performer can keep a steady tempo. In the original, these two measures are written as one measure with fermatas on each note.

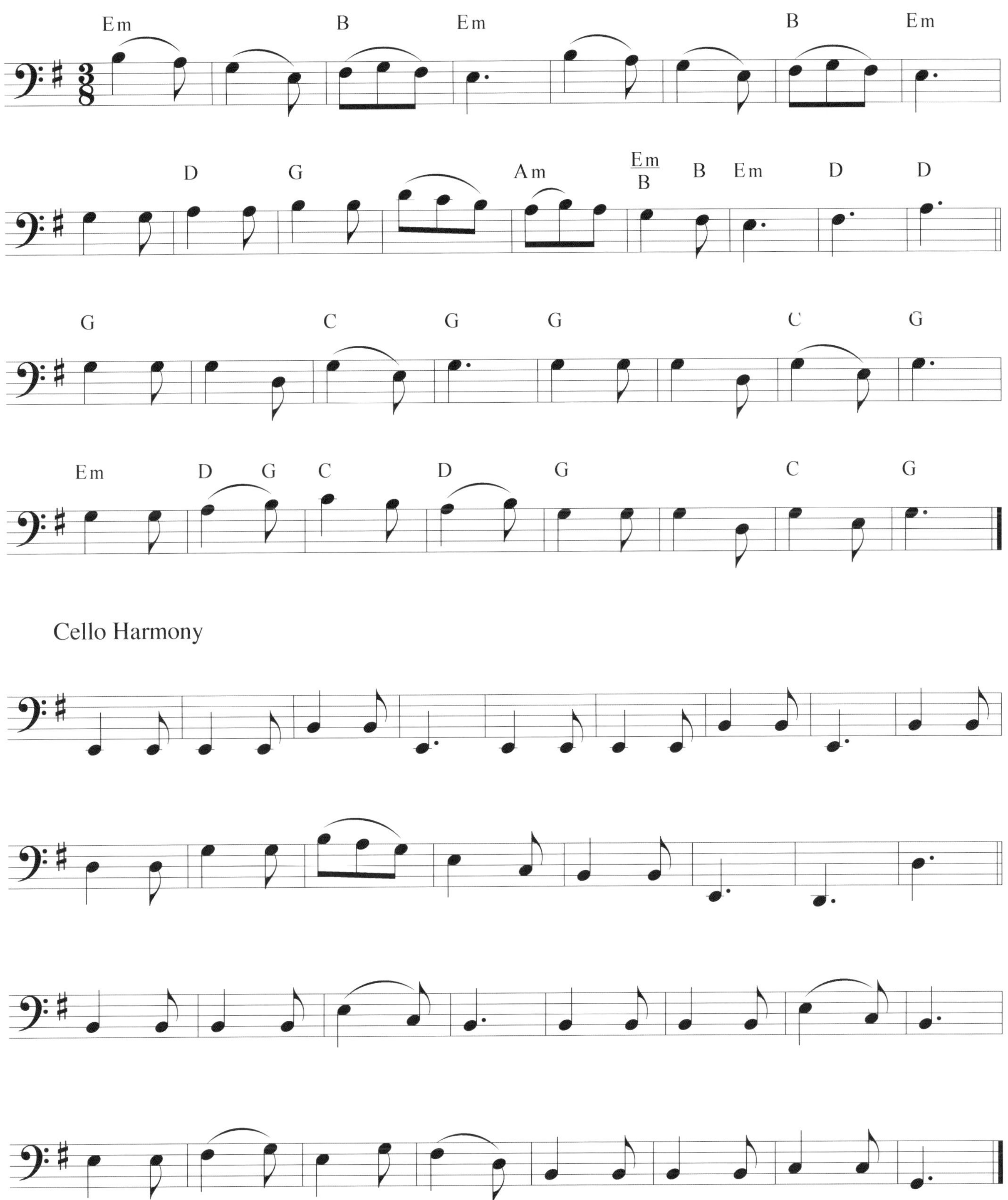

We Wish You a Merry Christmas

This traditional carol comes from the English "mummer" custom of caroling from door to door. This arrangement has the first part repeated making an overall AABA form.

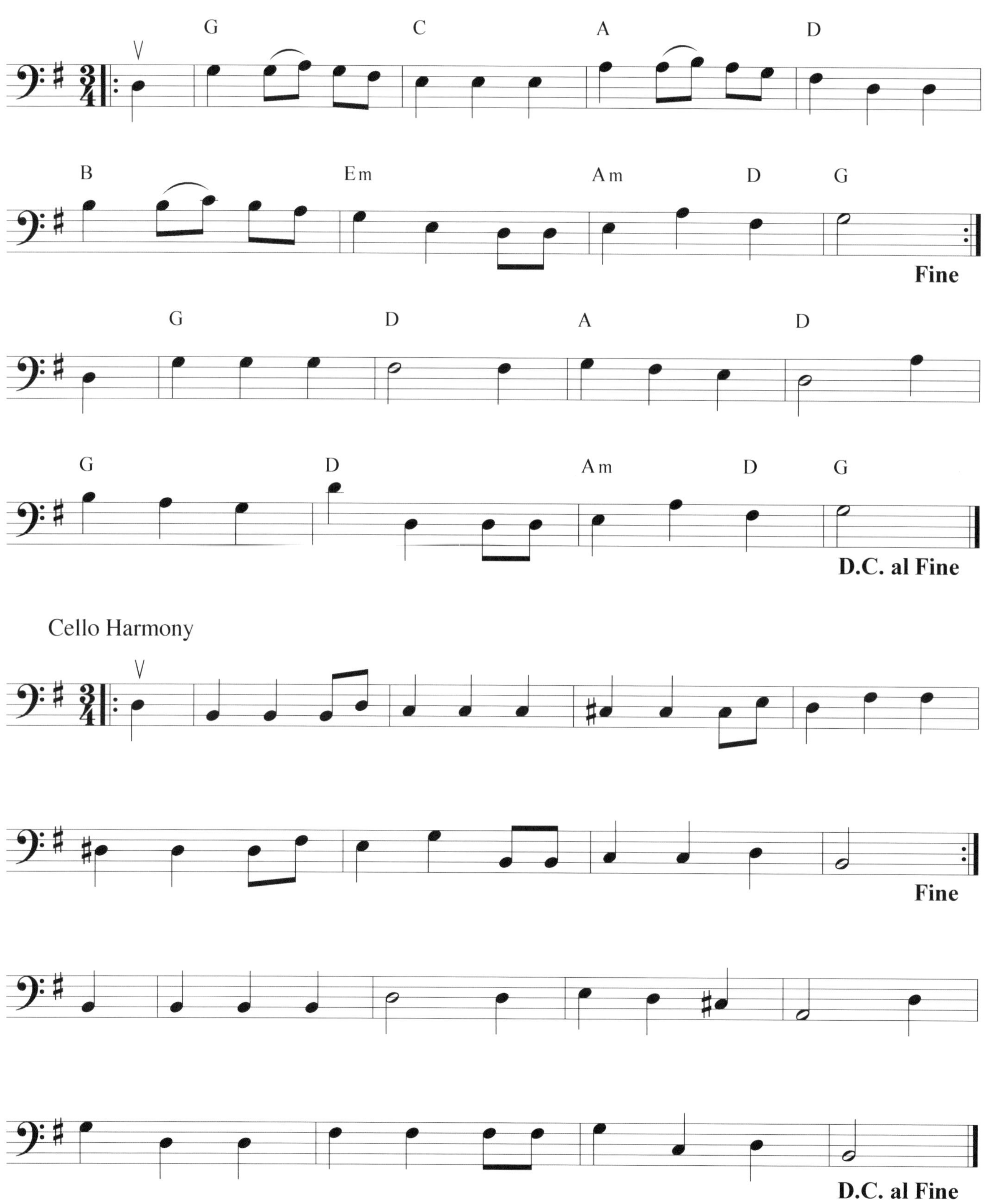

What Child Is This?

"Greensleeves", a traditional English tune, was first used as the melody for William Chatterton Dix's lyric around 1865. John Stainer arranged it with the following harmonies in 1871 in *Christmas Carols New and Old.*

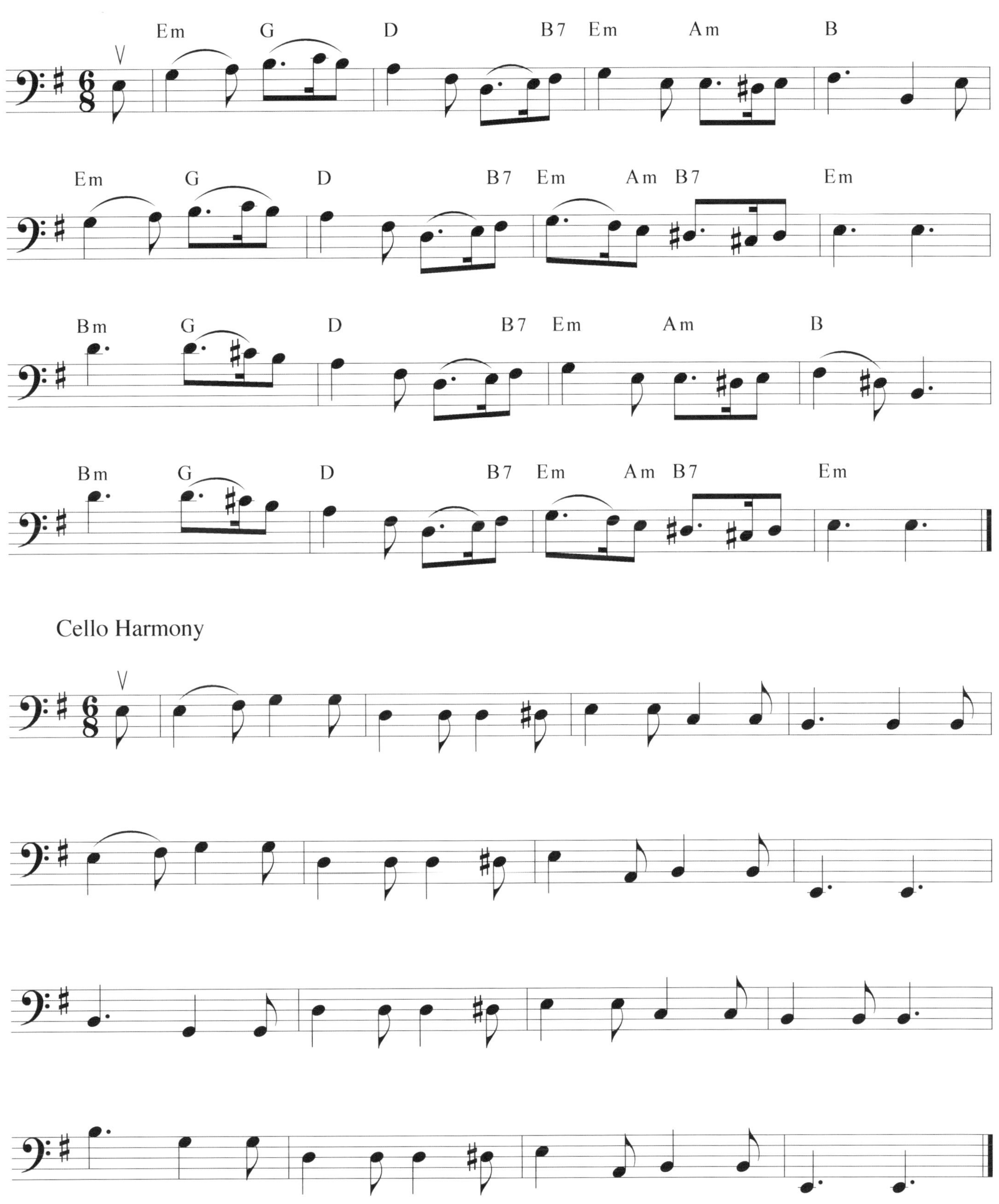

While Shepherds Watched Their Flocks

Nahum Tate and Nicholas Brady published this carol in 1696 in their *New Versions of the Psalms of David.* The text has been set to several tunes including this one by George Frideric Handel.

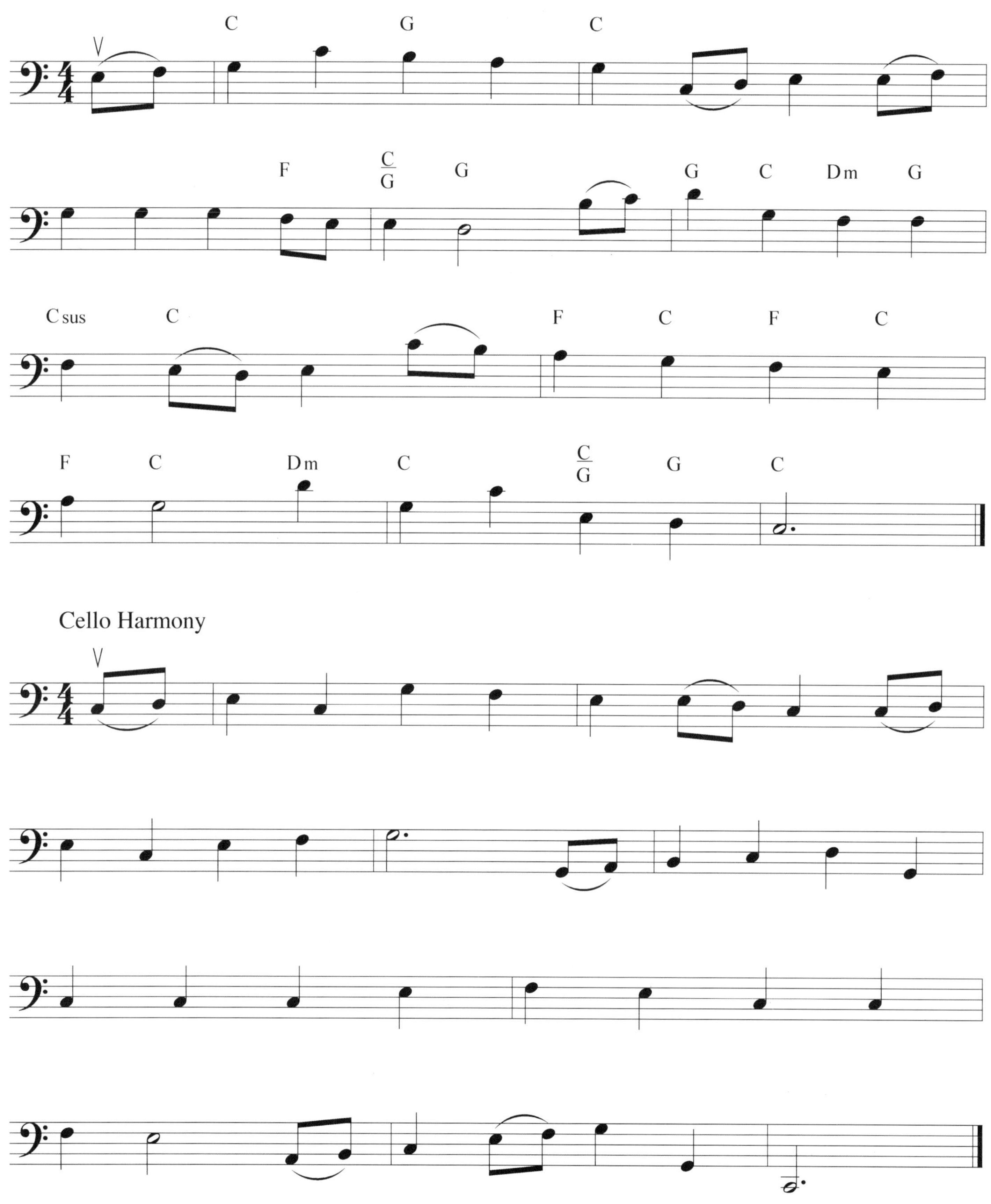